MW01196860

ABRAHAM KUYPER

Abraham Kuyper

A Pictorial Biography

Jan de Bruijn

Translated by

Dagmare Houniet

WILLIAM B. EERDMANS PUBLISHING COMPANY

GRAND RAPIDS, MICHIGAN / CAMBRIDGE, U.K.

Originally published in Dutch under the title

Abraham Kuyper: Een Beeldbiografie

© 2008 Uitgeverij Bert Bakker, Amsterdam

English edition published 2014 by

Wm. B. Eerdmans Publishing Co.

2140 Oak Industrial Drive N.E., Grand Rapids, Michigan 49505 /

P.O. Box 163, Cambridge CB3 9PU U.K.

Printed in the United States of America

20 19 18 17 16 15 14   7 6 5 4 3 2 1

Library of Congress Cataloging-in-Publication Data

Bruijn, J. de.

  Abraham Kuyper: a pictorial biography / Jan de Bruijn; translated by Dagmare Houniet.

    pages   cm

  Originally published in Dutch as:

  Abraham Kuyper: een beeldbiografie. Amsterdam: Bert Bakker, 2008.

  Includes bibliographical references and index.

  ISBN 978-0-8028-6966-1 (cloth: alk. paper)

  1. Kuyper, Abraham, 1837-1920.   2. Statesmen — Netherlands — Biography.

  3. Theologians — Netherlands — Biography.   I. Houniet, Dagmare, translator.

  II. Title.

  DJ283.K88B7713   2013

  284′.2092 — dc23

      [B]

                                                          2013033881

www.eerdmans.com

Contents

Introduction

Among historians there is little difference of opinion about the importance of the Dutch statesman and theologian Abraham Kuyper (1837-1920). Even those who are critical or disapproving of the man and his work will admit that Kuyper was a man of singular talents and a charismatic personality who had a profound influence on Dutch society. Apart from his contributions in ecclesiastical and theological matters, as a political reformer and Christian social thinker he is one of the founders of the modern political order as it exists in the Netherlands today; his importance is equalled only by that of the Liberal statesman Johan R. Thorbecke. In addition to this, he was the foremost architect of Dutch "pillarization" (in which the Netherlands was divided into three groups, or "pillars": Calvinist/Reformed, Roman Catholic, and Liberal/secular), which remained in place until well after the Second World War, and which, in current social debates, is increasingly valued as a model for integration. But it is his complex personality in particular that remains fascinating to this day.

In essence, Kuyper's aim was to turn Calvinism, which had once played a vital role in Dutch history and had contributed to making the nation great, into a vital and leading force in society again. At the same time he wanted it to answer the new questions and challenges of the time. Using the Calvinist principles he believed in, he involved himself intensely not only with such scholarly issues as the theory of evolution, the relationship between religion and science, and modernism in theology, but also with new social and political issues such as poverty, the educational system, the suffrage movement, women's emancipation, and colonialism. He worked tirelessly in the strong conviction that religion ought to play a formative role in all these areas. Unlike other prominent politicians of his time, Kuyper was much more than a political leader. He served as a minister and party leader, theologian and church reformer, journalist and spokesman of the people. Indeed, his life seemed like a stage for an ever-changing theatrical production, and in his capacity of director and actor he often both fascinated and confused the spectators.

This versatility was his strength and often made him elusive to his opponents, who accused him of overstepping the rules of the game by practicing politics in the church and theology in politics. But perhaps they were most irritated by his one-sidedness, which was a result of his polemical and inflammatory disposition. In the heat of battle Kuyper tended to simplify the issues and exaggerate opposing views, thus not doing justice to the viewpoints of his opponents. As editor-in-chief of the Liberal *Algemeen Handelsblad (General Trade Journal)* and one of Kuyper's opponents, Charles Boissevain revealed his ambivalence in an 1897 editorial devoted to "the first polemicist and party leader of the Netherlands": "[Kuyper"s] way of doing battle cannot be praised. Time and time again he leaves his readers in the dark about what the opponent has actually said. He informs them in as one-sided a way as possible. He is a man of the party down to his marrow and his pen, and especially in the past he has made the worst possible misuse of invectives and uncharitable expressions. . . . And yet: what a thinker, what a scholar he is, what a wealth of knowledge he has at his disposal. An incomprehensible man, whose contradictions we do not know how to cope with, but a rare man of genius!"

Indeed, the way in which Kuyper acted, however purposeful, was full of discrepancies and contradictions. While in his theological and social opinions he often harked back to the past, he also used all the means that the modern age had to offer. A significant scholar whose works fill half a bookcase, he also acted as an organizer and party leader with an eye for practical details. Feared for his sharp pen and polemical style, he was also the author of widely read devotionals that are surprisingly profound and pastoral. With his personal charm he was able to win over opponents, and then a day later rant and rave against them in the press. Although he moved in many different circles and saw much of the world in his travels, his lack of insight into human nature was often remarkable. Kuyper was an ideologue, a builder of systems with grand conceptions and fixed basic principles, but he was flexible enough to adjust his opinions if circumstances so dictated. He had a strong desire for security and harmony, but at the same time did not seem at ease without resistance and conflict. As a romantic, he valued purity more than concord, but at the same time he was enough of a tactician to carefully choose the right moment for confrontation or secession. He was a sensitive person full of self-pity and psychological stresses, but also a domineering personality who was well aware of his intellectual superiority and made little effort to conceal it. As a visionary leader of great rhetorical talent, Kuyper knew how to inspire his followers with high ideals, but as a power politician he was less than idealistic in practice.

In short, Kuyper was unpredictable, not an easy character to fathom. He had a complex personality, with multiple layers and often mutually opposing tendencies, desires, and feelings. In many ways he was a torn and troubled person, who did not live easily and experienced periods of deep depression. However, his faith gave him strength. That faith manifested itself on the one hand as a mystical desire, and on the other hand as an unremitting, almost compulsive desire for work and devotion to realizing his ideals.

The complex versatility of Kuyper's personality is reflected in his career. Beginning as a village minister of liberal persuasion, who initially seemed destined for a future as a church historian, Kuyper went into politics because of what became known in the Netherlands as the "school question" — the struggle for equal rights for Christian education. He became the emancipator of the Dutch Reformed "kleine luyden" ("little people"), who were considered less important politically and socially. In order to mobilize his followers, he founded the daily paper *De Standaard (The Standard)* in 1872, which he would lead for almost fifty years. He was also editor-in-chief of the influential church weekly *De Heraut (The Herald),* which disseminated his ecclesiastical and theological opinions. Kuyper was the founder of the first modern political party in the Netherlands, the Anti-Revolutionary Party (1879), and devoted himself to the extension of suffrage, which made Thorbecke's constitutional system accessible to ever broader ranges of the populace. By organizing the national petition of 1878, the Anti-Revolutionaries were at the forefront of the battle over the school question, and by the end of Kuyper's life their efforts would meet with success.

For more than twenty years Kuyper was a professor at the Free University, which he had co-founded in 1880. This was where the leaders of the Dutch Reformed and Anti-Revolutionary movement were formed. In church matters, his struggle for the maintenance of the orthodox creeds resulted in church schism leading to the establishment of the Reformed Churches in the Netherlands. Although this schism also extended to the political arena, only a few years later, thanks to a coalition with the Roman Catholics, the Anti-Revolutionaries were able to obtain a parliamentary majority that resulted in the formation of the first Christian coalition cabinet (1888-1891). With regard to social questions, Kuyper made a name for himself with his famous speech *Het sociale vraagstuk en de christelijke religie (The Social Question and the Christian Religion),* delivered at the Christian Social Congress of 1891, in which he expressed his criticism of the capitalist economic structure. However, later his reputation as a social reformer was severely damaged by the way in which he acted during the railway strike of 1903.

For Kuyper, his prime ministership (1901-1905) was without a doubt the pinnacle of his political career; he had completed the journey "from the parsonage to the turret." Thus his disappointment was all the greater when in 1905, after a fierce election contest, the parties in office lost their majority and Kuyper had to resign. It was a blow from which he would never fully recover, although he continued to play a role from the sidelines until shortly before his death in 1920.

This book attempts to offer a portrait of Kuyper's life and work in photographs and documents. A decision was made to present the material in the book chronologically, which means that at times several storylines run parallel to or across one another. To offer the reader at least something to go by, every chapter is preceded by a short survey of the principal developments and events of the time. The explanatory passages on each page attempt to clarify the connections further and offer background information.

Because this book is a non-specialist work meant for a broad public, systematic notes and glosses have been omitted. However, the sources of all the quotations have been included in the explanatory passages, and in a number of cases certain authors have been explicitly mentioned. The book contains a list of the most important works upon which this book was based. Also, at the time this book was first published in Dutch I was able to consult the then-unpublished English-language Kuyper bibliography compiled by Tj. Kuipers, which yielded rich rewards.

For the most part, the photographic and archive material included in the book come from the collections of the Historical Documentation Center for Dutch Protestantism at the Free University. In addition, a number of photographs have been made available by other libraries and archives; they are listed under "Sources of Photographic Material." I have greatly appreciated their cooperation. Finally I would like to thank my colleague Dagmare Houniet for her support and assistance.

J. DE BRUIJN

CHAPTER I

Early Years and Student Days, 1837-1863

Abraham Kuyper was born on 29 October 1837 in the small Dutch port town of Maassluis, near Rotterdam, as the son of the Dutch Reformed minister Jan Fredrik Kuyper and Henriëtte Huber, who before her marriage had been a governess and educator. He had two older sisters; after him, another boy and six girls were born, of whom four died in early childhood. Because his parents had limited means and lived on a modest minister's stipend, the children were raised frugally.

In April 1841 the family moved to Middelburg, the provincial capital of Zeeland, and in the summer of 1849 to the university city of Leiden, where Rev. Kuyper served as a minister of the Dutch Reformed Church until his retirement in 1868. From 1849 until 1855 his son Abraham attended the Stedelijk Gymnasium in Leiden, and went on to study theology in the same city from 1855 until 1862. Raised in a moderate orthodox environment, as a student he was influenced by the modernist movement in Dutch theology, which was centered in Leiden around professors J. H. Scholten and A. Kuenen. In September 1858 Abraham Kuyper became engaged to Johanna Schaay, the daughter of a Rotterdam stockbroker; after their marriage in July 1863, she would bear him eight children.

Abraham Kuyper was a brilliant and ambitious student who had a broad education at the academy and passed his exams with flying colors. In 1859-1860 he achieved a remarkable feat by winning the gold medal in a University of Groningen competition for his *Commentatio* (discourse), written in Latin, about the ecclesiology of the Protestant Reformers John Calvin and Johannes à Lasco. Unfortunately, his hard work on the 300-page manuscript exhausted him to such an extent that from February to July 1861 he had to discontinue his studies. It would not be the last time that Kuyper had to pay the price for his excessive passion for work.

Of great importance for the development in his thought during these years was the novel *The Heir of Redclyffe* by the English novelist Charlotte Mary Yonge, which he had received from his fiancée as a present in March 1862. The image in the book of the English church as a "mother" offering believers a sense of security made a deep impression on Kuyper, who in the long run was too much of a Romantic to find satisfaction in the rationalism of modernist theology. In September 1862 Abraham Kuyper completed his academic studies and received his doctoral degree in theology. In August 1863 he became a Dutch Reformed minister in Beesd, a village in the province of Gelderland, where he would remain until 1867.

The Rev. Jan Fredrik (Frederik) Kuyper (1801-1882), Abraham Kuyper's father. Rev. Kuyper was of humble origin: his father was a brushmaker in Amsterdam. He wanted to become a minister at a young age, but as his parents did not have the money to pay for his studies, when he was fifteen years old he turned to King William I for help, submitting a handwritten petition requesting financial support. The petition was rejected, but it shows that he (like his son in later years) did not lack initiative. Jan Frederik Kuyper became an employee at a merchant's office in Amsterdam and learned English in his spare time, at that time a language that was not spoken much in the Netherlands. This opened up new perspectives. At the request of the English minister A. S. Thelwall (1795-1863), who worked in Amsterdam at the time, he translated some minor English tracts for the Dutch Religious Tract Society. In 1823 he obtained a scholarship through the good offices of the secretary of the association, Rev. D. M. Kaakebeen, which enabled him to study theology in Amsterdam and Leiden (1823-1828). Afterwards he became a minister at Hoogmade (1828-1830), at Geervliet (1830-1834), at Maassluis (1834-1841), at Middelburg (1841-1849), and at Leiden (1849-1868). J. F. Kuyper was considered an adherent of the moderate-orthodox supranaturalistic school, whose adherents had a higher regard for peace and tolerance than for dogmatic certainty. He was to follow the later theological development of his son with some reservation.

Henriëtte Kuyper-Huber (1802-1881), Abraham Kuyper's mother. Her parents were of foreign extraction — Jean Jacques Huber was Swiss, his wife Christina Henriëtte was born in Liège — and they owned a large drapery store in the Leidsestraat in Amsterdam. Prior to her marriage Henriëtte Huber was a governess and a teacher at a boarding school for young ladies, and in her married life she taught her own children as well.

Abraham Kuyper wrote in *De Standaard* of Monday, 30 July 1906, "I never attended a public school or a Christian one. My father and mother taught me at home. Therefore, I owe them a great debt of gratitude. My mother was of Swiss origin and as a consequence was fluent in French. Father had a good command of English, and both knew Dutch well. They also taught me arithmetic and writing so that I certainly was not behind others who did attend school."

Het huis waarin Dr. A. Kuijper geboren is en welk met Amoveering
bedreigt wordt
Zuidvliet,   Maassluis.

The house in which Abraham Kuyper was born at the Zuidvliet in Maassluis, where his
father had been a minister since 1834. The house has been demolished and replaced by
newly built houses, upon which a commemorative plaque was added on the occasion
of the Kuyper commemoration of 1987. Unlike many other parsonages of the time, the
"minister's house" at the Zuidvliet does not look like a stately home. In Kuyper's parental home the family lived frugally, because it only had the minister's salary to live on.

The boxbed in which Abraham Kuyper was born on Sunday, 29 October 1837, at one o'clock in the afternoon. Kuyper's youngest sister, Jeannette Jacqueline Rammelman Elsevier-Kuyper, wrote in a booklet in which she recorded childhood memories (1921) that her parents were worried about little Bram's big head and were afraid that he had water on the brain. That was why they consulted a German professor who, after having examined the head, is said to have cried out: "Bewahre, das ist alles Gehirn!" ("Goodness gracious, it's all brain!")

Painting of the Grote Kerk in Maassluis where Kuyper was baptized by his father on 3 December 1837. The painting, made by J. W. Smith, was given to Kuyper in 1917 on the occasion of his eightieth birthday.

Certificate of baptism, Sunday, 3 December 1837. Initially the surname was alternately spelled as either Kuijper or Kuyper. The "y" was regarded as more distinguished.

The parental home at the Rotterdamse Kade in Middelburg, 1841-1849. "De Palmboom" ("The Palm Tree") is the fourth house from the right (with arrow). All the houses in this photograph were destroyed in World War II. Kuyper wrote in *De Standaard* on Monday, 30 July 1906: "In Middelburg the inclination (for the sea) fully revealed itself. During my school days I lived for the sight of ships and rigging, and at night I liked nothing better than to sit with the captain of some English coal barge and talk of the sea and sailing. I was determined to become a merchant captain by hook or by crook. It had even been decided that I should go to Amsterdam to be educated at the nautical college." The youthful Kuyper, at that time often called Bram, was said to bribe the crews of the ships in the harbor of Middelburg with his father's cigars so that they would listen to his "sermons."

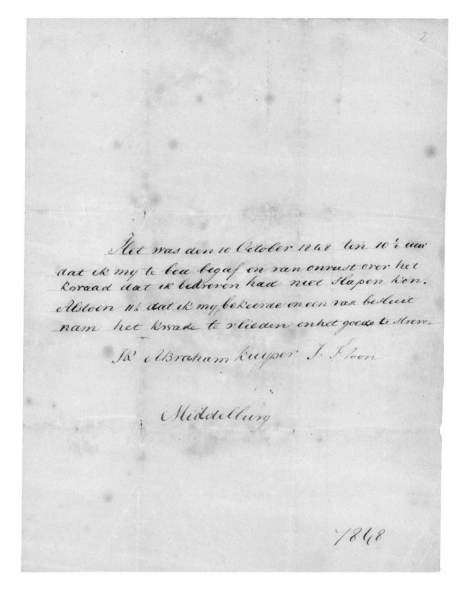

The oldest piece of handwriting by Abraham Kuyper is a solemn declaration about his conversion, a religious experience that he, as a boy of nearly eleven years old, committed to paper. The text reads, "It was on 10 October 1848 at 10:30 that I went to bed and could not get to sleep because of the evil I had committed. When it was 11:30 I was converted and made a firm resolve to banish evil and strive for good. I Abraham Kuijper J.F. son. Middelburg 1848." Alongside the text is written: "Aan den Vorst der vorsten uit een nedrig hart" ("To the Prince of Princes from a humble heart"), "Aan de God in den Hemel" ("To God in Heaven") and "Een gedachtenis die Heilig is" ("A holy remembrance").

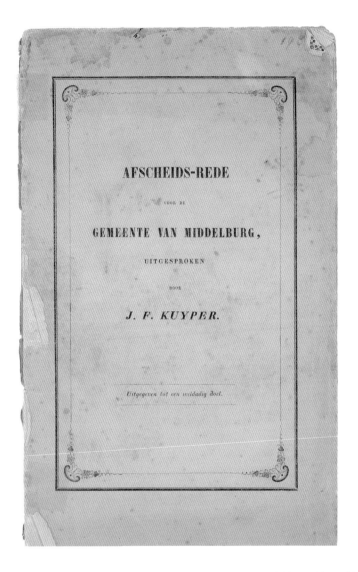

AFSCHEIDS-REDE

VOOR DE

GEMEENTE VAN MIDDELBURG,

UITGESPROKEN

DOOR

J. F. KUYPER.

Uitgegeven tot een weidadig doel.

Printed farewell-sermon by the Rev. J. F. Kuyper, delivered in Middelburg on 24 June 1849. On 6 December 1917 Kuyper wrote in the students' almanac of the Free University, "At first in Middelburg my father was regarded as being essentially orthodox. Under the leadership of the Rev. Thelwall, the English Methodist minister, he became a minister and consequently more of a supranaturalist. At first this did not matter much in Middelburg, as at the first half of that century orthodoxy and supranaturalism were considered for the most part identical. However, when at first Hasebroek and later on De Bruine took the pulpit in Middelburg, a split seemed unavoidable and my father felt he had lost too much of his congregation to remain in Zeeland's capital. For this reason he left for Leiden." According to Kuyper, his father's decision to accept the call to go to the university-city of Leiden was partly due to the fact that he was aware of his son's ambition to study theology after finishing university preparatory school.

Like many people in his time, Abraham Kuyper became acquainted with death at an early age. This photograph shows a lock of hair from his younger sister Louise Susanna, who died in Leiden on 4 December 1851, less than ten years old. Previously three other sisters had also died: Sophie (1840), Charlotte (1844), and Jacoba (1846).

The Hoogewoerd, one of the best-known streets in Leiden. The Kuyper family lived at number 315 (now 175). Rev. Kuyper bought the house for 2000 guilders. It had been abandoned for some time because it was thought to be haunted.

The restoration of the Roman Catholic hierarchy in the Netherlands in 1853 provoked fierce resistance amongst the Protestant majority of the population — the so-called April Movement — and resulted in the resignation of the Liberal Thorbecke cabinet. In the conservative-Protestant milieu in which Kuyper grew up, Thorbecke's fall was greeted with jubilation. Kuyper wrote in 1897, "It seems like only yesterday, the year was 1853, the year that Thorbecke was overthrown! He who now stands before you was by then the fiercest anti-papist you could imagine, and the April Movement made me into a violent anti-Thorbeckian. For I was brought up with the idea that Thorbecke and his followers had tried to undermine the honor and authority of the House of Orange. And the love, the warm inner loyalty to the House of Orange was so deeply rooted in my soul from a young age, that just one rumor was in itself enough to ensure that when finally on the evening of 20 April the news reached Leiden about how Thorbecke had been discharged, I, as if beside myself with joy, flew upstairs, rushed into my father's room and cried out, drunk with happiness: 'Father, Father, Thorbecke has fallen!'"

The Stedelijk Gymnasium (with stepped gable) in Lokhorststraat diagonally across from the Gravensteen in Leiden, where Abraham Kuyper received a thorough classical education from 1849 through 1855. The gymnasium (or university preparatory school) was the continuation of the old Latin School, which probably dated back to the second half of the thirteenth century. The oldest document referring to the school, a charter by Count Willem IV, dates back to 1324. The school building in the photograph was built in 1601. In 1838 the Latin School was turned into a gymnasium and in 1847 a second department was added, which taught a four-year course geared towards professions that did not require a classical education. In 1849 the school counted only sixty pupils, of which fifteen were in the (combined) first year.

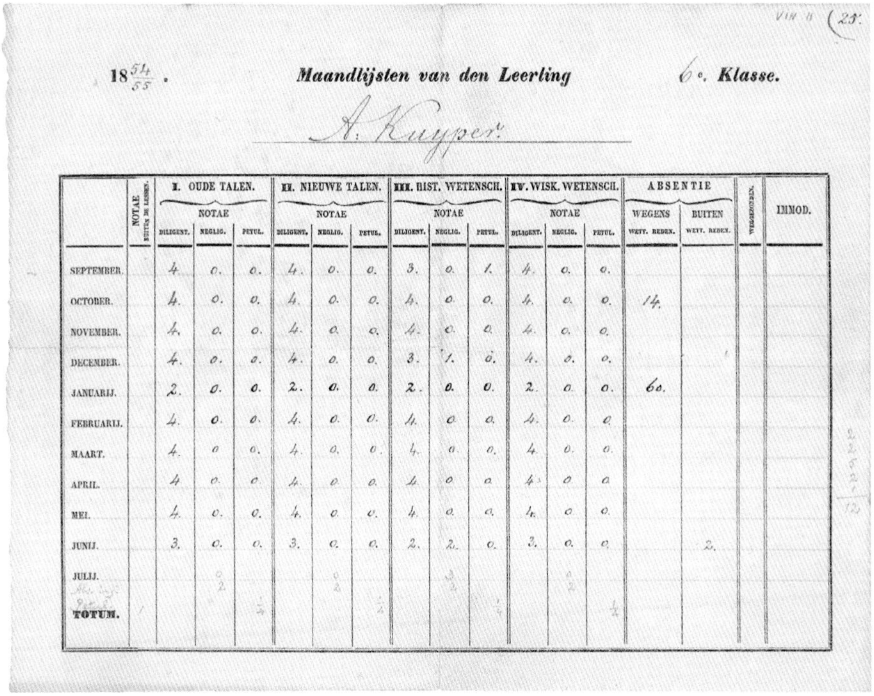

18 54/55 .   *Maandlijsten van den Leerling*   6°. *Klasse.*

A. Kuyper

| | NOTAE | I. OUDE TALEN. | | | II. NIEUWE TALEN. | | | III. HIST. WETENSCH. | | | IV. WISK. WETENSCH. | | | ABSENTIE | | | IMMOD. |
| | | NOTAE | | | NOTAE | | | NOTAE | | | NOTAE | | | WEGENS WETT. REDEN. | BUITEN WETT. REDEN. | | |
		DILIGENT.	NEGLIG.	PETUL.	DILIGENT.	NEGLIG.	PETUL.	DILIGENT.	NEGLIG.	PETUL.	DILIGENT.	NEGLIG.	PETUL.				
SEPTEMBER.		4.	0.	0.	4.	0.	0.	3.	0.	1.	4.	0.	0.				
OCTOBER.		4.	0.	0.	4.	0.	0.	4.	0.	0.	4.	0.	0.	14.			
NOVEMBER.		4.	0.	0.	4.	0.	0.	4.	0.	0.	4.	0.	0.				
DECEMBER.		4.	0.	0.	4.	0.	0.	3.	1.	0.	4.	0.	0.				
JANUARIJ.		2.	0.	0.	2.	0.	0.	2.	0.	0.	2.	0.	0.	60.			
FEBRUARIJ.		4.	0.	0.	4.	0.	0.	4.	0.	0.	4.	0.	0.				
MAART.		4.	0.	0.	4.	0.	0.	4.	0.	0.	4.	0.	0.				2.
APRIL.		4.	0.	0.	4.	0.	0.	4.	0.	0.	4.	0.	0.				2.
MEI.		4.	0.	0.	4.	0.	0.	4.	0.	0.	4.	0.	0.				
JUNIJ.		3.	0.	0.	3.	0.	0.	2.	2.	0.	3.	0.	0.		2.		12.
JULIJ.																	
TOTUM.																	

Abraham Kuyper had to get used to the classical school system after having been home-schooled; as a result in his first year, his grades were average. After that, things improved. As the best student *(primus)* of his class, there were several occasions at the end of the year when he was allowed to address the teaching staff of the Leiden gymnasium with the usual vote of thanks *(gratias)*. Depicted above are Abraham Kuyper's "month lists" dating from his final school year, with points *(notae)* for *diligentia* (accuracy), *negligentia* (slovenliness, neglect), and *petulantia* (impudence). This assessment system helped determine each student's ranking and admittance to the next school year.

The young historian Dr. R. J. Fruin (above left, 1823-1899) was one of Abraham Kuyper's teachers at the Leiden gymnasium. Appointed professor at Leiden University in 1860, he would continue to follow his former pupil's subsequent career with interest, although he had a higher regard for Kuyper's church-history work than for his political and ecclesiastical activities. During the elections of 1894 the conservative Fruin called Kuyper "the revolutionary leader of the Anti-Revolutionaries and radical democrats."

Kuyper was taught Dutch by the linguist L. A. te Winkel (above right, 1806-1868), who instilled in him a love for his own language. Te Winkel was a self-taught man and in 1855 became *doctor honoris causa* at the University of Leiden. For some time during the final school year he gave Kuyper private lessons in the Gothic language.

In the 1850s, the teaching staff of the Leiden gymnasium consisted of several other learned figures, such as the headmaster, Latinist and medievalist Dr. W. H. D. Suringar; the pro-rector Dr. W. G. Pluygers, librarian of the Leiden Academy and professor of classical languages; the Latinist Dr. J. E. Kiehl, who in 1855 was appointed professor at the Athenaeum in Deventer; the Dutch specialist and future head of the National Archives, Dr. L. Ph. C. van den Bergh; Dr. J. A. C. Oudemans, who would go on to become professor in astronomy in Utrecht; and Dr. C. A. X. G. F. Sicherer, who would later be appointed university lecturer in the German language at Leiden.

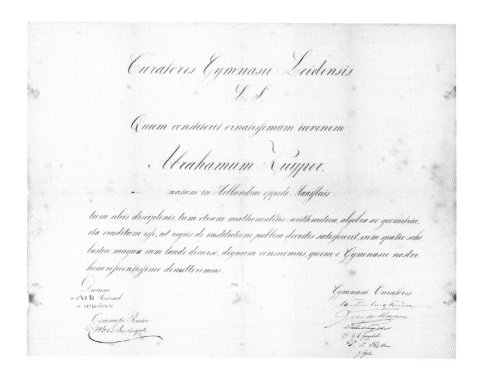

Abraham Kuyper's gymnasium certificate, 8 September 1855, with the grade *magna cum laude.* The highest distinction *(summa cum laude)* was reserved for his classmate H. W. (Hein) Stuffken, presumably because during his time at the gymnasium he had done the most homework during the holidays.

At his departure from the Leiden gymnasium on 8 September 1855, Abraham Kuyper spoke about "Ulfila, der Bischof der Visi Gothen und seine Gothische Bibelüber-setzung" (Ulfila, the Bishop of the Visigoths and his Gothic Bible translation). Kuyper's attention had been drawn to the figure of Ulfila (Wulfila) by L. A. te Winkel. It was typical of the religious climate in which Kuyper had been raised that he chose in favor of the Arian bishop Wulfila, who was defeated by his orthodox Catholic opponents and died a "Schlachtopfer religiöser Partheisucht" (a victim of political strife).

The Academy building on the Rapenburg in Leiden. During Kuyper's years of study the astronomical observatory was still in place on the roof. The observatory was pulled down in 1864.

Het Coll. Civ. Acad. Lugd. Bat. Supr.

VERKLAART DAT

de Heer A. Kuyper

LID IS VAN HET LEYDSCHE STUDENTEN-CORPS.

LEYDEN,
15 Junij 1862.

T.K. Halbertsma

loco Coll. Praeses.

On 16 July 1855 Kuyper enrolled as a student in Leiden. Students who intended to study theology *(studiis Theologiis destinatus)* first had to take preliminary examinations in the arts, which included Greek, Latin, Dutch, Hebrew, and Hebraic antiquities. Examinations in mathematics were also required. On 26 June 1857 Abraham Kuyper passed the examination with a *magna cum laude* and on 29 April 1858 he became a Bachelor of Arts *summa cum laude.*

Kuyper was a member of the Leiden students' union, but was only rarely able to participate in the university's colorful student life because of strapped finances. His name is absent from the student committees mentioned in the annual almanacs and the list of participants in the big masquerade held by the members of the "Studentencorps" on Monday, 11 June 1860, in celebration of the 285th anniversary of the university, even though no less than one-third of all the 500 students at Leiden took part in this historical procession.

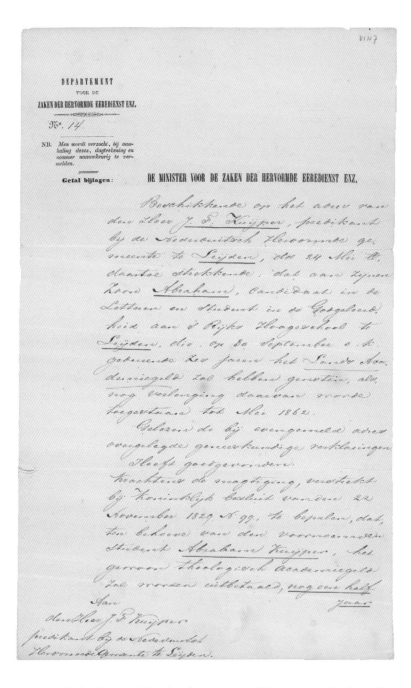

The award of national tuition fees for students of theology to Abraham Kuyper, 4 June 1861. Being a minister's son, Kuyper could only barely manage financially, and in order to fund his studies he was dependent on grants and earnings from private lessons. As a result, Kuyper became attuned to financial matters at an early age, which would prove useful in his later career, for example, in his dealings with publishers.

To save money, Kuyper lived with his parents during his student days, which oc-

casionally caused tensions between him and his father. On 27 October 1858 he wrote to his fiancée Johanna Schaay: "On coming home yesterday afternoon I found an invitation for a young couple's engagement-party which I could not decline. I had to be there at approximately six o'clock and did not return home until half past two in the morning. . . . I had a really good time last night, proposed toasts galore, and — just imagine — recited a verse, saw a little comedy, drank nice claret — in short I came home ringing the doorbell in high spirits, only to find — oh, it was frightful! — my old man in a nightcap glaring at me with a none-too-friendly face. It was quite a nuisance [for him] to stay up so long in the cold. But it could not be helped — in other words, there was not much I could do about it. I wished my parents good night and made my way to the sandman."

Among the professors whose lectures Kuyper attended were the Old Testament scholar Abraham Kuenen (1828-1885) and the theologian J. H. Scholten (1811-1885). They were the founders of the Modernist movement in Dutch theology, which flourished because of great doctrinal freedom within the Dutch Reformed Church. Kuyper was also greatly influenced by it during his student days. In his brochure *Het Modernisme, een fata morgana op christelijk gebied* (*Modernism, a Fata Morgana in the Christian Domain*, 1871) he wrote about the "electrifying" effect that Scholten and his enthusiastic colleagues had had on him. And on 3 March 1904 Kuyper, as prime minister, remarked in the Dutch parliament, "I came to the academy a religious young man, but after one-and-a-half years my conviction had changed into the most absolute intellectual rationalism."

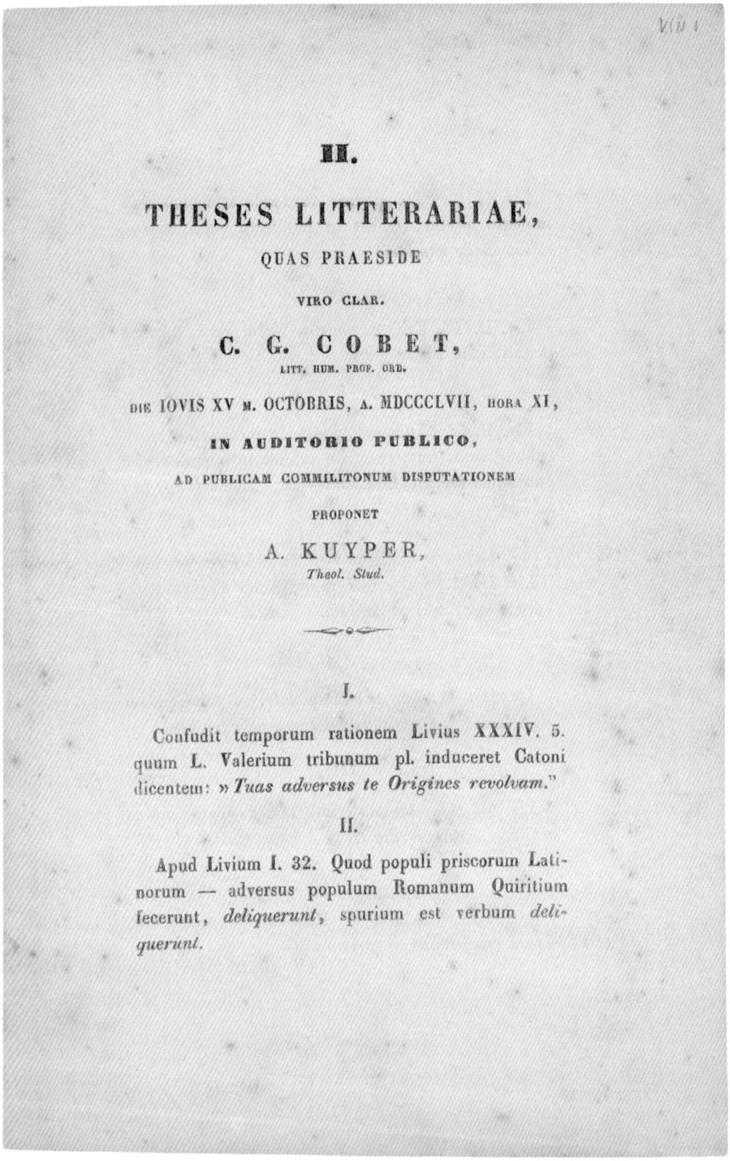

II.

THESES LITTERARIAE,

QUAS PRAESIDE

VIRO CLAR.

C. G. COBET,

LITT. HUM. PROF. ORD.

DIE IOVIS XV M. OCTOBRIS, A. MDCCCLVII, HORA XI,

IN AUDITORIO PUBLICO,

AD PUBLICAM COMMILITONUM DISPUTATIONEM

PROPONET

A. KUYPER,

Theol. Stud.

I.

Confudit temporum rationem Livius XXXIV. 5.
quum L. Valerium tribunum pl. induceret Catoni
dicentem: » *Tuas adversus te Origines revolvam.*"

II.

Apud Livium I. 32. Quod populi priscorum Lati-
norum — adversus populum Romanum Quiritium
fecerunt, *deliquerunt,* spurium est verbum *deliquerunt.*

In his second and third years Kuyper participated in the public disputations of the renowned classicist C. G. Cobet (1813-1889), which were organized for students of all the
departments who wanted to practice their Latin. Only a few students took part in this
literary debating society. The theses were usually provided by Cobet himself, and one
of the students had to defend them on the day of the disputation. During the academic
year 1857-1858 Kuyper acted as *defendens* in four of the fourteen meetings. The photograph shows a number of printed theses concerning the Roman writer Titus Livy, which
Kuyper defended on 15 October 1857. Owing to "a lack of participants," these disputations were phased out in 1859.

Having been taught at the gymnasium by the linguist L. A. te Winkel, at the university Kuyper attended the lectures of professor Matthias de Vries (1820-1892), who in cooperation with Te Winkel drafted the new Dutch spelling of 1863, which was named after them. De Vries also was editor of the *Woordenboek der Nederlandsche Taal (Dictionary of the Dutch Language)* and, as his teacher of Dutch language and literature, had a lasting influence on Kuyper's style.

Kuyper said in his 1892 oration *De verflauwing der grenzen (The Blurring of Boundaries)*, "In Leiden Matthijs de Vries has passed away, a man I am permitted to mention in our circles because he, more than any other professor, belonged *to the whole nation*. Where others may hold their tongue I feel the need, also in these circles, to dedicate a quiet word of thanks to his memory. Whatever power there might be in my language, whatever inspiration in my words, it is thanks to him. It was he, more than anyone else, who instilled in me the love of academic scholarship. For my entire development, I owe more than words can say to this loyal friend. I ventured upon teaching the Dutch language in our circles only because De Vries had inspired in my heart a love for our wonderful native language that can never die away." Between 1909 and 1912 Kuyper presided over the "State Committee for the Spelling of the Dutch Language," which in March 1912 chose in favor of the De Vries and Te Winkel spelling above that of R. A. Kollewijn.

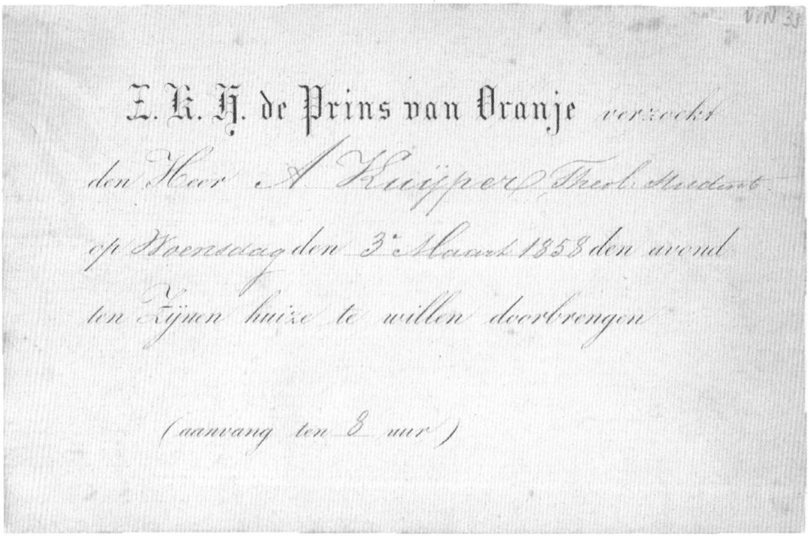

Z.K.H. de Prins van Oranje *verzoekt*
den Heer A Kuijper Theol Student
op Woensdag den 3e Maart 1858 den avond
ten zijnen huize te willen doorbrengen

(aanvang ten 8 uur)

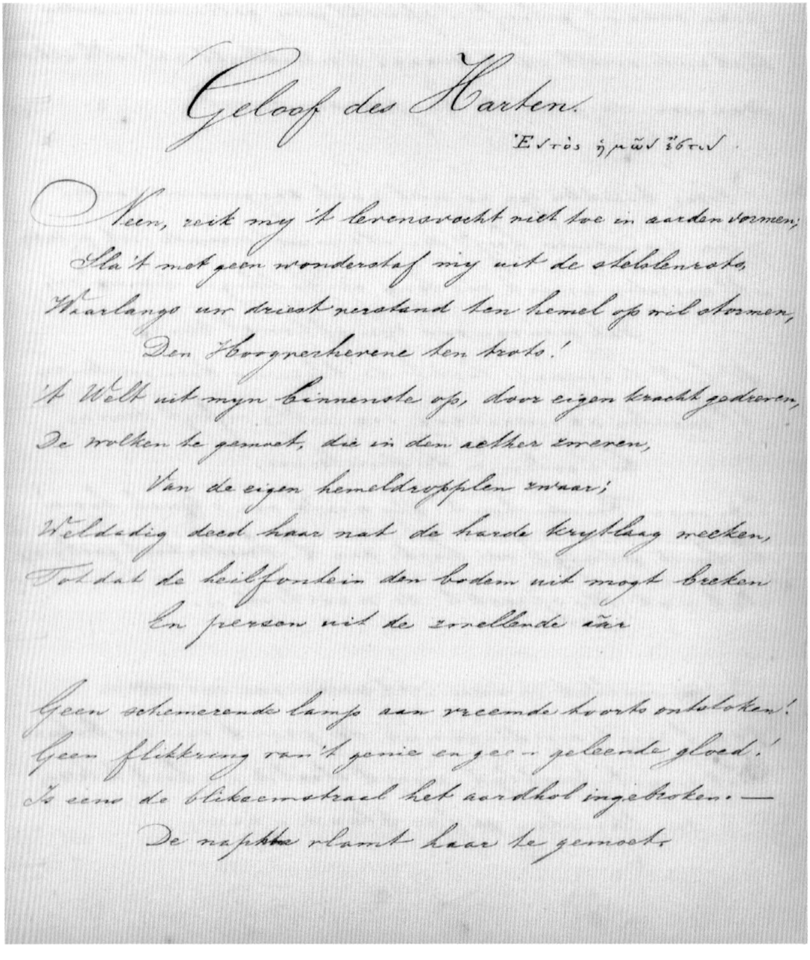

Geloof des Harten

Neen, reik mij 't levensvocht niet toe in aarden vormen,
Sla 't met geen wonderstaf mij uit de steenenrots,
Waarlangs uw dierst verstand ten hemel op wil stormen,
  Den Hoogverhevene ten trots!
't Welt uit mijn binnenste op, door eigen kracht gedreven,
De wolken te gemoet, die in den aether zweven,
  Van de eigen hemeldropplen zwaar;
Weldadig deed haar nat de harde krijtlaag weeken,
Tot dat de heilfontein den bodem uit mogt breken
  En persen uit de zwellende âer

Geen schemerende lamp aan vreemde toorts ontstoken!
Geen flikkring van 't genie en geen geleende gloed!
Zoo eens de bliksemstraal het aardhol ingebroken. —
  De naphta vlamt haar te gemoet

Invitation of the Prince of Orange addressed to Abraham Kuyper to "spend an evening at his house," 3 March 1858. Between 1856 and 1858 the Prince of Orange was enrolled as a student in Leiden.

Abraham Kuyper's poetry album containing verses by friends and relatives. "Faith of the Heart," by the theologian and poet Abraham des Amorie van der Hoeven Jr., who died young, was inscribed in the album by his college friend Johannes Petrus Mond, later an evangelical-Lutheran minister in Nieuwediep. On 6 April 1864 Rev. Mond married Abraham Kuyper's eldest sister Anna Christina Elisabeth (1834-1920); he died less than two years later, on 4 April 1866.

One of Kuyper's university friends was Isaäc Hooykaas (1837-1894), a supporter of the Modernist theological school, who after his studies and promotion in Leiden became a Dutch Reformed minister, but later joined the Remonstrants.

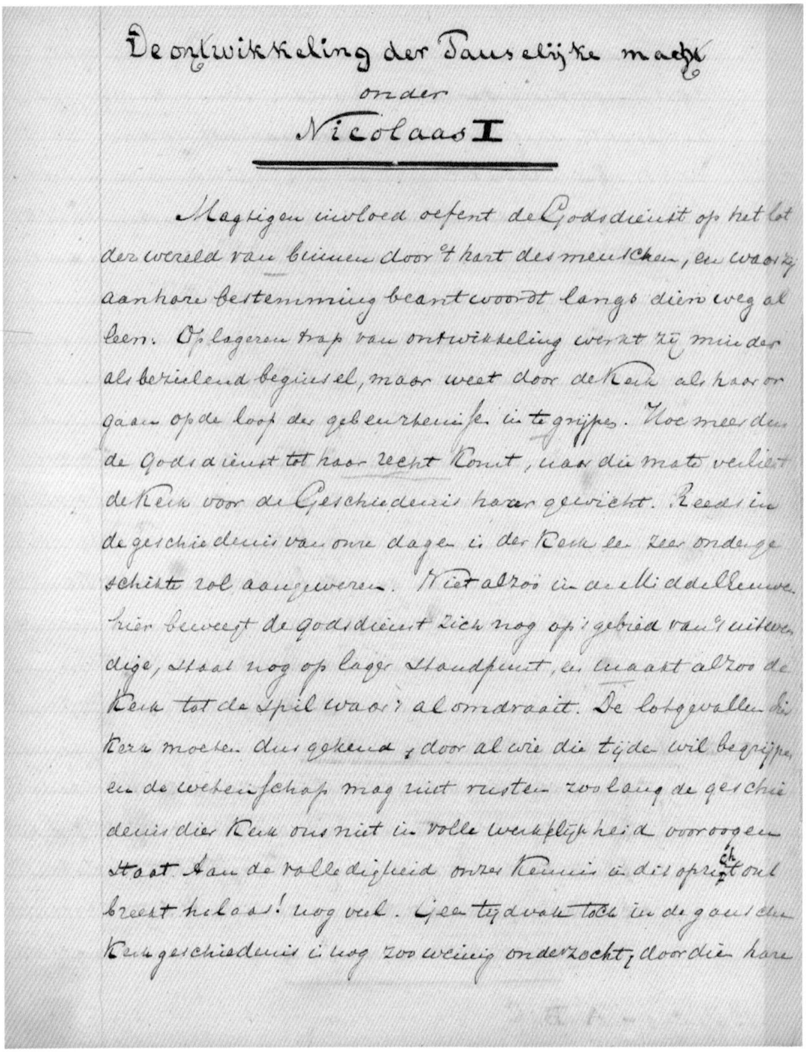
De ontwikkeling der Pauselijke magt
onder
Nicolaas I

Magtigen invloed oefent de Godsdienst op het lot der wereld van binnen door 't hart des menschen, en waar zij aan hare bestemming beantwoordt langs dien weg al leen. Op lageren trap van ontwikkeling werkt zij minder als bezielend beginsel, maar weet door de Kerk als haar orgaan op de loop der gebeurtenissen in te grijpen. Hoe meer den de Godsdienst tot haar regt komt, naar die mate verliest de Kerk voor de Geschiedenis haar gewicht. Reeds in de geschiedenis van onze dagen is der Kerk een zeer ondergeschikte rol aangewezen. Niet alzoo in de Middeleeuwen, hier beweegt de godsdienst zich nog op 't gebied van 't uitwendige, staat nog op lager standpunt, en maakt alzoo de Kerk tot de spil waarom 't al omdraait. De lotgevallen dier Kerk moeten dus gekend, door al wie die tijden wil begrijpen, en de wetenschap mag niet rusten zoolang de geschiedenis dier Kerk ons niet in volle werkelijkheid voor oogen staat. Aan de volledigheid onzer kennis in dit opzicht ontbreekt helaas! nog veel. Geen tijdvak toch in de gansche Kerkgeschiedenis is nog zoo weinig onderzocht, doordien hare

After earning his Bachelor of Arts, on 24 November 1858 Kuyper enrolled as a student of theology, which was a popular study in those days. Of the 487 students in Leiden in 1858/1859, 162 studied theology. In January 1859 Kuyper submitted a master's thesis entitled "The Development of Papal Power under Nicolas I," which, surprisingly enough, he had written for the linguist Matthias de Vries, and not for the church historian N. C. Kist. Kuyper had little regard for the latter. In his lengthy thesis (150 pages), Kuyper also discussed the role of the church in society and the relationship between church and state. He understood the domineering nature of the ninth-century pope. Given Kuyper's later attitude in church matters, the thesis contains some surprises, including this: "He, Pope Nicholas, was the power that had to keep the church under control, had to force it to promote the happiness of mankind. As the head of Christ's church, he had to cripple every power that thwarted it."

Walter Damry

Engagement photograph of Johanna Hendrika Schaay, September 1858.

In the summer of 1858 Abraham Kuyper met his future wife Johanna Hendrika Schaay, daughter of the Rotterdam stockbroker Jan Hendrik Schaay and Henriëtte Sophie Susanne Leopold. In 1917 Kuyper's youngest sister, Mrs. Rammelman Elsevier-Kuyper, described to her nephews and nieces how the two had met: "At the age of sixteen, your mother, Johanna Schaay, came to stay with her Uncle Verhoef, who owned a grocery store in Oegstgeest; her aunt, who lived in Leiden and who visited my parents frequently, came with Miss Schaay to have a drink at our place during the week of the fair; your mother was a beautiful, very charming girl. She soon developed a friendship with Aunt Kee and came to stay with us a month later, wearing long dresses for the first time. She looked most lovely and captured all hearts by storm. No wonder that the young student could not resist so much charm, and soon the engagement was a fact."

The first letter Abraham Kuyper wrote to his fiancée Johanna Schaay, September 1858. On 14 September 1858 Bram proposed to the sixteen-year-old Johanna, and on 27 September her parents approved of the engagement — on the condition that it would only be announced after Johanna's confession of faith at Easter, 1859. However, the joyful news could not be kept a secret for long.

On 10 November 1858 Johanna wrote to Bram: "Here the news is spreading like wildfire; there is only one family Mother did not tell, and they came to congratulate us

yesterday. My old man did not comment on the publicity in Leiden, but he was hardly in a position to do so, as he had given us permission to take a walk together." Bram answered on 12 November: "The publicity of the Schaay-Kuyper engagement in Leiden is going *de plus fort en plus fort.* Wednesday night I was visiting Prof. Scholten for the customary cup of tea . . . and there, surrounded by a great number of unknown fools, was congratulated about you by the great man himself. By last night everybody knew; they did not congratulate me but talked about it as a *fait accompli et annoncé.* And even in Rotterdam the news has spread. Boy oh boy, it is going well!"

Jan Hendrik Schaay (1802-1863), Johanna Schaay's father, was not an easy gentleman to get along with, keeping unrelenting discipline over his underage daughter, and not easily persuaded by his future son-in-law.

Johanna Schaay to her fiancé, September 1859: "Father called you a headstrong person . . . [saying] that you acted positively against his wishes and then managed to explain matters in such a way that in the end you were right." Kuyper's own father called him an *"animal disputant,"* because he liked to be difficult.

Henriëtte Sophie Susanna Schaay-Leopold (1809-1882), Kuyper's mother-in-law.

Abraham Kuyper wanted his young fiancée to develop herself, because by marriage she would move from "a commercial background into academic circles." The hundreds of letters he wrote during their engagement (1858-1863) are full of admonitions and advice. Already in one of his first letters, dated 18 October 1858, he wrote: "If I enumerated all the grammatical mistakes you make in your letters I would frighten you — but alas, that's an obstacle for all young girls. When you are here again we shall go over them together; it's easier that way."

A characteristic fragment from the letter of 2 December 1860: "But equally sacred to me is the obligation to point out to you, with love but in all seriousness, the failings you innocently confess in self-delusion. Jo! Is my guidance, at least in this area, worth no more to you? Should you be so cruel as to tell me that I *hurt your feelings* when all I do is to try to elevate you from the position in which you were placed by your education and for which you are really too good? Withdraw; retract that cruel word that you cannot mean. . . . It sounds sad to me when I hear the girl I love like my own soul make a fuss about a work by Sue, while about Shakespeare I hear her say: I don't like it. Just reflect awhile on what can be said of such taste. Is this one thing not proof enough that you are still greatly lacking in education?"

The French reformer John Calvin, 1509-1564.

From April 1859 until April 1860 Kuyper worked on an essay contest organized by the University of Groningen, in which a comparison had to be made between the ecclesiology of John Calvin and the Polish reformer John à Lasco. Kuyper's attention had been drawn to this contest by his tutor De Vries, who knew from experience that winning an academic prize could be a promising start to a scholarly career.

In his autobiographical work *Confidentie (Confidential,* 1873) Kuyper wrote that he wanted to give up the contest at first because the works of à Lasco were hard to find. At the advice of De Vries, however, he turned to the latter's father, the learned minister Abraham de Vries (1773-1862), who turned out to have a collection of Lasciana at his disposal "richer than any library possessed or still possesses in all of Europe." To Kuyper, this surprising discovery was a sign from God: "Seriously, one must be overcome by such a surprise during one's own struggles in life to know what it means to meet with one of God's miracles on one's life-path. . . . Need I add that because of this, my work on this contest took on a sacred and hallowed character that had been lacking in my studies so far?"

The Polish reformer John à Lasco (1499-1560) led a roving life, serving as pastor in the refugee-churches in England and on the continent. Many of à Lasco's works were destroyed by the Jesuits.

In working on the Groningen competition, Kuyper also met the internationally famous church historian and exegete Eduard Reuss (1804-1891), professor at Strasburg. Reuss helped him obtain French literature about Calvin and personally transcribed a work for him by à Lasco, which was kept in the Strasburg city library and could not be lent out. In return Kuyper sent Reuss extensive information for his bibliography of editions of the Greek New Testament.

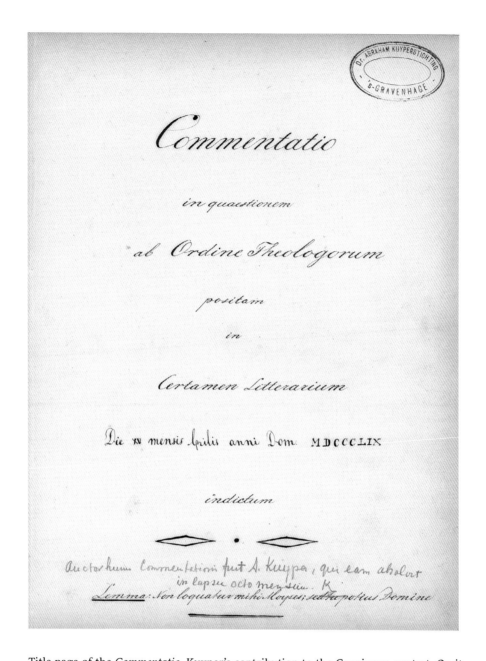

Commentatio

in quaestionem

ab Ordine Theologorum

positam

in

Certamen Litterarium

Die xv mensis Aprilis anni Dom. MDCCCLIX

indictum

◇ • ◇

Auctor hujus Commentationis fuit A. Kuijpa, qui eam absolvit in lapsu octo mensium. K.
Lemma: Non loquatur mihi Moyses; sed potius Domine

Title page of the *Commentatio*, Kuyper's contribution to the Groningen contest. On it Kuyper noted that it had taken him eight months to write. To make a fair copy of the Latin manuscript, of which the text alone (excluding footnotes) ran to 267 pages, took several months because the copyist had difficulty reading Kuyper's handwriting. The manuscript was submitted on 4 April 1860, one week before the due date.

On 15 June 1860, Kuyper received word from W. Muurling (1805-1882), dean of the theological faculty in Groningen, that Kuyper's "outstanding work" had been awarded a gold medal.

Certificate that went with the gold medal of the Groningen competition. Kuyper, having undergone the necessary examination by the faculty, received it in Groningen on 11 October 1860. On that same day Kuyper's future ally, the Hon. A. F. de Savornin Lohman, received an honorable mention for his answer in the contest concerning legal studies.

Abraham Kuyper to his fiancée, 11 October 1860: "This morning I received my medal; it is very beautiful and worth 96 guilders. The judgment of the faculty was very good, as good as I dared to hope for. Yesterday's examination went well, although they gave me a hard time by asking about the controversial theological issues that exist between Leiden and Groningen. Yesterday night I had supper with Prof. Hofstede de Groot, which was rather difficult too, but came off well. After the award we went to the university senate, where all the curators and professors were present. Oh! If only you could have been with me today, that would have been pure bliss."

In 1865, when he was a minister in Beesd, Kuyper sold the gold medal for 121 guilders. He promised his wife that he would use it to buy a silver tea set, but according to one biographer it was probably used to purchase a rare à Lasco edition.

The Dutch writer and freethinker Multatuli (pseudonym of Eduard Douwes Dekker, 1820-1887), who in his novel *Max Havelaar* expressed sharp criticism of the colonial administration in the Dutch East Indies. Kuyper gave the book to his future in-laws for the feast of St. Nicholas. As appears from a letter Jo wrote, the present was well received, so that on 10 December 1860 Bram was able to write back: "That *Max Havelaar* gave satisfaction genuinely pleases me. You should certainly read it yourself, my dear girl! But not too hastily, as the style is beautiful."

In later years Kuyper no longer wanted to have anything to do with Multatuli, because he "deprived my only brother, who gave his life in the Dutch East Indies for his country, of his faith." Herman Kuyper, born on 2 October 1843 in Middelburg, served in the military in the Dutch East Indies, where he died on 24 April 1874.

Kuyper as a student, around 1860.

In writing his thorough and well-documented *Commentatio,* even though he had only started to study theology in the autumn of 1858, Kuyper accomplished an impressive feat. It radically changed his vision on the position of the church. In his thesis about Nicholas I he had still assumed that the role of the church in society would steadily decline because it had for the greater part fulfilled its historic task of developing humanity. However, in the *Commentatio* he emphasized the increasing importance of the church. In doing so, Kuyper developed a vision of the church that was original in many ways. As biographer Jasper Vree wrote, "What the twenty-two-year-old now had in mind, following Schlei-ermacher, was a church in which the pivotal role was reserved not for the institution but for the organism of believers led by the Spirit of Christ: that would conquer the world for God. Unlike most of the established churches, his ideal church was social, democratic, and financially independent of the state. Moreover, it originated from below, from the local congregation. Female members of the congregation also counted: they had both suffrage and — in the capacity of deaconess — responsibility. . . . As this church came to function better, the role of the state could become smaller."

His intensive studies for the *Commentatio* took a heavy toll. Kuyper had to interrupt his studies from February through July of 1861, as the ambitious and diligent student had strained his nervous system to the limit during the preceding years. For therapy during this period, he constructed a wooden model of a sailboat, which he named after his fiancée. During his illness Kuyper was allowed to stay with Johanna's family for a couple of months. The respite concluded with a journey to Germany with the Schaay family.

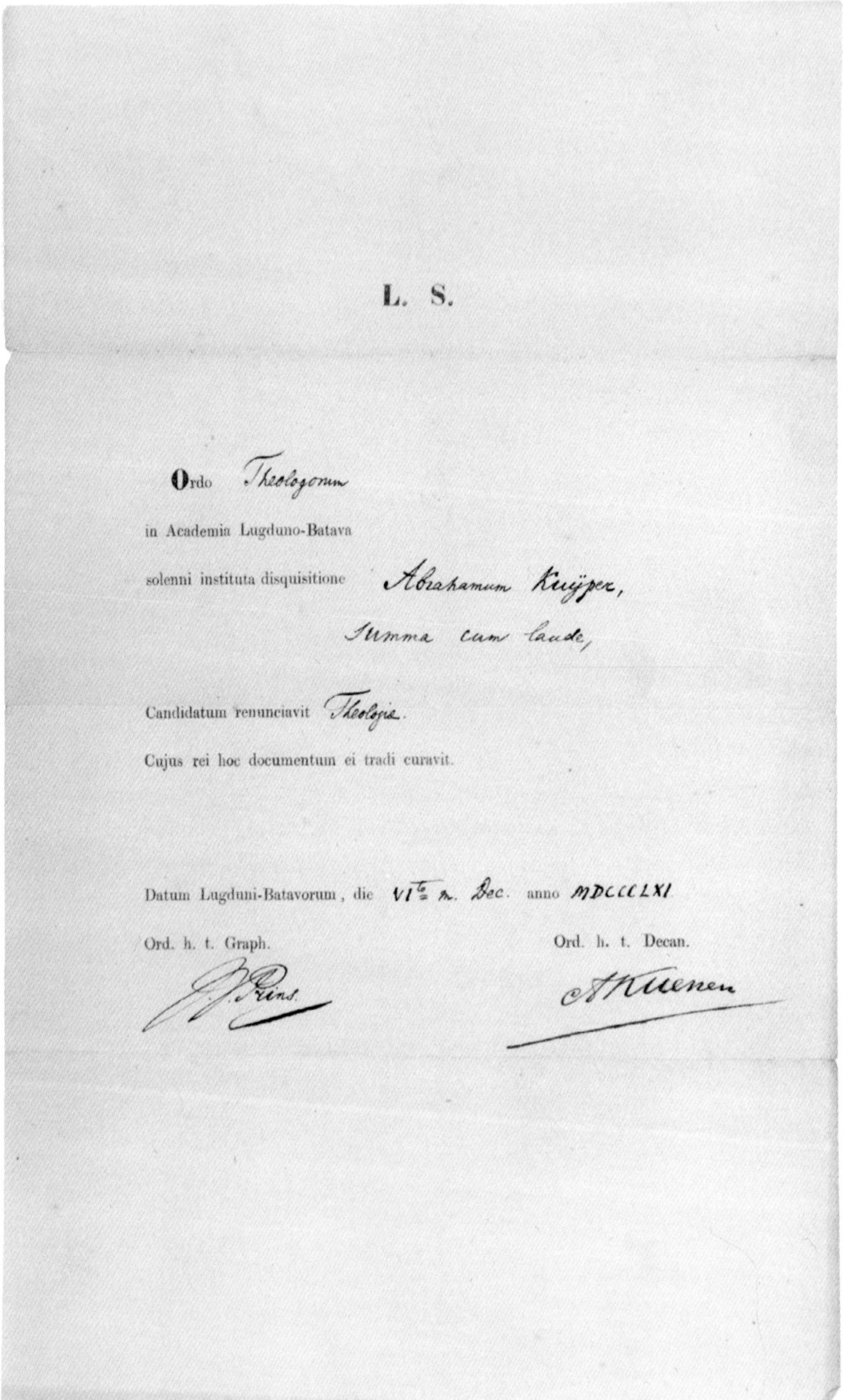

L. S.

Ordo *Theologorum*

in Academia Lugduno-Batava

solenni instituta disquisitione   *Abrahamum Kuyper,*

                    Summa cum laude,

Candidatum renunciavit *Theologia.*

Cujus rei hoc documentum ei tradi curavit.

Datum Lugduni-Batavorum, die *VI^{ta} m. Dec.* anno *MDCCCLXI*

Ord. h. t. Graph.   Ord. h. t. Decan.

J. Prins.   *A. Kuenen*

After his recovery Kuyper was able to resume his studies. On 6 December 1861 he took the qualifying examination in theology. Being very ambitious, he was worried beforehand that a less favorable *judicium* would damage his reputation as a prize-winner, but to his satisfaction he was again awarded a *summa cum laude*.

Kuyper to his fiancée, 6 February 1862: "A dream of undisturbed pleasure, pleasure through activity, Jo! That's what I expect of the future. I am not a fanatic, my dear girl, but I live in the atmosphere of the ideal. Oh, do the same; that's how to enjoy life to the full! It's a bitter disappointment when cold reality wakes us out of that dream, but nevertheless I enjoy the dream. Believe this: love for the ideal gives so much strength."

Kuyper gave his first probation sermon as a candidate in theology at the Baptist church in Leiden, on 11 January 1862; the invocation is shown above. On 7 May 1862 Kuyper took the candidate examination for the Provincial Church Administration of South Holland and was admitted to the ministry. At that point he was eligible to receive a call as minister, but he would have to wait for well over a year before he was called. Meanwhile, in many places where he gave "trial sermons," people preferred a more orthodox minister, something Kuyper had not yet become. As he wrote to his fiancée on 7 December 1862: "Oh, Jo! It's so tedious — wherever I go, all I hear are references to an orthodox minister, and not being one myself, I feel so dejected."

While Kuyper prepared himself for life at the parsonage, his fiancée presented him with a book that deeply impressed him: *The Heir of Redclyffe,* by the English novelist Charlotte Mary Yonge (1828-1901). She belonged to the circle of the Oxford Movement, the nineteenth-century high-church reformation movement within the Church of England. Later in *Confidentie* (1873) Kuyper wrote that the novel "for me, although not having equal value, ranks next to the Bible in significance." He felt a strong affinity for one of the characters, the confident Philip, who came to see the error of his ways; but he was also deeply moved by the image of the Church of England as described in this book: the mother church in which the faithful found a sense of security. "Such a church I never saw or knew. Oh, to have such a church, 'a mother who guides our steps from our youth!' It became the thirst of my life."

Abraham Kuyper at his promotion to doctor of theology. On 20 September 1862 Kuyper rounded off his theological studies by defending a dissertation about the ecclesiology of Calvin and à Lasco. For this dissertation, which included the historical part of his (unpublished) treatise for the Groningen competition (the *Commentatio*), Kuyper received the judicium *summa cum laude.*

The complete text of the *Commentatio* was not published until 2005, with an English preface by Jasper Vree and Johan Zwaan.

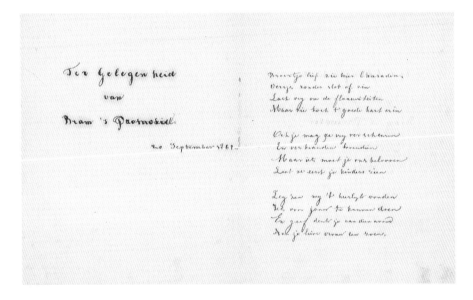

Abraham Kuyper's promotional certificate, with the signatures of his supervisor J. H. Scholten, P. L. Rijke (rector), J. J. Prins (secretary), W. A. van Hengel, A. Kuenen, and L. W. E. Rauwenhoff.

Verse by Abraham Kuyper's sisters on the occasion of his doctorate.

As he had announced in the preface to his dissertation, Kuyper had plans to continue his church history studies. As early as 22 September 1862, the young and promising doctor signed a contract with the famous publishers Martinus Nijhoff (The Hague) and Frederik Muller (Amsterdam) for the publication of à Lasco's collected works, a biography of à Lasco, and the history of the "churches under the Cross," the oldest Reformed churches in and around the Netherlands. Kuyper did not write the last two books, because within a few years his church history research was pushed aside to make way for his ecclesiastical and political activities.

As a first downpayment, the publishers printed 400 copies of Kuyper's dissertation free of charge. According to the contract, Kuyper was to receive 350 guilders and fifteen presentation copies for the publication of à Lasco's *Opera Omnia*.

Church Pastor, 1863-1874

In addition to his pastoral duties in Beesd (1863-1867), Kuyper continued with his church history studies by collecting texts and letters for a publication of works by à Lasco. To that end he kept in touch with all the important European libraries and regularly traveled abroad to do research. In the spring of 1866 Kuyper's two-volume publication of the *Opera* by à Lasco was published, which established his name in academic circles.

In Beesd, Kuyper turned away from the rationalistic movement in theology and converted to Calvinist orthodoxy. With its melancholy nature and strict logic, Calvinism answered the deepest needs of his sensitive and restless personality. Romantic in nature, with an inclination towards the extreme and the ideal, he sought and found in Calvinism "the power of the absolute," which would be a guiding principle in his life henceforth.

After his conversion Kuyper joined the Dutch Anti-Revolutionary movement, which rejected the humanistic and secular principles of the French Revolution and under the leadership of Guillaume Groen van Prinsterer opposed Liberal domination in both church and politics. As early as 1867 Kuyper involved himself in the struggle by publishing a brochure in which he championed the democratization of church suffrage and openly came down on the side of the orthodox movement within the Dutch Reformed Church. That same year he became a minister in Utrecht, and in 1870 in Amsterdam. It was a quick rise within the informal hierarchy of the Dutch Reformed Church to the top rung of important city congregations, the highest posts a minister could achieve at that time in the church.

In Utrecht and Amsterdam Kuyper passionately threw himself into the church struggle. He argued for the maintenance of the classical Reformed creeds and against the Dutch Reformed Church's centralized structure of government, which he believed paralyzed church life and hindered necessary reforms.

From the outset Kuyper singlemindedly sought confrontations, not only against the Modernist movement but also with other orthodox groups, which he accused of being "neither this nor that," "conservative," or "disloyal." In particular he took the moderate-orthodox or "ethic-irenical" movement to task. In numerous brochures and eventually in the church weekly *De Heraut*, Kuyper attacked his opponents, who in turn complained about his fierce and "demagogic" way of doing battle.

In addition to his church activities, Kuyper got involved in the "school question," an important point of contest for the Anti-Revolutionaries after the Education Act of 1857 made state elementary schools more or less religiously neutral in character. The Anti-Revolutionaries fought for the establishment of doctrinally orthodox Christian schools.

On this point Kuyper chose a position based on principle, but with polarizing results. In Utrecht in 1869 it led to a rift with the moderate-orthodox movement, which did not want to forfeit church influence on public education entirely, while Kuyper and Groen van Prinsterer wanted to expose state schools as clearly *neutral* schools, in order to make room for the extension of Christian education.

Through the school struggle Kuyper entered into politics. As early as May 1871 he was put forward as a candidate for the second chamber, but not elected. The following year he was involved in the foundation of the Anti-School-Law Union, which soon started coordinating election campaigns for the Anti-Revolutionaries. The most important event for the cause was the foundation in 1872 of the national Anti-Revolutionary daily newspaper *De Standaard*, of which Kuyper (then still a church minister) took political leadership. His election as a member of the second chamber in January 1874 completed his transition into politics. From then on Kuyper was a politician first and foremost, although he remained tirelessly involved in church matters.

Written call from the Dutch Reformed parish of Beesd, "approved" by the lord of the manor of Beesd, O. W. A. Graaf (Count) van Bylandt van Mariënweerd.

On Good Friday, 3 April 1863, Kuyper preached in Beesd in the Betuwe region, and by 6 April the consistory had sent a promise of the call, which was officially confirmed on 8 June 1863. Having given sermons all over the country for a year, Kuyper gladly accepted the call. Moreover, it offered a handsome salary. In addition to a small allowance granted by the government, he received an annual sum of 2400 guilders from "the rented lands of the parsonage."

S. S. ———

De kerkeraad der Hervormd Gemeente te Beesd, heden
wettig bijeengekomen ter zake van de beroeping van eenen
Herder en Leeraar naar de kerkelijke verordeningen;
Gezien de acte van agreatie van den Hooggeboren Heer
Graaf van Bijlandt van Mariënwaerdt;

Heeft goedgevonden te beroepen, gelijk hij beroept bij deze
tot Herder en Leeraar dezer Gemeente den Eerwaarden Heer
Abraham Kuyper, Theol. Doctor en Candidaat tot den H.
dienst bij het provinciaal kerkbestuur van Zuid Holland,
en zulks op zoodanig tractement en zoodanige emolumenten
als aan deze Standplaats verbonden en in anexe opgave
vermeld zijn,

De kerkeraad deze beroeping ter kennis van den Eerwaarden
Heer Abraham Kuyper brengende, verlangt dat hij deze
beroeping, geagreerd door den Hooggeboren Heer Graaf
van Bijlandt van Mariënwaerdt, bereidvaardig aanneme,
en na de approbatie van het daartoe bevoegde kerkelijk
gezag, en het noodige bewijs van wege den Koning ten aan
zien der gelden van 's lands wege aan de Standplaats
verbonden verkregen te hebben, ten spoedigste tot deze gemeente overkome, om door leer en voorbeeld, bestuur en
opzigt, alles te doen wat een Herder en Leeraar, overeen
komstig Gods Heilig woord, volgens de verordeningen der
Nederlandsche Hervormde Kerk betaamt; Inzonderheid
door het verkondigen van het Evangelie en de bedie
ning van den H. Doop en van het H. Avondmaal op de
bij de Gemeente vastgestelde tijden; het verhooren der kran
ken; het bezoeken der gemeente leden aan hunne huizen
en door het onderwijzen van de Bijbelsche en kerke
lijke geschiedenis en van de geloofs en zedeleer van de
Christelijke Godsdienst in Catechisatien, gedurende het
gansche jaar wekelijks te houden; ———

Terugzij

The Dutch Reformed parsonage on the Voorstraat in Beesd.

    With the prospect of a secure social position, Kuyper's marriage to Johanna Schaay could now also be solemnized. It took place on 1 July 1863 in Warmond, the place of residence of the Schaay family. Johanna's father could not attend the ceremony due to a serious illness but had expressed the wish that the marriage should be celebrated while he was still alive. He died in Warmond on 6 July.

The Dutch Reformed Church of Beesd with its late-Gothic tower.

    On 9 August 1863 Abraham Kuyper was installed by his father during the morning service as a minister in Beesd. In the evening Kuyper gave his inaugural sermon based on 1 John 1:7: "But if we walk in the light, as He is in the light, we have fellowship with one another."

Mariënwaerd House, where O. W. A. Graaf (Count) van Bylandt van Mariënweerd (1794-1882) lived. He had been the church warden for almost forty years and, as lord of the village, traditionally had great influence. The mayor of Beesd, J. W. F. Snethlage, himself a descendant of an old family of Dutch Reformed ministers, also served as the count's bailiff.

There were regular disputes between Kuyper and van Bylandt, because the latter was not used to being contradicted. For his part, Kuyper did not always handle things tactfully, and with his commanding personality sometimes presented the count with a *fait accompli* instead of negotiating with him first.

Kuyper as a minister in Beesd around 1865.

Johanna Kuyper as a young minister's wife. In Beesd their two eldest children were born: Herman Huber on 22 July 1864 after a difficult delivery, and Jan Hendrik Frederik on 12 February 1866.

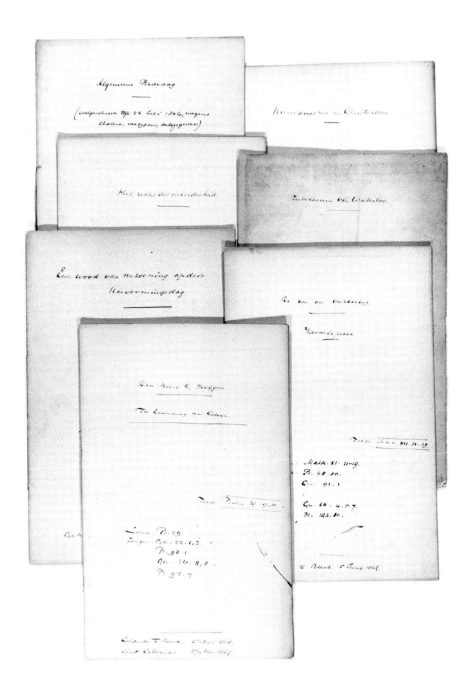

A number of Kuyper's sermons delivered in Beesd: "General Day of Prayer Called for on 22 July 1866 Owing to Cholera, Cattle-Typhoid, and Threat of War"; "Humanism and Christianity"; "The Rights of the Minority"; "Waterloo Jubilee"; "A Word of Reconciliation on Reformation Day"; "The Hour of Temptation"; and "Rest in the Lord: In memory of Calvin." At first Kuyper wrote his sermons out in full; later on he improvised on the basis of a few points.

As a minister in Beesd Kuyper continued to collect works and letters for his two-volume
à Lasco publication. For that purpose Kuyper kept in touch with all the important European libraries and regularly travelled abroad to do research, using copies of his dissertation as calling cards. The photograph shows a circular by Kuyper dated March 1863,
addressed to libraries and archives with a request to report works and letters of à Lasco
that they held.

First letter to Kuyper from the Anti-Revolutionary leader Guillaume Groen van Prinsterer, director of the Royal-House Archives, 14 October 1864. Kuyper had called on Groen's aid in an attempt to borrow one of à Lasco's manuscripts from the secret archive at Koningsberg in order to copy it. Earlier, the Prime Minister of Prussia, Otto von Bismarck, had personally given permission for consultation. Groen declared himself willing to help. Kuyper thanked him with the following words: "For a country parson in an out-of-the-way place, it's extremely difficult to exert the necessary pressure for such an enterprise."

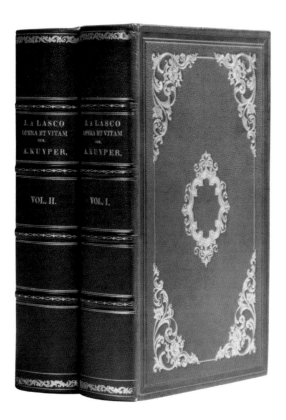

In March 1866 Kuyper's publication of à Lasco's *Opera* was published in two volumes with a total of 1540 pages, including an introduction of 120 pages. The work on the publication was completed on 9 December 1865.

The photograph shows the deluxe edition of the *Opera*, offered by Kuyper with a cover letter dated 30 April 1866 to George V, King of Hanover, out of gratitude for the latter's help in East Frisia (then part of the Kingdom of Hanover; on October 1866 the kingdom was annexed by Prussia) during his research. The work is now kept in the Johannes à Lasco Library in Emden. In the catalogue of the great à Lasco exhibition at Emden in 1999, the *Opera* elicited the following comment: "It remains the most important collection of source material with regard to à Lasco, containing almost all of the Works and more than 120 letters written by him."

Kuyper's publication of à Lasco's work established his name in academic circles and was received with much acclaim by the church press. R. J. Fruin, who had meantime been appointed professor of Dutch history at Leiden, wrote a letter to his former pupil on 20 March 1866 in which he thanked him for sending him the *Opera*: "Especially in collecting your materials you have shown unusual perseverance and courage, which are rewarded and justified by the result. . . . Even for me, merely a spectator, it is a pleasure to see how the opuscula and the opera, which were hidden in all kinds of libraries from Petersburg to Dublin, were brought together and are now united in your publication."

Kuyper's turn to orthodoxy, which would so influence the rest of his life, came about in Beesd. Having familiarized himself with the works of Calvin and à Lasco through his studies in church history, he now discovered as a young minister that Calvin's theology was still alive among the laborers and farmers of Beesd. Kuyper wrote in *Confidentie* (1873): "Calvin still existed, however misshapen, in those simple laborers, who had hardly even heard of his name, and Calvin had taught in such a way that people, centuries after his death in a foreign country, in a remote forgotten corner, in a small room with a flagstone floor, with a common laborer's mind, still understood him. For that riddle there was only one solution. . . . *Calvin had established a church* and he had by *this consistent church structure* bestowed blessing and peace in properly disposed minds."

An important part in his conversion was played by a young woman, Pietje Baltus (1830-1914), who at first refused to talk to the new minister, and in doing so made him think. The photograph shows her in later life. On the occasion of her death Kuyper wrote in *De Standaard* of 30 March 1914: "Even when Dr. Kuyper had become a minister, she wanted nothing to do with him. This would just be another one of those half-grown, half-committed, half-baked, half-winged church wreckers. In short, she did not want anything to do with him. And this was understandable, in the sense that Dr. Kuyper was known as 'orthodox' at the time of his arrival in Beesd, but in a way that was so strongly Ethical that he tended to be anti-Reformed. All the same, they did meet, and this meeting brought about such a change in Dr. Kuyper's conviction that he saw at once *the power of the absolute* in this woman, and this made him break with all half-heartedness. He then made the acquaintance of the spiritual legacy of the fathers. [The Canons of] Dort, which had first repelled him, now attracted him. He caught rays of light from Calvin. That simple woman had bent the line of his life from a *halfway* position to a *whole* one, and it consistently remained Dr. Kuyper's grateful confession that in meeting her he had, for the first time, been brought to where he now felt he had to be."

The theologian and cultural philosopher Dr. Allard Pierson (1831-1896), Walloon clergyman and in later life professor at Heidelberg and Amsterdam.

Kuyper's conversion to orthodoxy was advanced not only through his contacts
with the humble believers of Beesd, as he himself later suggested in his romanticized
version in *Confidentie*. He was also greatly impressed by the pamphlet *Dr. Pierson in His
Last Parish* of 17 October 1865, in which the well-known minister from Rotterdam, Allard Pierson, explained his decision to leave the ministry: increasingly he regarded the
church as an obstacle for the development of humanity. In stating this, he directly contradicted the vision that Kuyper had set down in the *Commentatio*. From the pulpit in
Beesd in the months that followed, Kuyper continually addressed the issues that Pierson
had raised and pointed out the importance of the church for modern society.

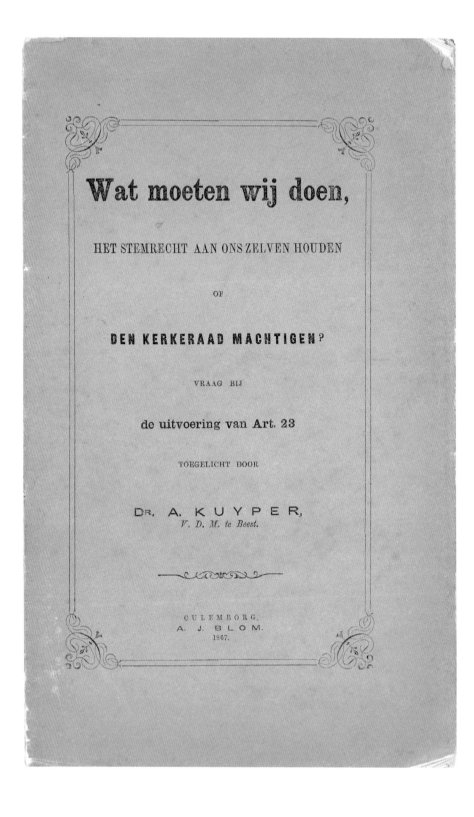

Wat moeten wij doen,

HET STEMRECHT AAN ONS ZELVEN HOUDEN

OF

DEN KERKERAAD MACHTIGEN?

VRAAG BIJ

de uitvoering van Art. 23

TOEGELICHT DOOR

Dr. A. KUYPER,
V. D. M. te Beest.

CULEMBORG,
A. J. BLOM.
1867.

In April 1867 the publisher Blom in Culemborg published Abraham Kuyper's first church pamphlet, in which he openly came down on the side of the orthodox movement in the Netherlands Reformed Church. The pamphlet discussed the pressing question of church suffrage, which was of great importance in the governance of local Netherlands Reformed congregations. On 1 March 1867 the "New Synodical Regulation for the Appointment of Elders and Deacons and Calling of Ministers by the Male Members of the Congregation" came into effect, which elaborated on Article 23 of the Church Regulations of 1852. This article stipulated that henceforth church officers might be elected by the male members of the congregation, instead of by self-perpetuating elite boards.

Kuyper immediately recognized that the new regulation could be used to weaken the ecclesiastical establishment. Although he believed that the suffrage of Article 23 was questionable on principle ("general suffrage in the spirit of Article 23 is the crown of modern individualism, the modern idea of the state transplanted to the terrain of the church"), he welcomed it as a means for choosing orthodox consistories and forcing "illegal" church boards to abdicate.

The publication of Kuyper's pamphlet attracted much attention in church circles and led to closer ties with Groen van Prinsterer, who praised the work as "the most remarkable thing to see the light of day on this burning question."

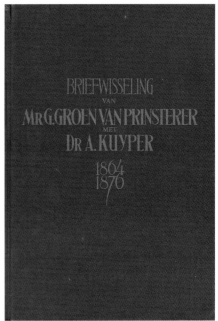

Guillaume Groen van Prinsterer (1801-1876), leading man of the Réveil (a 19th-century Protestant spiritual awakening) and leader of the Anti-Revolutionary or Christian-Historical movement. After the constitutional revision of 1848 Groen opposed in Parliament, and further afield, the dominance of the Liberals under J. R. Thorbecke's leadership and developed a political program on which Kuyper could later build. Groen exerted his greatest influence through his numerous political, church, and historical works, with which he managed to reach "the people behind the voters," the "little people" who would later become the backbone of the Anti-Revolutionary Party.

The edition of the *Briefwisseling (Correspondence)* between Groen van Prinsterer and Kuyper presented on the occasion of the Kuyper commemoration in 1937. Kuyper was to work closely with Groen van Prinsterer until Groen's death in 1876. Although the initial contact between Groen and Kuyper occured in 1864 in connection with Kuyper's à Lasco publication, the correspondence really got under way in 1867 after Kuyper published his pamphlet on Article 23. In spite of all the differences of opinion between the patrician Groen and the more populist Kuyper, publicly they pulled together because, as Groen aptly put it, "When our friends turn on each other with drawn swords, the Philistine's victory is ensured."

Kuyper as a minister in Utrecht, around 1868.

After the publication of the pamphlet on Article 23 brought Kuyper to their attention, the orthodox consistory of Utrecht issued a call to Kuyper in June 1867. Kuyper accepted it with a sense of relief. He was attracted by the prospect of becoming a minister in a university town that was also one of the strategic sites of church life at the time, but he had also outgrown Beesd in a number of ways. In his farewell sermon there on 3 November 1867, he pointed out that "from the moment that I fully associated myself with the wonderful orthodox plenitude of the Gospel, I noticed that from more than one quarter there developed a dislike of me that came close to hatred and condemned my endeavors, because I looked for rather than avoided conflict where my principles were concerned, and always fought to the end, without pulling punches, out of a sense of duty."

The literary figure Nicolaas Beets, minister in Utrecht, proved to be pleased with Kuyper's "bold decision" to answer the call to Utrecht: "You took this decision with the Lord. He will not hide His approval — of that I am sure."

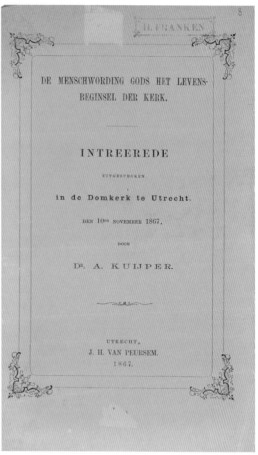

A bust of Nicolaas Beets (1814-1903), made by his son Cornelis Beets. He owed his national renown as a literary figure to the *Camera Obscura*, a collection of realistic and mildly ironic sketches about Dutch bourgeois life of his time, which he had written as a young man and published in 1839 under the pseudonym Hildebrand. After entering into the ministry, he wrote mainly edifying poems. Beets was professor of theology at Utrecht from 1874 to 1884.

Kuyper's introductory sermon as a minister in Utrecht, 10 November 1867. During his years in Utrecht, Kuyper wholeheartedly threw himself into ecclesiastical conflict. In his introductory address he spoke prophetic words: "The parting of the ways has come, and the only remaining question concerns the ruin of the once-beautiful church of our fathers, upon which our opponents, through our own fault, now have as much claim as we. . . . We must face the bitter truth that the church that was built with the blood of our fathers is lost to us forever if our opponent believes that maintaining his claim to ownership is worth the effort. . . . In any case, whether we prepare to restore the church or establish a new church, we have been called to build."

The Domtoren, as seen from the Mariaplaats in Utrecht, the highest church tower (110 meters) in the Netherlands. In the Middle Ages the city was the seat of the Archbishop of Utrecht. During the Republic, Utrecht with its university (founded in 1636) became an important center for orthodox Calvinism. In the nineteenth century the theology faculty in Utrecht was known as orthodox, while the faculty in Leiden became known for its Modernist orientation, with the faculty in Groningen, or "Groningen School," being identified with a position between the two.

STATUTEN

DER

„MARNIX-VEREENIGING"

opgericht te Utrecht 1 April 1868.

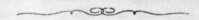

ART. 1.

Er is te Utrecht een Vereeniging gevestigd voor de uitgave van de oudste oorkonden van de geschiedenis der Nederlandsche Hervorming. Zij draagt den naam van **Marnix-Vereeniging.**

ART. 2.

Lid der Vereeniging is ieder, die ten haren behoeve, vóór den 1sten Juli van elk jaar, bij haar Thesaurier een contributie van *f* 10.— voldaan heeft. Het lidmaatschap is verbindend tot wederopzegging toe.

ART. 3.

Zij treedt in werking zoodra het getal harer leden tot 250 geklommen is.

ART. 4.

Zij heeft een bestuur van vijf leden, waarvan één Bestuurder-Directeur, die eenmaal des jaars (in de maand Januari), en voorts zoo vaak hem dit noodig dunkt, het advies zijner medebestuurders inroept. Een door bestuurders gekozen Secretaris-Thesaurier voert de correspondentie en het geldelijk beheer en doet op de jaarlijksche bestuurs-vergadering rekenschap.

Statutes of the Marnix Society, 1 April 1868.

Kuyper was the driving force behind the foundation of the Marnix Society "for the publication of the oldest testimonies of the history of the Dutch Reformation." From 1868 until 1874 he was the chairman of this society, which was named after the Calvinist writer and politician Philips van Marnix, lord of Sint-Aldegonde (1540-1598). In 1871 Kuyper himself published the society's first volume: *The Protocols of the Consistory of the Dutch Congregation in London, 1569-1571.*

171

N. 23.   **1868.**

PREDIKBEURTEN

BIJ DE GEREFORMEERDE GEMEENTE TE UTRECHT.

Voormiddag ten half 10. Namiddag 2. 's Avonds half 6 Ure.

OCTOBER.

Z. M. D. W. D. V. Z.
4. 5. 6. 7. 8. 9. 10.

EERSTE AVONDMAAL.

ten 9 Ure,

in de DOM- JANS- en NICOLAI-KERK.

DE 37. ZONDAG

DOM-KERK.

Voormiddag BERVOETS.
's Avonds KUYPER.
Nabetrachting op het H. Avondmaal.

JANS-KERK.

Voormiddag BÖSKEN.

JACOBI-KERK.

Voormiddag FELIX.
Namiddag SCHIJVLIET.

BUUR-KERK.

Voormiddag Garnizoen SCHIJVLIET.
Half twaalf ure ONDERWIJZ. G.

NICOLAI-KERK.

Voormiddag VAN HOOGSTRATEN.
Namiddag BERVOETS.
Nabetrachting op het H. Avondmaal.

Maandag Avond, ten zeven Ure.
Bedestond voor de Uitbreiding van het Evangelie.
WALE-KERK S. ULFERS.

Dingsdag Morgen ten half 10 Ure.
BUUR-KERK S. H. J. DE WOLFF. Pred. te Blaauwkapel.

Dingsdag Avond ten 8 Ure Bedestond voor Israel
lokaal Maliebaan No 202. P. HUET, Reizend Pred.

Woensdag Avond ten half 6 Ure.

TWEEDE VOORBEREIDING.

BUUR-KERK BERVOETS.

WALE-KERK
ZONDAG 4 October 1868.
Voormiddag ten 10 Ure NOLST TRENITÉ.

Voor particuliere rekening
gedrukt bij H. MELDER, op
de Oude Gracht, bij de
Gaardbrug te UTRECHT.

List of preaching engagements of the Reformed church in Utrecht, October 1868. At this time Utrecht had ten Dutch Reformed parishes. The Reformed membership counted about 35,000 souls in 1867, 58 percent of the almost 60,000 inhabitants; 36% of the population was Roman Catholic. The balance between Protestants and Catholics in Utrecht did not differ substantially from the national pattern.

The house at the Catharijnekade (now nr. 4) in Utrecht where Kuyper lived from 30 October 1867 until 1 May 1869. Kuyper lived with his family in one half of this historic building, the half to the right of the front door.

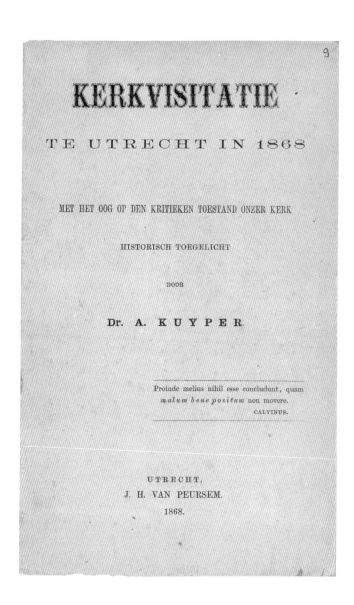

KERKVISITATIE ·

TE UTRECHT IN 1868

MET HET OOG OP DEN KRITIEKEN TOESTAND ONZER KERK

HISTORISCH TOEGELICHT

DOOR

Dr. A. KUYPER.

Proinde melius nihil esse concludunt, quam
malum bene positum non movere.
CALVINUS.

UTRECHT,
J. H. VAN PEURSEM.
1868.

During his years as a minister in Utrecht, Kuyper forcefully expressed his opinions regarding church matters of the day. In September 1868 he published his pamphlet *Church Visitation in Utrecht* after the orthodox consistory of Utrecht had refused to cooperate with the annual inspection by the classis. Kuyper defended the consistory's position on the grounds that the higher bodies of church government were no longer faithful to the historic creeds.

Although Kuyper had been enthusiastically welcomed in Utrecht as a defender of orthodoxy, his radical position and polemical style of writing eventually met with a great deal of resistance. For his part, Kuyper thought that many orthodox believers were too passive and too defensive, in particular in their attitude towards the church hierarchy and Modernism.

As leaders of the Utrecht Apologetical School, professors J. I. Doedes (1817-1897) and
J. J. van Oosterzee (1817-1882) belonged to the more moderate-orthodox movement.
They defended "the basic truths of the Scripture" against Modernism but also distanced
themselves from Kuyper's assertively Reformed theology, which they considered to be
an anachronism.

In 1897 Kuyper wrote the following about his time in Utrecht: "But what did I find?
Everywhere, petty sentiments. All the leading men locked up in the stronghold, only
thinking of possible weak defenses, waiting for the first shot to be fired, and then when
it finally came, firing back as best they could, while the outer rings of the faith were
offered up to the enemy. . . . And during all of this, a complete lack of unity in the plan
of defense, the one defender fighting against and being resentful of the other, all one
mixed-up confusion and no longer any ideal to strengthen the spirit and wrest from the
enemy not only theology and church, but also social and political life. That position,
those tactics, the whole situation in the stronghold, repulsed me. . . . Perhaps a little
recklessly, that was when I became a *sniper* and waged battle at my own *risk*. It was not
enough for me to defend the stronghold under attack, but I decided to make a sortie.
Not seeing a way forward through apologetic work, I decided to attack, and threw grenade after grenade towards the opponents."

The Groningen professor Petrus Hofstede de Groot (1802-1886) was the principal representative of the Groningen movement. This school of theology called into question traditional Christian dogmas and was opposed to the obligation to adhere to church doctrine, but also did not feel at home with the intellectualism of Modern theology. It looked for the source of faith in religious feeling and focused attention on Christ, in whom God raises people to find their true destiny. They believed that the ethical ideals of Christianity were of great importance for nurture and education. The ministers of the Groningen movement played an important part in the development of Dutch church and social life. Well into the nineteenth century, they exerted great influence in the church and in church government.

Dr. J. H. Gunning (1829-1905), minister in The Hague (1861-1882), professor at Amsterdam's City University (1882-1889) and at Leiden University (1889-1899).

Gunning was the most important representative of the Ethical movement within the Dutch Reformed Church. Strongly Christocentric, the Ethicals emphasized the personal experience of faith. They set less value upon matters such as the church as an institution, the Confessions, and the obligation to adhere to church doctrines — which for the strictly Reformed believers were very important. In doctrine there were considerable differences between Ethicals and the Reformed, particularly on the points of election and higher criticism. Supporters of the Ethical movement were often called "ethical-irenical" because they did not want to act as a party in the church, and strove for the restoration of spiritual life through "medical" means by preaching the Word and the working of the Spirit. They rejected Kuyper's actions and those of his supporters, which were laced with "politics" and the struggle for power. For his part, Kuyper accused the Ethicals of being "weak" and "disloyal." In the long run Gunning severed relations with Kuyper, because he thought that Kuyper's way of fighting was demagogic and reprehensible.

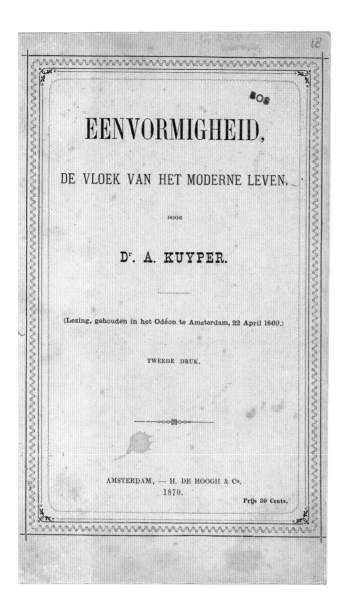

On 22 April 1869, in the concert hall Odéon in Amsterdam, Kuyper delivered his famous speech *Uniformity, the Curse of Modern Life*, one of the "grenades" with which he shelled his opponents at this time. Shortly before, in his pamphlet against the "Public Welfare Movement," he had thrown his first grenade, because the Society for Public Welfare glossed over differences in religious matters.

In *Uniformity*, an essay in cultural criticism, Kuyper denounced the false aim of uniformity, as it manifested itself in all kinds of areas (church, state, school). As an alternative he elevated the organic unity as intended by God, which took into account the variety and multiformity of life. In church matters he argued for a federation system as "the only way . . . to unite freedom and unity without being detrimental to the truth."

Dr. Carl Schwartz (1817-1870), founder in 1850 and until 1864 editor of the orthodox weekly paper *De Heraut*. Under his successor, the Utrecht minister G. Barger, the paper languished. On 9 July 1869 Kuyper published his first article in *De Heraut*, about the church inspection in Utrecht. Soon he became a regular contributor to the paper, not only on church and theology, but also about political issues such as the School Law, suffrage, and higher education.

On 6 January 1871 Kuyper was appointed editor-in-chief of *De Heraut*, which meant that he had at his disposal a publication of his own. On 22 March 1872 the paper was turned into the daily newspaper *De Standaard*, which until December 1877 subsumed *De Heraut* as a Sunday edition. On 7 December 1877 *De Heraut* was published again as an independent church weekly with Kuyper continuing as its editor-in-chief.

Dr. A. W. Bronsveld, 1839-1924.

In addition to Gunning, Kuyper during these years had conflicts with other Ethical theologians, such as his fellow minister from Utrecht, Dr. Nicolaas Beets, who at first had so encouraged Kuyper to come to Utrecht, and the Haarlem minister Dr. A. W. Bronsveld. From 1868 onward, Bronsveld opposed Kuyper's beliefs with regard to church and political issues in his theological monthly *Voices for Truth and Peace,* an important organ of the Ethical movement. He was opposed to the founding of the Free University, was against the Doleantie [church split from the Netherlands Reformed Church], and, because of his anti-Roman Catholic convictions, was fiercely opposed to the political coalition of Anti-Revolutionaries and Roman Catholics. Bronsveld strongly defended the historical rights of the Dutch Reformed Church, and in later years became a member of the Christian-Historical Union, the party consisting mainly of Dutch Reformed Church members who had split off from Kuyper's Anti-Revolutionary Party. Ironically, his daughter-in-law Mrs. S. Ch. C. Bronsveld-Vitringa became the first female member in Parliament for the Roman Catholic State Party in 1922.

Kuyper came into conflict with the Ethical-Irenicals not only in church matters, but also regarding the school question. For years, general education was a bone of political contention. After the Anti-Revolutionaries had failed in their aim to make elementary public education more expressly Christian through the Education Act of 1857, they started to work towards the expansion of independent Christian schools. To that end the Society for Christian National Schooling (CNS) was founded, with members coming from both Confessional-Reformed and Ethical circles.

On 18, 19, and 20 May 1869 the general assembly of the CNS took place in the Hall of Arts and Sciences in Utrecht. Being held so soon before the parliamentary elections in June, it was meant as a political demonstration. The meeting was chaired by Groen van

Gewijzigd Schoolwet-program van de Christelijk-Nationale richting.

J.VANNOOP.SC.   2257

UILENSPIEGEL: *»Drommels! ik dacht in de Vereeniging voor Christelijk Nationaal Onderwijs te zijn, maar ik zie, dat 'k in het Concilie verzeild ben!"*

Prinsterer, but Kuyper, being a minister in Utrecht, opened proceedings with a speech in which he rejected the Education Act of 1857 because it ran contrary to the "people's conscience." Later a heated argument arose between Kuyper and Beets about the attitude one should take with regard to public education. Groen and Kuyper clearly wanted to portray the state schools as being *neutral*, in order to create room for the expansion of independent Christian education. Beets, however, pointed out that state schools, in accordance with the law, also had to teach "Christian virtues," and pleaded for the preservation and intensification of their Christian character. After the assembly had accepted Groen's proposal to remove the word "Christian" from the Education Act, prominent Ethical-Irenical members such as Beets, Daniel Chantepie de la Saussaye, and J. J. Van Toorenenbergen resigned from the CNS. In 1870 Chantepie established the periodical *Protestant Contributions*, which as an organ of the Ethical Movement was particularly opposed to Kuyper.

After the meeting of May 1869 the discussions within the CNS carried on as before, and beginning in October Kuyper fiercely defended himself in *De Heraut*. That in the meantime his actions had also attracted national attention is apparent from a caricature in the first edition of *Uilenspiegel*, a satirical liberal magazine, published by Nijgh and Van Ditmar in Rotterdam as of the spring of 1870. It was the first published caricature of Kuyper.

This caricature, drawn by the well-known illustrator J. M. Schmidt Crans, shows Beets fighting with Groen and Kuyper. The caption reads: "By gum! I thought I was at the Union for Christian National Schooling, but I see that I have ended up in the Council." The text refers to the First Vatican Council (1869-1870) in Rome, where in the spring of 1870 fierce debates took place about the doctrine of papal infallibility.

Letter by Gunning to Kuyper dated 18/25 December 1869, in which he criticized Kuyper's articles in *De Heraut*. Gunning wrote that Kuyper's reasoning was too "abstract-logical": "The consequence is that this way of thinking is completely *correct* but not *true*. It drives the opponent *into a corner*, where he, being of the *same mind*, does not know how to reply, but this way of thinking does not *convince* him. The regular person understands *perfectly* the issues that lawyers deal with. And yet, when discussing *spiritual* matters in a legal context, a lawyer may drive him to the wall (as *you* do to your opponents) and thus make him bitter, but he does not *convince* them. Only the higher tone does that, the ἔλεγχος of the Holy Spirit, which so often, even in your legal arguments, flows from your *heart* in waves! . . . There are many who dislike you and let you pass by *in silence*. As far as I am concerned, I love you more than I am prepared to say. I will *continue* to do so even if you express reservations about my point of view in the light of your logic, as we have grown accustomed to over the years."

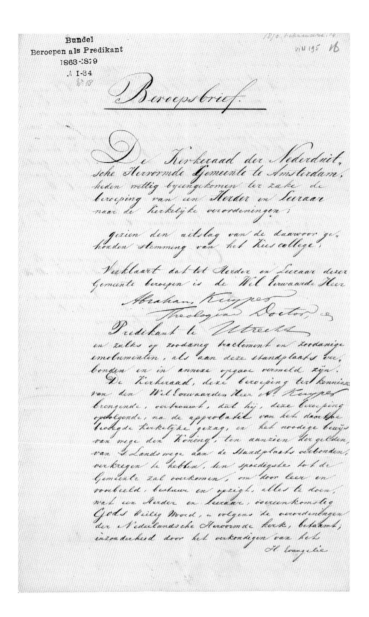

Written call of the Dutch Reformed congregation in Amsterdam, 14 February 1870.

Kuyper was the first minister to be called to Amsterdam under the new demo-cratic election process, which had been established in 1867. Kuyper was elected by 202 votes, while his colleague from Utrecht, J. W. Felix, received 110 votes, and a minister from Rotterdam, W. J. Gorissen, got 16. Kuyper accepted the call on 6 March 1870 after hesitating for some time. He was disappointed in the weak cooperation of the ortho-dox clergymen in Utrecht, and hoped that Amsterdam would supply him with a bet-ter foundation for his objective of church reform. In his farewell address *Conservatism and Orthodoxy* (31 July 1870), he warned the Utrecht congregation against burying "our wonderful orthodoxy in the treacherous pit of false conservatism."

According to a letter of 15 February 1870, Kuyper's father described the call to Amsterdam as most honorable, but also expected that his son would only take the decision after "difficult days of struggle." Kuyper indeed hesitated for a long time before accepting because he feared opposition from orthodox quarters there too. There were also financial complications, which were solved after mediation by Dr. H. F. Kohlbrügge.

Dr. H. F. Kohlbrügge (1803-1875) in 1853.

Originally a Lutheran theologian, Dr. H. F. Kohlbrügge had been refused membership in the Dutch Reformed congregation in Utrecht in 1830 because of his orthodox
convictions. Since 1846 he had been pastor of the independent Reformed congregation
in Elberfeld, Germany. His works, which were widely read in the Netherlands, also influenced Kuyper. In *Confidentie* (1873) Kuyper wrote that he had come to Calvinism "in
part owing to Kohlbrügge's solidly muscular, deeply thought words of wisdom." The
two had first met in 1864 when Kuyper was preparing to publish the à Lasco *Opera*;
Kohlbrügge had the highest regard for à Lasco. Characteristic of Kuyper's trust in Kohlbrügge, he travelled to Elberfeld on 19 February 1870 to discuss the call to Amsterdam
with him.

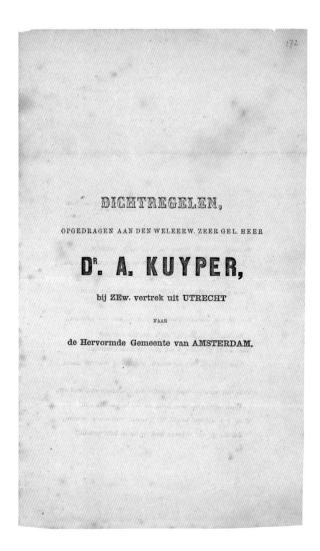

DICHTREGELEN,

OPGEDRAGEN AAN DEN WELEERW. ZEER GEL. HEER

D^R. A. KUYPER,

bij ZEw. vertrek uit UTRECHT

NAAR

de Hervormde Gemeente van AMSTERDAM.

Many members of the Utrecht congregation were sorry to see Kuyper leave for Amsterdam. This excerpt from the "Verses" by "Johannes" was dedicated to Kuyper on 31 July 1870. The poem shows how great the differences of opinion in church matters were:

> Remove, with your brethren who have remained loyal to Christ,
> As much as you can the wretched overgrowth,
> With which the still gentle pasture of God is so infested,
> and so destroy the power of the newly burgeoned weed.

> Now thrives that parasite, arisen from "foolish delusion,"
> Bedewed, cultivated by the breath of the age.
> But God is with the man who, bold and undaunted,
> As much as possible and wherever he can, rids it from the earth.

The Nieuwe Kerk, dating back to the fifteenth century, the most important building of the Dutch Reformed Church of Amsterdam.

In his inaugural sermon *Rooted and Grounded,* delivered in the Nieuwe Kerk on 10 August 1870, Kuyper referred to the church as an organism and an institute. The first characteristic was neglected by the Modernist theologians, he argued, while the Ethical theologians had too little eye for the institutional side. However, both aspects were inextricably bound up with the essence of a free church — free of state interference and centralized church government. In his sermon Kuyper argued for the "liberation" of the Dutch Reformed Church: *"We must rebuild or move.* . . . The false ties of the unreformed church government will ultimately burst if we but quickly adopt the slogan that lies within the autonomy, that is to say, in the 'independent administration and self-rule of the congregation.'"

According to Kuyper the church not only had a spiritual task, but also a social one: "The great social issues of 'vice and overpopulation,' of 'labour and poor relief' are not regarded as peripheral to our church." Kuyper's early interest in the situation of the workers also appears from the foreword that he wrote for the pamphlet (translated from the German) *The Labour Problem and the Church,* which was published in March 1871. A year later in *De Standaard* of April and May 1872, immediately after its foundation, he published a series of eleven articles about "the social question."

Letter from Kohlbrügge to Kuyper, 3 January 1871.

Kuyper flung to the winds Kohlbrügge's pastoral advice not to take upon himself too much work meant for publication. In January 1871 Kuyper became editor-in-chief of *De Heraut,* which was given a new programmatic subtitle: "For a Free Church and Free School in a Free Netherlands."

Kohlbrügge had good reason to worry. With his busy schedule Kuyper often demanded too much of himself, which resulted in all kinds of physical and psychological maladies. On several occasions he had to stop working to go abroad and rest.

HET MODERNISME

EEN

FATA MORGANA OP CHRISTELIJK GEBIED

LEZING

DOOR

DR. A. KUYPER.

AMSTERDAM,
H. DE HOOGH & Cº.
1871.

Kuyper fought the battle against Modernism on several fronts. In August 1871 his speech *Modernism, a Fata Morgana on the Christian Scene* appeared in print, after he had delivered it in various places throughout the country in March and April.

Before having the speech printed, he had visited Allard Pierson in Heidelberg in April 1871. Despite their differences of opinion, Kuyper appreciated Pierson as "a logical, principled thinker, who . . . shares with me antipathy against the lukewarm, Laodicean half-men."

What typifies Kuyper's personality in this context is the excerpt from *Modernism* in which he describes how, on 6 May 1791, Edmund Burke ended his personal friendship with Charles Fox in the English Parliament after the latter had defended the principle of the French Revolution, which for Burke was "a monster of destruction." "As soon as principles gain ground that run counter to your most deeply held convictions, then to struggle is your duty, peace has become a sin to you, and you must attack those principles at the expense of the sweetest peace . . . with all the fire of your faith," according to Kuyper.

Kuyper as a minister in Amsterdam, 1872.

On a completely different level, Kuyper had to struggle against Modernism in his own congregation in Amsterdam. There was a growing opposition between the orthodox members of the consistory, who had been elected after 1867, and the Modernist ministers, who had been called under the old regulations. By establishing a "consultative body" of orthodox consistory members, which regularly held preliminary consultations, Kuyper was able to influence the decision-making process of the church consistory. In his Pamphlet *The Offense of the Seventeen Elders* (October 1872), Kuyper defended the decision of orthodox elders to avoid "as much as their office allowed" the church services of Modernist ministers.

Groen van Prinsterer in later life.

Because of his cooperation with Groen van Prinsterer, Kuyper became more and more involved in the political Anti-Revolutionary struggle. At the same time Groen gradually retreated from the front lines, leaving the leadership increasingly to Kuyper. "My parliamentary role is played out. I no longer feel up to such a task," Groen wrote to Kuyper on 10 January 1871. Three months later he characterized their relationship as follows: "Each one of us has his *own position*. You as a participant in the struggle, as a *leader* of journalism on the battlefield. As a man of action and of *practice*. . . . I, on the other hand, the *leader* (inasmuch as this is to be desired) only on matters of *principle*."

Kohlbrügge's house in Elberfeld.

During the parliamentary elections of June 1871 Groen, as "leader on matters of principle," took a hard line and jolted existing arrangements, just as he had done in 1869 at the meeting of the CNS. He refused to cooperate in the reelection of the incumbent Anti-Revolutionary members of Parliament because he believed that they had identified too much with the Conservatives and had not sufficiently supported independent Christian schooling. He publicly recommended only three Anti-Revolutionary candidates who in his opinion were truly Anti-Revolutionary, among whom was Kuyper. Although none of them were elected, by keeping to his principles Groen van Prinsterer did influence the future course of the Anti-Revolutionary movement, which freed itself from the "deadly embrace of Conservatism."

Because Kuyper had not been elected, he was saved from having to make the difficult decision whether to accept the seat in Parliament while still being fully involved in the church struggle in Amsterdam as a minister. Once again Kuyper travelled to Elberfeld to consult with Kohlbrügge. During their long conversation on 19 May 1871 the latter did not give concrete advice, although he did imply that he was skeptical about Kuyper's political inclinations: "I quietly made it quite clear to him that he was arguing too much with the world in mind." Despite Kuyper's disappointment in this meeting, their personal relationship remained good. On Kuyper's invitation Kohlbrügge gave a sermon in the Zuiderkerk in Amsterdam on 12 November 1871 and stayed for a few days with the Kuyper family.

The first edition of the Anti-Revolutionary daily paper *De Standaard*, published on 1 April 1872 with Kuyper as editor-in-chief.

Thanks to the abolition of the newspaper tax on 1 July 1869, the fiscal obstructions for publishing newspapers were removed. In the same year a failed attempt was made to found a Christian national daily paper, for which Kuyper designed a platform — a prelude to his later political program. In 1871 the *De Heraut* society decided to turn that weekly into a national daily, with the intention of defending and disseminating

Anti-Revolutionary principles. Except for one interruption in the year 1876-77, Kuyper would remain editor-in-chief until his death.

The inaugural date of *De Standaard* was characteristic of Kuyper's sense of historical symbolism: 1 April 1872 was the 300th anniversary of the day the Sea Beggars had taken the city of Den Briel, a turning point in the fight against Spanish domination. In his front-page article Kuyper placed the spiritual and political task of *De Standaard* in this historical context.

Budget for editorial costs, drawn up by Kuyper, from the early days of *De Standaard*. Despite its small staff and limited circulation, *De Standaard* developed into an influential organ upon which Kuyper, with his talent as a journalist, made his personal mark. In particular his short, sharp commentaries, also known as "three-stars" or "asterisks," which appeared in the paper practically every day, were famous. In addition to his longer lead articles, Kuyper wrote approximately 16,800 "three-stars" for *De Standaard*.

Thorbecke with his German wife Adelheid Solger.

On 4 June 1872 the Liberal statesman J. R. Thorbecke, who had controlled Dutch politics since 1848, died. Kuyper commemorated him in *De Standaard* of 7 June 1872 by writing an "in memoriam" that ended with the words: "Our thoughts multiply as we stand at his grave; we prefer to sum them up not in adulatory tributes for the statesman who was taken from our midst, but in humble thanks to our God for both the *blessing* and the *trial* that befell us in Thorbecke."

Thorbecke's old opponent Groen van Prinsterer wrote in a letter to Kuyper on that very same day: "Just a word to thank you for your splendid article in today's *De Standaard*. The graciousness of this masterpiece will perhaps not be recognized by our harshest opponents, but it will be felt."

J. Voorhoeve H.Czn, 1811-1881.

After the debacle of the 1871 elections, Kuyper argued in *De Heraut* for a national organization of Anti-Revolutionaries. Although the electoral federation that he had in mind would take years to materialize, in the autumn of 1872 the Anti-School-Law Association (ASV) was founded. The driving force behind the foundation of the ASV was the real estate agent J. Voorhoeve, who had been inspired by the successful example of the British Anti-Corn-Law-League (1838). As a one-issue organization with a low subscription fee, the ASV soon expanded among all sectors of the population. Throughout the country local chapters were established. The propaganda in *De Standaard* also played an important role. In 1873, upon Kuyper's suggestion, it was decided that the general board of the ASV would take the lead during the elections and would advise the local electoral associations. Years later the ASV was incorporated into the Anti-Revolutionary Party, but until 1879 it played an important role in elections and in the great school-petition of 1878.

Een dag op de graven! Een dag van rouwe! Heel de kerk der Hervormden aan alle plaatse der aarde treurt!

Ze kan haar martelaren niet vergeten, want ze belijdt een „gemeenschap der heiligen," die in het graf niet sterft, niet wegslijt met den loop der eeuwen en te nauwer klemt om het bloed, dat vergoten werd.

Ze zwoer het haar dooden, en dien eed breekt ze niet, dat ze in haar sombere historie den vinger rusteloos houden zou bij die bladzij vol afgrijzen, met zwarter kool dan één geteekend; een bladzij in den pestwalm der hel geblakerd en bedropen met het zwartst verraad. Een bladzij, waarbij het boek der Martelaren, ook al trok ze haar vinger terug, nog, om wraak schreiend, van zelf zou openvallen, en die, weigerend haar vlekken te doen verbleeken, met een stemme des bloeds, als wierd het pas gister vergoten, voor God en al het schepsel zal blijven klagen, zoolang de leste klacht nog niet in 's menschen borst verstomt.

Die nu nog strijden in Gods kerk op aarde, willen eens de martelaren daarboven in het verheerlijkt aangezicht staren, zonder van de lippen der Coligny's, der Rohans, der de Beauvais, der Pardaillans, ach, wie noemt ze ons bij duizenden? het zaligheidbannend verwijt te hooren: „Gij hebt vergeten het bloed, door ons gestort voor den Heer!"

"A day on the graves! A day of mourning!" Opening words of Kuyper's pamphlet St. Bartholomew's Eve (1872), published in remembrance of the so-called "blood wedding" in Paris of 24 August 1572, when many Huguenots lost their lives. The pamphlet was an offprint of a half-dozen Standaard articles written by Kuyper during a polemic with the Roman Catholic magazine De Maasbode. Eighteen months later, with Catholic support, Kuyper was elected as a member of the second chamber of Parliament, the first sign of the future cooperation between Anti-Revolutionaries and Roman Catholics.

D. Chantepie de la Saussaye, 1818-1874.

After the confrontation between Groen and Kuyper with Beets and Chantepie de la Saussaye at the meeting of the CNS in 1869 and the split of Groen and Kuyper from the conservative Anti-Revolutionary members of Parliament in 1871, a new conflict arose between Kuyper and the supporters of the Ethical movement in September 1872, at the Zeist Missionary Conference. The leadership and the speakers at the conference were predominantly Ethical and Groningen theologians. When Kuyper expressed his disapproval of this, there was an uproar. As chairman of the conference, Chantepie was so irritated by Kuyper's behavior that he publicly broke off all relations with him.

In Amsterdam support for Kuyper was growing. On the occasion of his thirty-fifth birthday on 29 October 1872, 190 friends and members of his congregation offered Kuyper the house at Prins Hendrikkade 183 as a gift. The house was named after its commemorative stone and called "Mount Sapphire." After he and his family had moved into the house in May 1873, Kuyper delivered a sermon in de Nieuwe Kerk on 18 August on Isaiah 54:11: "I shall lay thy foundations with sapphires." In October the sermon was published under the title *Our House*, and Kuyper sent it to all the donors.

Kuyper was obliged to sell the house in 1876, when he had to leave the country because he was overworked. In 1968 the house was demolished to make way for the construction of the Y Tunnel.

First page of the list of donors of "the Mount of Sapphire," showing small and large contributions. Groen van Prinsterer donated 1250 guilders. The notary G. Ruys, who had taken the initiative for the collection, contributed 400 guilders. The largest sum (3000 guilders) was given by the Amsterdam real estate agent Th. Sanders Jr., a wealthy man who owned the Hartenstein estate near Oosterbeek. Later he also donated 25,000 guilders to help with the founding of the Free University.

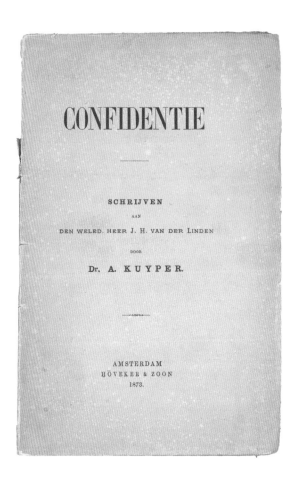

Title page of Kuyper's autobiographical work *Confidentie* published in April/May 1873 in the form of an open letter to a member of the Amsterdam consistory, J. H. van der Linden.

In *Confidentie* Kuyper discussed his polemic with Gunning about the interpretation of scripture and defended his handling of church politics in Amsterdam. He outlined his ideal of a democratically administered, free and independent Reformed church, which would no longer be dependent on the government. In this context he compared the Dutch Reformed Church of Amsterdam with the churches that had emerged from the Secession of 1834. He pointed out that the latter, without government support, were in much better shape both financially and spiritually.

Confidentie has become well known because in it Kuyper describes his spiritual evolution and conversion in a very personal and rather romanticized way, including the providential discovery of the works of à Lasco, the impression *The Heir of Redclyffe* made on him, and his acquaintance with Pietje Baltus in Beesd. On later occasions Kuyper would recount the past differently, which led to the criticism that he consciously changed his life story to suit the needs of the moment. However, there is no reason to doubt the facts he reported.

CHAPTER III

Political Life, 1874-1880

After a period of increased political activity, Kuyper himself was elected as a member of the second chamber of Parliament by the constituency of Gouda in January 1874. After his election, which he accepted after considerable hesitation, he resigned his office as a pastor. Kuyper's first term in Parliament (1874-1877) was not a success. Although he did not avoid debates, his position in the chamber was too isolated to be able to achieve anything. He was the odd man out, not only because of his political opinions, but also because of the way in which he operated, which was unusual in the parliamentary culture of those days. After having exhausted himself in the previous years, the mental pressure of this "lonely post" now became too much for him. He fell out of balance, as was evident also in his euphoric reaction to the revival meetings at Brighton, England, in May and June of 1875. Back in Parliament he was barely able to control himself. In February 1876 Kuyper had to discontinue his work in Parliament and for *De Standaard* by reason of complete exhaustion. He went abroad to recuperate and would stay there for over a year.

Notably, Kuyper's greatest successes occurred right after his most serious crisis. After his return to the Netherlands in April 1877 he gave up his seat in Parliament in order to devote himself to building up the Anti-Revolutionary movement, which, owing to Groen's death (1876) and his own illness, had reached an impasse. For the time being, Kuyper was more in his element outside Parliament. The School Bill of the Liberal cabinet of Johannes Kappeyne van de Coppello, which threatened the cause of Christian education, provided him the opportunity to demonstrate his talents as a journalist and organizer. Together with his most important supporter, the Hon. Alexander F. de Savornin Lohman, in 1878 he organized the great national petition against the School Bill; after a fierce and intensive campaign the petition was signed by more than 300,000 people. Despite this success the School Bill was still implemented.

However, the national petition campaign gave the Anti-Revolutionary organization a solid base. In April 1879 the Anti-Revolutionary Party (ARP) was founded in Utrecht, whereby 21 local electoral associations joined to form one national alliance with a common program, which Kuyper provided with a massive commentary, *Our Program*. He himself became party chairman, and he led with a firm hand. The ARP was not only the first modern political party in the Netherlands, but distinguished itself from the existing Liberal and Conservative factions by its specifically Christian foundations. Its establishment heralded the pillarization of Dutch society, which was based on the "antithesis" between confessional and non-confessional parties and organizations.

De strijd te GOUDA bij de Stembus.

Tusschen deze twee partijen is geen plaats meer — ook niet voor de thuisblijvers

On 21 January 1874 Kuyper was elected to Parliament by the constituency of Gouda. He defeated his Liberal opponent H. C. Verniers van der Loeff in the second round with 1504 of the 2756 votes cast, partly owing to the support of the Roman Catholics. According to the caricature in *Uilenspiegel* of 17 January 1874, the Liberal candidate in Gouda represented the cultured aims of freedom and progress, while Kuyper, who had been supported much more by the commoners' vote, could be expected to bring division and religious hatred.

"A prophet in doubt," caricature from the Liberal weekly *De Nederlandsche Spectator*, 7 February 1874. Written in the style of the book of Revelation, the caption read: "And a view unfolded, and I saw two precious barrels/And I had to chose between two barrels/ The lord of the vineyard had ordered me to oversee one/and had called to me about the other/And my mind was wondering, whether I should support the one barrel/and let the other just roll away/or whether I should support the other and let the first one fall to pieces."

As in 1871 Kuyper again hesitated for a long time before accepting his election, and he turned to Groen van Prinsterer and others for advice. His father was not very pleased with his son's election to Parliament, because he valued, as did many people in those days, the spiritual office of pastoral ministry above the worldly office of people's representative: "Think carefully seven times and then a further seven times before you give up your distinguished, holy, and blessed position as the minister of the congregation in Amsterdam." However, his old college friend Isaac Hooykaas, who in the meantime had become a Remonstrant minister in Rotterdam, wrote to him: "In your whole religious attitude and history it seems to me lies *much* more the statesman than the man of the church. . . . There would be a sense of forcing things, something unnatural, if you declined." On 16 March Kuyper resigned as a minister, since by law clergy were not permitted to be members of Parliament at that time (in 1887 the law was changed). On 20 March 1874 he was sworn in as a member of the second chamber of Parliament.

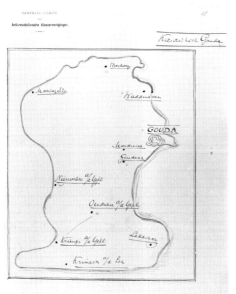
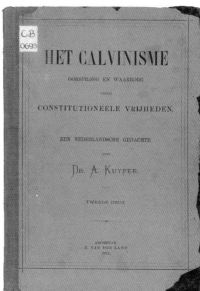

Small map of the electoral district of Gouda, drawn by Kuyper himself. At that time the second chamber of Parliament (similar to the American House of Representatives or the British House of Commons) was elected through a constituency voting system in which the right to vote could be exercised by only 10 percent of the male population. Every two years there were recurring elections for half of the seats in the chamber. The first chamber had less power and was elected in stages by the members of the Provincial Councils. In 1874 the second chamber numbered eighty members: 38 Liberals, 16 Conservatives, 16 Roman Catholics, and 10 Anti-Revolutionaries. Kuyper was chosen to fill the vacancy left by Groen's brother-in-law, the Anti-Revolutionary M. A. F. H. Hoffman, who for health reasons had resigned as a member of Parliament.

In November 1873 Kuyper delivered an important historical oration for students of the University of Utrecht; it came to be regarded as his political statement of principles. The speech was published in June 1874 as *Calvinism: Source and Stronghold of Our Constitutional Liberties*. In it Kuyper argued that not the French Revolution, but the Reformation had brought the people real freedom. After all, long before 1789 the Calvinist principle of freedom of conscience had spread throughout the Dutch Republic, in Great Britain and in the United States, where human rights and the acknowledgment of God as the highest governing force had been included in the Declaration of Independence (1776). As heirs of this political tradition of Calvinism, which in its nature was democratic and progressive, the Anti-Revolutionaries had to have an eye for "the needs of our time" and develop a political and a social program that could meet those needs.

Aanblik van de Tweede Kamer,

nadat dr. Kuyper zitting zal hebben genomen.

Kuyper was the first pastor to be elected as a member of the second chamber of Parliament, which *Uilenspiegel* pointed out in this caricature on 21 February 1874.

Kuyper indeed cut a strange figure in the second chamber of that time. He was not a lawyer like most members of Parliament, who were usually recruited from among the administrative elite. He clashed with the prevailing parliamentary culture not only because of his views but in particular because of how he acted. In a room filled with notables and members of the aristocracy, Kuyper, as "tribune of the people" with a bourgeois background, did not feel at ease. The tempestuous minister was the odd man out amid the polite calm that was characteristic of the parliamentary debates of that time. Fellow MPs thought that he was bombastic and accused him of rejecting "Chamber music" for excessive pounding at "the broad keyboard of the popular conscience." As one opponent wrote, "Whenever he spoke, he spoke well but without adhering to the traditional form. Perhaps he was the first to sense that he lacked the subtlety and the distinguished tone that could have enabled him to follow in Groen's footsteps and play first fiddle at the Binnenhof. Thus he hung the bow, which was too fine for him, up on the wall and placed himself willingly behind the booming reed organ."

Chamber of the lower house of the Dutch States General. On the left in the middle, the chairman's seat with canopy; on the right, directly opposite, the cabinet table. The members of Parliament were in the habit of speaking to the chamber from where they sat. The speaker's platform (with sound equipment) was not introduced until much later. Because some members of Parliament were not clearly audible, often a circle of listeners would form around the speaker.

On 29 April 1874 Kuyper delivered his first speech in Parliament, regarding the bill submitted by Liberal MP Samuel van Houten to abolish child labor. Kuyper sympathized with the social import of the bill, but voted against it because of reservations about its practical implementation.

The Conservative J. Heemskerk Azn. (1818-1897), leader of the cabinet from 1874 to 1877 and 1883 to 1888. Although his Conservatives were in the minority, because of dissension among the Liberals Heemskerk was able to become Prime Minister in August 1874. Heemskerk was a formidable opponent to both the Liberals and the Anti-Revolutionaries. He introduced the Higher Education Bill in 1876, which a few years later enabled the establishment of the Free University. A bill concerning primary education, submitted on 21 December 1876, did not get onto the agenda because the cabinet had to resign the following year after the Liberal election victory.

Minister Heemskerk and the Higher Education Act, caricature in *De Nederlandsche Spectator*, 3 April 1875.

With his new Higher Education bill, Heemskerk wanted to end the situation whereby the theological faculties of the state-funded universities had the exclusive right to educate ministers for the Dutch Reformed Church, which ran contrary to the separation of church and state. Originally Heemskerk had planned to abolish the theological departments altogether, but he changed his mind.

Kuyper was also critical of the power of the theological faculties, because he believed that the "paganizing" influence of the Liberal state was as detrimental to theological studies as it was to primary education. As early as December 1872 he had pointed this out in a series of articles about "Our Universities" in *De Standaard*, and had argued for a "free" Protestant university that would be independent of both church and state. With this plan he offered a solution to the dilemma facing many orthodox theologians: a scholarly but "unbelieving" faculty or an orthodox but limited seminary. In his series of articles Kuyper was reacting to the inaugural address that D. Chantepie de la Saussaye delivered in Groningen, *The Place of the Science of Theology in the Encyclopedia of Sciences*, in which Chantepie defended the theological faculties.

In *De Standaard* of December 1875 Kuyper's idea of a free Protestant university was again put forward by Gunning, after which Kuyper called for exploratory consultations between the orthodox and the Ethicals about this issue. Although the disunity within Ethical circles in particular was too great to make consultation possible, it inspired *Uilenspiegel* to publish this caricature on 15 January 1876. In the foreground to the right, Kuyper is talking to the court jester Uilenspiegel, who ridicules the "great plans" for a free university. The figures in the left foreground are shown wearing the outdated 17th century pastor's robes, which the magazine used to indicate the reactionary nature of Kuyper's plans.

Jhr. Mr. A.F. de Savornin Lohman

Johannes Kappeyne van de Coppello (1822-1895), leader of the Liberals in the second chamber, was an astute and provocative politician who saw parliamentary debates as sparring matches. In a debate with Kuyper about amendments to the School Act on 8 December 1874, Kappeyne made the following remarks about the supporters of private education: "If they say that the minorities will have to be subjugated, I am almost inclined to say: 'Well, let the minority be subjugated, because then it is the proverbial fly in the ointment and has no right to exist in our society.'" Kuyper replied, "If ever the day comes when at this ministerial table a cabinet sits that puts forward this speaker's program as the government's program, then I will call out: Take from the Dutch coat of arms *the Lion*, the image of the proudest freedom, and replace it with the *Eagle with the lamb in its talons*, the symbol of tyranny!" As Kuyper put it in *De Standaard* of January 1876, the education policy of the Liberals was geared towards secularization, "towards the severance of every bond with eternity . . . towards rejection of the doctrine of immortality in the state school."

A. F. de Savornin Lohman (1837-1924), descendant of a line of Groningen regents and judge at the court of justice in 's-Hertogenbosch when he was introduced to Kuyper by Groen van Prinsterer in the spring of 1875. Shortly before, Lohman had become well known through the publication of his book *Authority and Freedom*, in which he outlined and defended the principles of Anti-Revolutionary constitutional law. With Kuyper, Lohman would lead the opposition against the School Act in the years that followed.

Kuyper's first letter to Savornin Lohman, 9 March 1875. The formal salutation "Your Honor" would soon be replaced by the more intimate "Dear friend" or "Dearest brother."

Het Restitutiestelsel.

(OP HET KANTOOR VAN EEN BELASTING-ONTVANGER.)

«Zooals mijnheer ziet, heb ik zeven kinderen. Daar geen van allen school gaat, spaar ik de gemeente heel wat geld uit. De heeren zullen wel willen uitrekenen hoeveel dat bedraagt, en als het dan mijnheer gelegen komt, zou ik graag het sommetje ontvangen...»

In the existing educational system, the public schools were financed by public funds, while private schools had to be paid for by the parents themselves. This meant that these parents were in fact assessed twice, because by paying taxes they were already funding public schools. Moreover, owing to the existence of private schools, the government was able to spend less on public education. With a view to the latter point, Kuyper and Lohman argued for "restitution" of the money that those parents saved the government by sending their child to a private school. In *Uilenspiegel* of 17 April 1875, this notion of restitution was ridiculed: "a poor man with seven children is asking the tax collector for a refund."

Kuyper during a ten-day meeting that was held in Brighton, England, from 9 May to 7 June 1875, organized by the American revivalist Robert Pearsall Smith (1827-1899). Eight thousand participants attended the conference in Brighton, of which half came from the continent. Kuyper, who at this time was already on the brink of becoming over-taxed, was deeply impressed by the inspiring meetings in Brighton. When asked to express his opinion of the conference in biblical terms, he chose the words from Psalm 23: "My cup runneth over." Upon returning to the Netherlands he reported at length about the Brighton revival in *De Standaard*. Also during missionary local festivals in 's Heer-Arendskerke, Boekenrode, and Winschoten in June and July, Kuyper told about the spiritual revival in Brighton as, for him personally, a "Bethel experience." During a debate in Parliament about the school question he quoted a verse written by the American revivalist composer Philip Bliss:

Dare to be a Daniel,
Dare to stand alone,
Dare to have a purpose firm,
Dare to make it known!

In the autumn of 1875 Kuyper's euphoria about the Brighton movement suddenly changed into depression, accompanied by mental and physical ailments. He took showers, tried to keep his "strongly affected nerves" under control with cold compresses to the head, and even went horseback riding in the mornings, but nothing helped. Seriously

overworked, in February 1876 he had to discontinue all activities. On the advice of his physician, he went abroad to convalesce. For more than a year he alternated between the south of France, Italy, and Switzerland, not returning to the Netherlands until April 1877. In order to pay for the sojourn abroad, the house on the Prins Hendrikkade was sold.

From Marseilles Kuyper wrote to his wife on 20 February 1876: "I can clearly feel how much more I have been harmed than [my physician] presumed. O Jo, God only knows how much I suffered in Holland. Whenever I think of how they literally murdered me, I burst into tears. . . . I resort to reading Job. I understand Job so well." Jo stayed on in Holland at first, but later joined her husband with their children. Besides the two elder sons, Herman and Frederik, the family now numbered three more children: Henriëtte Sophia Susanna (born in Amsterdam on 1 October 1870), Abraham (born in Amsterdam on 14 November 1872), and Johanna Hendrika (born in The Hague on 6 March 1875). Their sixth child, Catharina Maria Eunice, was born in Nice on 30 November 1876.

Kuyper as a mountaineer, Switzerland 1876. The mountains had a soothing influence on his nerves. Kuyper subsequently saw to it that every year in the summer he stayed abroad for two months to recuperate in peace and quiet. He strictly kept to this annual round. Another way to prevent further depressions was the strict timetable that Kuyper imposed on himself. Although his daily regime was almost compulsive in nature, it did keep him from having any more serious relapses. Furthermore, it was also conducive to Kuyper's staggering literary output, which he maintained until he was well advanced in years.

Gravestone of Groen van Prinsterer and his wife in the churchyard "Ter navolging" in Scheveningen. Groen died on 19 May 1876 at the age of 74 after being sick for a number of weeks. In March of that year two other prominent Anti-Revolutionaries (member of the second chamber J. W. van Loon and the vice-president of the Council of State, Æneas Mackay) had also died. With Kuyper abroad because he was seriously ill, the future of the Anti-Revolutionary movement did not look promising at that time.

As editor-in-chief of *De Standaard* Kuyper was replaced by Lohman. This saved the newspaper, which during these years faced an uncertain future. In a letter from Nice on 6 October 1876, Kuyper wrote Lohman that he had saved *De Standaard* from an "almost certain death": "and if I may offer you some word of thanks for your uncommon dedication and affection, then receive my assurance that it will continue to be my highest aim *to stand as one in heart and hand with you before our nation's people.*"

In February 1877 Kuyper visited the Netherlands, but had not sufficiently recovered to be able to stay there. A visit to Mrs. Groen van Prinsterer totally upset his nerves again, he wrote to Lohman. According to a caricature in *De Nederlandsche Spectator* of 10 February 1877, his opponents did not want him to return to politics too quickly. The subtitle was taken from the tragedy *Gijsbreght van Aemstel* by the Dutch poet Joost van den Vondel (1587-1679) and reads: "Doorman: 'Oh Jesus, come to our aid, this is a bad sign.'"

After his final return to the Netherlands in April 1877 Kuyper resigned his seat in Parliament in order to commit himself fully to the construction of a national Anti-Revolutionary movement. Once more he took upon himself the chief editorship of *De Standaard* and led the Anti-Revolutionaries during the biennial parliamentary elections in June 1877. The results were disappointing. Winning an additional six seats, the Liberals gained a majority in the second chamber, while the Conservatives and the Anti-Revolutionaries each lost three seats.

To give the political action of the Anti-Revolutionaries a firmer basis, in the autumn of 1877 Kuyper wrote a political program, which, after having been shown to a number of prominent supporters for consultation, was published on 1 January 1878. The photograph shows the printed design of the program, drafted by Kuyper, with notes by Lohman, November 1877. In addition to Lohman, B. J. L. Baron de Geer van Jutphaas, professor of law in Utrecht, was consulted, as was B. J. Gratama, professor of law in Groningen.

First issue of *De Heraut* at its republication as a church weekly, 7 December 1877.

In December 1877 the Sunday issue of *De Standaard* was again changed into a separate church weekly, *De Heraut*, also edited by Kuyper. From then on church issues were discussed in *De Heraut* and political issues in *De Standaard*. In making this distinction Kuyper hoped to prevent a situation in which the political position of the Anti-Revolutionaries would be weakened by the church struggle, which in the meantime continued unabated in *De Heraut*.

Although after his return Kuyper had made it known that he would not re-enter the pastoral ministry, as editor-in-chief of *De Heraut* he continued to influence developments in the Dutch Reformed Church. In addition to commentaries on church issues, Kuyper wrote a devotional for *De Heraut* every week. The devotionals were later published as collections. His larger theological treatises were also usually first run as a series in *De Heraut* before being published as books.

Fragment of the national petition, drafted by Kuyper, 3 June 1878.

After the Liberal election victory of June 1877, the Conservative Heemskerk cabinet was succeeded by a Liberal cabinet under the leadership of Kappeyne van de Coppello. On 11 March 1878 this cabinet introduced a bill that made higher demands on the furnishing of school buildings and the quality of primary education. The ensuing costs would have to be paid for by the (unsubsidized) private schools themselves. This meant that private education would end up in a financially worse position than it already was. The bill was sharply opposed by the Anti-Revolutionaries and Catholics, but was passed on 28 July by the second chamber and on 7 August by the upper house. At the instigation of Kuyper, Lohman, and De Geer van Jutphaas, a national petition was now organized requesting the king not to sign the bill: "Never, Your Majesty, place your royal signature under such a bill."

The Reformed historian and apologist J. C. Rullmann wrote the following about Kuyper's part in the national petition: "During the three months that preceded the opening of the petition drive, the editor-in-chief of *De Standaard* showed his talents as a strategist in the most unforgettable way. Day after day he battled against the opposition's papers. And at the same time he made the strings of the nation's conscience vibrate in such a way that the whole nation, insofar as it had not yet recklessly betrayed its Christian character, raised its voice for the palladium of its Christian school that had been seriously threatened by Kappeyne's bill."

„TOT DEN KONING GAAN.”

De *finale* van het volksconscientie-concert.

"Going to the king." Caricature in *Uilenspiegel* of 5 July 1878, in which Kuyper's supporters are depicted as donkeys.

The Liberals accused Kuyper of unconstitutional agitation. After all, his request to the king not to sign a bill that had been passed by both Chambers ran contrary to the Constitution of 1848, which had bestowed political power on parliament. Although Kuyper disputed this accusation, his articles in *De Standaard* left no room for doubt. "To the King! Not to the Chambers!" was the headline above the editorial of 15 July in which Kuyper wrote: "The States General are there for us, *not we for the Chambers*, and as soon as those Chambers place more importance on their own game than on issues of national importance, then *eo ipso* the nation is released from any obligation towards the States General." The leading article in *De Standaard* of 25 July ended with the words: "Away with such an indecent constitution! Away with such an *unscrupulous* system!" Kuyper argued that the second chamber lacked legitimacy because it was not representative of the people as a whole, but only represented a Liberal "electoral aristocracy."

In the week of 22 to 26 July 1878, which had started out with a nationwide "hour of prayer," the popular petition was signed by more than 305,000 people, while 164,000 signatures supported a similar Roman Catholic petition. These figures are all the more noteworthy if one takes into account that there were only about 122,000 enfranchised voters at that time.

On 3 August 1878 the national petition was presented to King William III at the royal palace Het Loo. Kuyper was not a member of the deputation because the king had let it be known that he did not want to receive him. The delegation was led by the former Anti-Revolutionary member of the second chamber P. J. Elout van Soeterwoude. He delivered an "excellent speech by heart" lasting twenty minutes, to which the king listened most attentively, as *De Standaard* assured its readers in an account on 7 August. After the king had accepted the "written plea" and had in turn spoken kind words, he was applauded by the delegation who cheered: "Long live the King! Long live Orange!" (The royal house of the Netherlands originated in the nobility of the House of Orange-Nassau.)

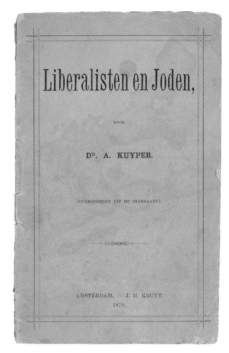

Liberalisten en Joden,

DOOR

Dr. A. KUYPER.

(OVERGEDRUKT UIT DE STANDAARD).

AMSTERDAM. — J. H. KRUYT.
1878.

Jhr Mr P. J. ELOUT VAN SOETERWOUDE.

P. J. Elout van Soeterwoude (1805-1893), member of the second chamber (1853-1862) and a member of the Council of State (1864-1874), was an old political friend of Groen van Prinsterer. In 1879 he became a member of the second chamber for a short time once more. He also played an active role in establishing the Free University.

Although the king (in accordance with his constitutional position) signed the School Act on 17 August 1878, the national petition had far-reaching effects. It speeded up the rapprochement between the Anti-Revolutionaries and the Roman Catholics and gave a strong impulse to the growth and expansion of the Anti-Revolutionary organization.

Characteristic of the intensified political antagonism was the series of articles *Liberalisten en joden (Liberals and Jews)*, which Kuyper published in *De Standaard* in October 1878. In these articles he pointed out the Jewish influence on Liberalism, which had made it anti-Christian in nature. That same month, the articles were published as a pamphlet in order to refute the "thoroughly false" and "slanderous" criticism that they had been written "to fan the flame of Christian hatred against the Jews and to tamper with their civil rights."

The Hall Arts and Sciences on the Maria Square in Utrecht, where two important meetings took place in short succession directly related to the national petition. Here on 23 January 1879 the union "A School with the Bible" was founded, which was to become very important for the extension of Protestant-Christian education. Lohman acted as the first chairman of the union. Henceforth, every year on 17 August (the day on which the King had signed the School Law) a nationwide collection for Christian education was held. In 1879 this "union collection" raised 40,000 guilders; by 1882 the proceeds had risen to 100,000 guilders.

A few months later, on 3 April, the Anti-Revolutionary Party (ARP) was founded in the same building, when twenty-one local electoral associations joined together in a nationwide network with an executive board (central committee) and a joint program. The ARP was the first modern political party in the Netherlands, which gave the Anti-Revolutionaries an organizational and programmatic lead over other political factions. Kuyper was elected chairman of the central committee and would continue to fill this position until 1918, with an interval from 1905 to 1907. Although the ARP had a democratic structure, which was based on the Presbyterian model of church government, Kuyper exerted much influence as its political leader and ideologist.

As the list shows, most electoral associations were called "The Netherlands and Orange," in order to express the historic ties between the nation and the Royal House of Orange which had started during the Dutch war of independence against Spain, 1568-1648.

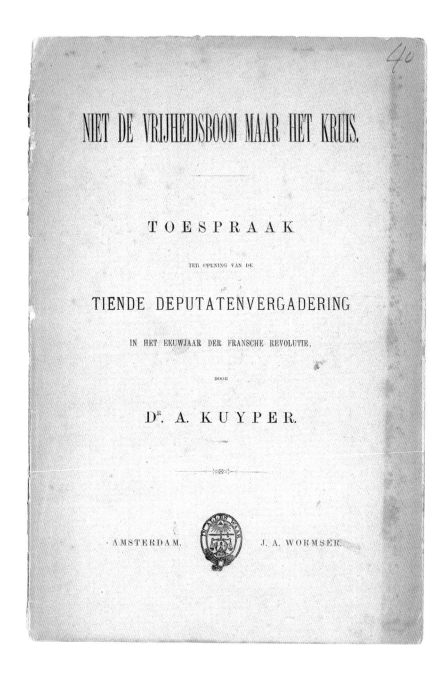

NIET DE VRIJHEIDSBOOM MAAR HET KRUIS.

TOESPRAAK

TER OPENING VAN DE

TIENDE DEPUTATENVERGADERING

IN HET EEUWJAAR DER FRANSCHE REVOLUTIE,

DOOR

D^R. A. KUYPER.

AMSTERDAM, J. A. WORMSER.

One of the speeches to the delegates that Kuyper gave during his years as party chairman, *Not the Liberty Tree but the Cross* (in 1889, the centennial of the French Revolution).

The meeting of delegates, the highest organ within the ARP, consisted of the deputies of the local electoral associations and usually convened before the parliamentary elections. They chose the members of the central committee and agreed upon the platform for the next election. In his fiery and compelling speeches to the deputies Kuyper would give a summary of the political situation and inspired his followers.

During the inaugural meeting of the ARP, the political program, already published on 1 January 1878, was formally accepted. Subsequently, Kuyper wrote a lengthy commentary on it in *De Standaard* and published it as a book in March 1879 under the title *Our Program*. For years both program and commentary would serve as a guide in Anti-Revolutionary politics.

The photograph shows a beautifully bound copy of *Our Program* as offered to the Anti-Revolutionary politician L. W. C. Keuchenius upon his departure from the Dutch East Indies to Holland, after he had been elected as a member of the second chamber in 1879.

L. W. C. Keuchenius (1822-1893) had already been a member of the second chamber from 1866 to 1868. In 1866 he proposed the motion rejecting the appointment of the minister of colonies, Pieter Mijer, Governor-General of the Dutch East Indies. After 1879, as a specialist in colonial affairs, Keuchenius argued for missionary work and campaigned in the second chamber against the Billiton contract (1882/1883), which had become a burden to the treasury. From 1889 until 1890 he was the minister for colonies in the first cabinet of Roman Catholics and Anti-Revolutionaries.

Along with Keuchenius and Elout van Soeterwoude, De Savornin Lohman was also elected to the second chamber in 1879. He was instrumental in forming the Anti-Revolutionary Parliamentary Club, which held regular meetings and as much as possible set out a common policy that benefited the unity of purpose in the chamber.

CHAPTER IV

The Free University, 1878-1888

In addition to organizing the national petition and the establishment of the ARP, another issue demanded much of Kuyper's attention: the foundation of the Free University. During Kuyper's stay abroad because of illness, Heemskerk's Higher Education Act was passed. In the new Act the theological faculties of the universities had not been abolished, as had originally been planned, but while their old name of "theology" was preserved, they were converted into departments of religious studies. The direct link between the Dutch Reformed Church and the state was replaced by the system of the "duplex ordo," whereby a distinction was drawn between scholarly education and ministerial training. In addition to the professors who were appointed by the state, who were expected to study religion as a scientific phenomenon and offer doctrinally neutral education, vocational education in official and doctrinal subjects would be given by "church" professors appointed by the Dutch Reformed synod and paid by the state. Heemskerk's Act further authorized the establishment of privately-owned universities which would not be funded by the state. This provision paved the way for the establishment of a free university, independent of the state, for which Kuyper had already pleaded in *De Standaard* of December 1872.

The reorganization of theological education once again led to discord in orthodox circles. While Kuyper and his supporters worked on plans for an independent free university, Ethical and Confessional theologians wanted to keep in place the state universities. They argued for the installation of special chairs in the theological faculties to supplement the education that was already in place. The second bone of contention concerned the character of the proposed new university. At an earlier stage Kuyper had supported the idea of a free university, in which orthodox members of all sorts could cooperate, but he now considered this broad approach outdated.

In the years 1878-1880 Kuyper definitively went in the direction of a university based on strictly Reformed principles, an aim that demanded a great financial and organizational commitment and also went hand in hand with continual polemics. Kuyper first attacked Gunning in 1878, because he had been nominated to become "church professor" in Utrecht, which would reduce the chances for Kuyper's own university. In 1879 and 1880 he also engaged in historical arguments with the Confessional theologians Bronsveld and Van Toorenenbergen about the establishment and principles of the Free University. He also attacked the Dutch Reformed synod, because it had been biased in the way it had appointed church professors, and had made it quite clear that it did not believe in Kuyper's university.

Despite this turbulent early history, the Free University was opened on 20 October 1880 in the Nieuwe Kerk in Amsterdam. Here Kuyper as professor and first rector delivered his great speech *Sphere Sovereignty*. In addition to educating orthodox ministers, the Free University would play an important role in the training of lawyers and teachers, which went towards strengthening the organizational framework of the Anti-Revolutionary movement. In the first years, however, the university was no more than a theological school with modest means and few students and an offense to the scientific and theological establishment.

As a professor of theology at the Free University (1879-1901) Kuyper wrote his principal theological works on numerous subjects in dogmatics, ethics, liturgy, church history, and church order, all in a systematic and clear way. As of 1881 Kuyper was also professor in the faculty of arts, where he lectured in literature, linguistics, and aesthetics. Characteristic of his broad range of interest is that in his second rectorial address in 1888 he discussed "Calvinism and Art," a theme that at that time was hardly ever discussed in Calvinist circles.

Kuyper was not an armchair academic. Much of what he wrote was dictated by everyday reality, as had already become apparent from his church-historical polemics with Bronsveld and Van Toorenenbergen. In the church struggle of the 1880s, he presented himself as the champion of the classical Reformed tradition, as defined in the Netherlands at the Synod of Dordrecht (1618/1619). On other occasions, however, he did not let tradition get in his way, instead effortlessly adapting it to the demands of the moment. It goes without saying that the old Calvinism had to be adapted so that it could fulfill a vital role in modern times, but the neo-Calvinism that Kuyper created was an arsenal full of weapons that could be deployed at his convenience in every field and against any opponent. It was in any case flexible enough to serve as a crowbar to open up the national Dutch Reformed Church, and in addition (almost simultaneously) to forge a political alliance between Anti-Revolutionaries and Roman Catholics.

** Slippendraagster aan Amsterdam onthouden.

Wijlen de Minister Heemskerk heeft aan de Synode (?) van de Ned. Herv. Kerk salaris voor een *slippendraagster* aan elk der drie Rijksuniversiteiten toegezegd, als aanvulsel van de romp-faculteit, die er voor de Theologie is gesticht.

Altijd op meer belust, vroeg de Synode ook geld voor zulk een *slippendraagster* bij de Gemeentelijke Universiteit te Amsterdam.

Heemskerk zou waarschijnlijk ook dat hebben toegestaan.

Kappeyne weigerde.

Die weigering strekt hem tot eer.

After the implementation of the Higher Education Act of 1876, the old Athenaeum Illustre in Amsterdam was granted university status in October 1877. In imitation of the state universities, this City University also wanted to appoint two Dutch Reformed Church professors. From Kuyper's scornful comments in *De Standaard* of 4 December 1877, it appeared that he did not favor the new way in which the theological curriculum was organized, with a "rump faculty" and church professors as "lackeys." According to Kuyper, the implementation of the duplex ordo was "the bitter fruit of political bungling."

The Higher Education Act enabled the establishment of private universities, but these would not be funded by the state. Already in December 1877 Kuyper and a number of supporters decided to make preparations for the establishment of a "free" university based on Reformed principles. The photograph shows the white double residence of Kuyper's sympathizer, the brewer Willem Hovy, at the Niewe Herengracht in Amsterdam where planning meetings took place.

Dr. J. H. Gunning Jr. as a minister.

The re-organization of theological education again led to disagreements between the Ethicals and the Orthodox. While plans were being made for the Free University, Kuyper grasped the old disputed point of Higher Criticism to distance himself from the Ethical movement. The victim was his long-time friend and sometime collaborator J. H. Gunning. As an Ethical-Orthodox minister, Gunning had been nominated to become a church professor in Utrecht, but at that time also published the first installments of his book *The Life of Jesus* in which he called the stories about Jesus' nativity "holy legends." Although Gunning almost immediately revoked his point of view, he was fiercely attacked by Kuyper in *De Heraut* of 3 February and denounced as not being orthodox. The result was that Gunning withdrew from the Utrecht nomination because he felt that Kuyper had discredited him.

Christelijk-historische gewetensvrijheid.

De conscientie, *ook al mist zij het vermoeden van achtbaarheid niet,*
g e e n grens — voor de onverdraagzaamheid.

[Zie het Program van het Centraal-comité.]

GUNNING-GALILEÏ. — *»En tòch is het legende!!..."*

Caricature from *Uilenspiegel* of 23 February 1878 in which Gunning is depicted as a second Galileo who is forced by Pope Kuyper to tear up *The Life of Jesus* while muttering the words: "And still it is legend!!" The illustration does not do justice to the real course of events, because Gunning himself pulled back from what he had said. However, Kuyper's role was most controversial, because he had written his fierce article in *De Heraut after* Gunning had informed him about his retraction in a personal note. Thus he prevented Gunning, who was well-loved among the Orthodox, from becoming a professor at a state university, which would not have done the Free University any good.

When later that year the Dutch Reformed synod appointed the church professors, there was only one Orthodox theologian among them — who was not even appointed to teach doctrinal subjects — in addition to a Modernist and four theologians of the Groningen School, which still had a lot of support at the synod. This biased policy of selection helped Kuyper's efforts to establish the Free University; he could now point out that the ministerial training at the state universities was not in good hands.

W. Hovy.   Dr. F. L. Rutgers.

Willem Hovy, 1850-1915.

The Society for Higher Education on Calvinist Principles was founded at Utrecht on 5 December 1878 to make it possible to found the Free University. The wealthy Amsterdam brewer Willem Hovy took upon himself the task of raising funds for the new university. At its opening on 20 October 1880, he was able to present a starting capital of "one hundred thousand guilders in gold," one-quarter of which came from his own account. From 1879 to 1896 Hovy was chairman of the Association's board of governors, but he resigned after Lohman was dismissed as professor in law at the Free University.

The theologian F. L. Rutgers (1836-1917) also played an important role in the establishment of the Free University. As a minister in 's-Hertogenbosch he had come into contact with Kuyper through Lohman in 1877. He became a permanent member of staff of *De Heraut* and in 1878 a minister in Amsterdam. In part through Rutgers' efforts, Lohman would also associate himself with the Free University as a curator, although he had grave objections to the way Kuyper fought with the Ethicals.

Dossier "Oprichting van de Vrije Universiteit, 1878–1880" 9

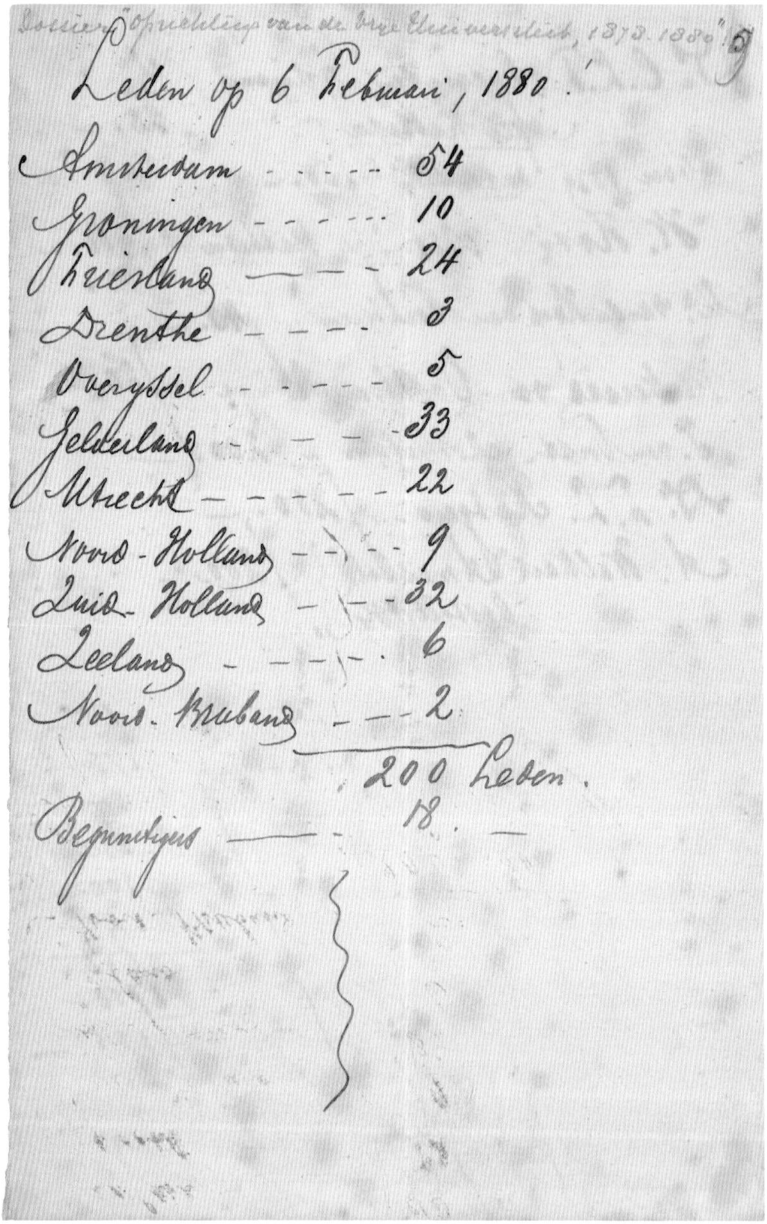

Leden op 6 Februari, 1880.

Amsterdam	54
Groningen	10
Friesland	24
Drenthe	3
Overijssel	5
Gelderland	33
Utrecht	22
Noord-Holland	9
Zuid-Holland	32
Zeeland	6
Noord-Brabant	2
	200 Leden.
Begunstigers	18.

On 6 September 1879, Kuyper and Rutgers were appointed as professors in the Theological Faculty, which was yet to be founded. In early November Kuyper and his family moved to Amsterdam. As the children had scarlet fever, the journey was made by barge with a large placard on the bow that read "Infectious disease scarlet fever."

In February 1880 the Society for Higher Education on Calvinist Principles counted 200 members. In the following months, Kuyper, Rutgers, and Keuchenius travelled throughout the country to recruit members and benefactors for the Society.

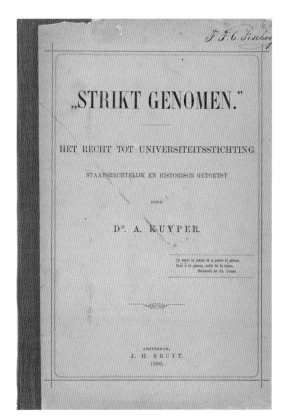

In 1879-80 Kuyper debated fiercely with the Evangelical-Confessional theologian and church historian J. J. van Toorenenbergen and the Ethical-Orthodox minister A. W. Bronsveld about the establishment and principles of the Free University. Both had objections against the exclusively Reformed character of the university. Kuyper battled against Van Toorenenbergen in his pamphlets *The Leiden Professors and the Executors of the Legacy of Dort* (April 1879) and *Revision of the Revision Legend* (December 1879), and against Bronsveld in the pamphlet *Plea for a Double Corrigendum* (February 1880) and in the book *Strictly Speaking: The Right to Found a University Tested Constitutionally and Historically,* which was published in September 1880 shortly before the opening of the Free University.

In January 1880 Van Toorenenbergen was appointed professor in church history at the City University of Amsterdam, which Free University supporters saw as an attempt to make that institution acceptable to orthodox students. Kuyper openly accused Van Toorenenbergen of thwarting fundraising activities for the Free University. Van Toorenenbergen apparently persuaded Groen van Prinsterer's widow, just before her death, not to give generous financial support to plans for a Reformed university; she donated only one thousand guilders.

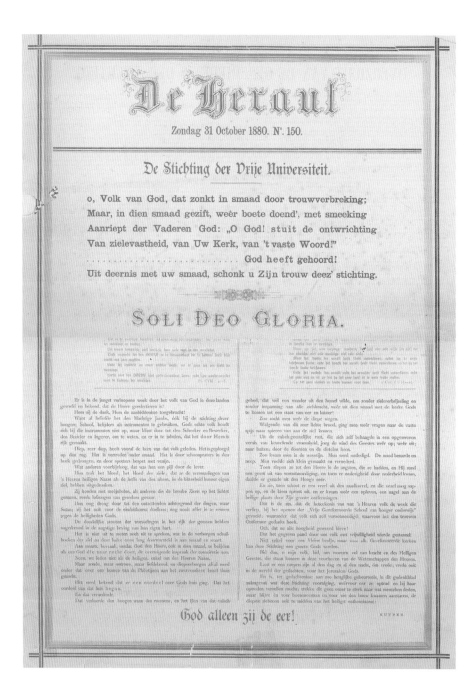

Festive cover of *De Heraut* on the occasion of the opening of the Free University, 19-21 October 1880, in Amsterdam. The director of ceremonies was Kuyper, who, as the first rector, delivered the inaugural address on 20 October in the pulpit of the Nieuwe Kerk — his famous *Sphere Sovereignty* address.

Dr A·Kuyper op 20 October 1880.

Kuyper in the chancel of the Nieuwe Kerk delivering his speech, as drawn by J. H. Isings (1884-1977). In front of the railing of the chancel were draped burgundy velvet curtains, while the specially converted podium had been covered with a sober gray carpet. Characteristic of Kuyper's sense of publicity, he had arranged for a special bench for journalists on the podium, so that they would have a good view of the events.

To the left of the pulpit is Elout van Soeterwoude, who had presented the starting capital of 100,000 guilders on behalf of forty founders, and next to him, in a robe, F. L. Rutgers. Rutgers wore the robe of his father, who had been a professor in Leiden. In its choice for the professorial robe, the Free University adopted the model worn in Leiden, where Kuyper and Rutgers had both studied.

Interior of the Nieuwe Kerk in Amsterdam, with the chancel where the opening of the Free University took place.

In his inaugural address Kuyper set out the principle of sphere sovereignty, an important element in his organic vision for state and society, in which the autonomy of circles within society was to be protected against the "revolutionary" drive for an omnipotent state. Science also had its own sphere of life, in which the truth was sovereign and which might be corrupted "neither under the tutelage of the state nor under church restraints." "And so it is entirely within the Reformed spirit that we now ask for the sovereignty of our principle in our own scholarly sphere. We may not make a pact of neutrality with learning that proceeds from another principle, or sit at the same university table." The Free University was founded on the Christian principle that was revealed in the Bible as God's Word, and that placed Christ as "all-sovereign" at the center of history: "There is not an inch in the entire field of our human life, over which Christ, who is sovereign over all, does not declare: 'mine!'" Kuyper did not conceal the fact that the foundation of the Free University was a gamble: "For I do not exaggerate: it is contrary to all that is called great, contrary to a world of scholars, contrary to a whole century . . . that we undertake the establishment of this school."

SOUVEREINITEIT

IN EIGEN KRING.

REDE TER INWIJDING

VAN DE

VRIJE UNIVERSITEIT,

den 20sten October 1880 gehouden,
in het Koor der Nieuwe Kerk te Amsterdam,

DOOR

DR. A. KUYPER.

AMSTERDAM,
J. H. KRUYT.
1880.

Kuyper's inaugural address, *Sphere Sovereignty*. The speech appeared in print the very same day.

Robert Fruin commented at length on Kuyper's speech in a letter of 7 December 1880: "Dear Colleague. It is a real pleasure to address you, who were at one time my disciple, with this title. For a long time you have deserved to be included among professors, and your oration, which I was most interested to read, amply proves your right to the position that you have achieved. Not that I would affirm your speech: you don't expect that from me, anyway. On the contrary, in my opinion you have done history a disservice. . . . However, I read your spirited and enthusiastic words with great pleasure and I hope with all my heart that you will be permitted to follow your aspirations freely, which may be more modern than you think, without being hindered too much by the traditions of your party. . . . I, for my part, long for argument, and the more the better: in this way I separate the false from the true in my mind's eye and become more convinced of the truth. This is why I am truly glad for the awakening of both the Catholics and the Calvinist Anti-Revolutionaries, because action calls for reaction, and the fortitude of the Modernists has been considerably weakened since their victories. . . . I was very sorry to have missed you when you visited recently. I never leave a conversation with you without having learned something."

Staff of the Free University, with the Minerva that the Seceder weekly paper *De Bazuin* characterized as "heathen." Kuyper rejected the reproach as "iconoclastic fanaticism" and pointed out in *De Heraut* that Minerva, a symbol of learning, also appeared in the works of Reformed theologians such as Voetius. There was also criticism of the fact that after the inauguration of the university, wine had been served at dinner. Against this "mania for the abolition of drinking a glass of wine at a dinner party," Kuyper remarked that his enemies "said of the banquet that those Reformed were not the sort *to water down their wine*. That's true. From the chocolate kettle and the milk-and-water bottle one does not breed a race of bold Calvinists."

In de collegekamer der Vrije Universiteit op Gereformeerden grondslag.

Professor. — Let wel op, dat er buiten de leer, die ik u onderwijs, geen andere leer is dan uit den Booze. Uw streven zij het daarom vóór alles, ieder te verketteren en te verdoemen, wiens begrippen ook maar een haar van de uwe — of liever van de mijne afwijken.

In its first year the Free University counted eight students, all of them in theology. That was more than the single student depicted in the political cartoon above, appearing in *Uilenspiegel* on 21 February 1880. Still, the number of students remained small at first because the career prospects for the university's graduates were limited. The diplomas of the Free University as a private institution were not legally recognized until 1904. If the Free University wanted graduates to obtain an academic title with *effectus civilis*, they had to repeat their academic exams at the Amsterdam's City University or at a state university. Moreover, in 1882 the Dutch Reformed synod decided that theological candidates of the Free University were not allowed to become ministers within the Dutch Reformed Church.

Philip J. Hoedemaker (1839-1910), professor in theology at the Free University (1880-1888). The portrait was painted by Rein Pol on the occasion of the Hoedemaker commemoration (1989) at the Free University.

At first Hoedemaker was a critical ally of Kuyper, but he resigned his position as a professor after the Doleantie and became a minister in the Dutch Reformed Church once more. With his theocratic beliefs, Hoedemaker also exerted influence in the political arena. Unlike Kuyper and Lohman, who believed in the separation of church and state, Hoedemaker argued for a Christian state, one that took God's Word into account and where the Word was proclaimed by a church that played an important role in the public domain.

Two professors from the early days of the Free University: to the left the classicist J. Woltjer (1849-1917); to the right the legal scholar D. P. D. Fabius (1851-1931).

Kuyper and Rutgers together with Ph. J. Hoedemaker formed the Theological Faculty, which was formally constituted on 8 December 1880. With Woltjer's accession to office on 8 October 1881, the Faculty of Arts and Philosophy was also established, in which Kuyper and Dr. F. W. J. Dilloo (appointed on 8 June 1880) also served. Fabius accepted his position on 21 October 1880. The Law Faculty was founded with the inauguration of Lohman on 6 June 1884.

The house at the Prins Hendrikkade 173 in Amsterdam where Kuyper lived from 1 July 1880 until 9 October 1900. During the early years this residence also housed the office of the Free University. Kuyper rented the house from Hovy.

In the early years the lectures of the Free University were held in rooms at the Scottish Missionary Church on the Erwtenmarkt (now: Amstel 56) in Amsterdam, whose façade bore words from Mark 16: "Preach the Gospel to all creatures." For years this former French playhouse had also housed the Scottish Seminary, founded for the education of missionaries to the Jews. The poet and great figure of the Réveil Isaäc da Costa (1798-1860) also taught at this seminary, which was open to young men from both national church and Seceder circles.

The Rev. S. J. du Toit, 1847-1911.

Kuyper hoped to attract students from the Boer republics of South Africa to the Free University. Since 1879 he had corresponded with the minister and journalist S. J. du Toit, who after the Transvaal War of Independence (1880-1881) became superintendent of education there. Although du Toit sympathized with Kuyper, he refused to send students bound for the Netherlands for their higher education exclusively to the Free University. Only after 1900 did the influx of South African students get well underway. Curiously enough the first of them was du Toit's son, the future writer and poet J. D. du Toit (Totius) (1877-1953), who enrolled at the Free University in 1900 and took his doctoral degree in April 1903, defending a doctoral thesis about Methodism under the supervision of Kuyper's son H. H. Kuyper.

*Prof. Kuyper. — Jonge-
luî, ik moet even naar
Londen. Oom Paul ver-
langt mij te raadplegen...*
Gereformeerd student. —
Professor zal dus ook over
Transvaal den baas gaan
spelen?
*Prof. Kuyper.— Den baas
spelen? Jongmensch, je
veroorlooft je hoogst onge-
paste uitdrukkingen...*
Gereformeerd student. —
Nu, u moet me dat woord
zoo kwalijk niet nemen,
professor... Ik bedoel, dat
professors invloed zich nu
ook al tot de Transvaal
schijnt te gaan uitstrekken.
Natuurlijk kan dit niet
anders dan de Gerefor-
meerde zaak ten goede
komen, en daarom zal elk
goed anti-revolutionair er
zich in verheugen. Ik mag
lijden, dat professor er ook
in slaagt oom Paul *Ons Program* aan te smeeren...
*Prof. Kuyper. — Ik heb ook nog andere plannen, jonge vriend!
Ik hoop mijn invloed op onze vrienden de Doppers ook dienstbaar
te maken aan de belangen onzer universiteit.*
Gereformeerd student. — Dat is goed, professor... wij studenten
zullen de Kaffertjes als broeders ontvangen.

The Transvaal War of Independence in South Africa (1880-1881) aroused great enthusiasm in the Netherlands for the Boers, who were of Dutch descent and successfully
fighting against the powerful British. Kuyper fully supported the case of the Boers in *De
Standaard*, and in May 1881 joined the central board of the Nederlands-Zuidafrikaanse
Vereniging (the Netherland-South African Society). In November 1883 he stayed in
London for two weeks at the request of Du Toit to advise the Transvaal deputation,
which consisted of President S. J. P. Kruger, General N. J. Smit, and Du Toit. Despite
their successful negotiations/talks with the British government, Kuyper's interference
with the Transvaal was ridiculed in *Uilenspiegel* of 3 November 1883.

DE UITTOCHT VAN „ONS CHRISTENVOLK".

Juiste voorstelling van de verwezenlijking van dr. Kuyper's dreigement
in *Plancius*.

"The exodus of 'our Christian people'" caricature in *Uilenspiegel* of 29 March 1884, in reaction to Kuyper's Plancius speech.

During the visit of the Transvaal delegation to the Netherlands, Kuyper played an important role. He delivered the official speech during the meeting of 11 March 1884 in the Plancius building on the Plantage Kerklaan in Amsterdam, where the delegation had been invited as guests by the Protestant Labour Association Patrimonium. In his glowing speech he praised the free and orthodox Transvaal, which he said could well become a future sanctuary for Calvinist Dutchmen if the constriction upon freedom in their native country continued. At the end of his speech, Kuyper handed over to General N. J. Smit, one of the heroes of the Spitskop battle, a Transvaal flag with the embroidered motto: "In God we will do brave deeds!" But first Smit had to shake Kuyper's right hand and solemnly swear "that, whatever the future might bring, this flag may never fall into the hands of the Brits."

Kuyper as professor at the Free University.

Kuyper was Rector Magnificus at the Free University four times. (Instead of a president, the head of a Dutch university is usually designated as the Rector Magnificus.) Although his first inaugural address about modern higher criticism (1881) was theological in nature, in 1888 he discussed the relationship between Calvinism and art, while in later inaugural addresses he discussed broader philosophical questions.

Kuyper wearing a daytime dressing-gown in his study, Prins Hendrikkade 173.

After his nervous breakdown in 1876-77 Kuyper kept to a fixed daily schedule, which changed only rarely over the years. The day started with short morning devotions with members of the family and servants, followed by breakfast. Between nine and twelve he wrote his lead articles, and afterwards until lunch the "asterisks," for *De Standaard* — according to his daughter Henriëtte, his "favourite work." After lunch, he traded his dressing gown for a formal coat, in which he gave lectures, held meetings, and dealt with correspondence. The time after dinner was used for lighter work, such as correcting proofs.

Kuyper also saw to it that he took a two-hour walk every day, a habit that he maintained until he was quite old. Kuyper, who was not a regular churchgoer, used Sunday mornings for his other "favourite work," writing his devotions for *De Heraut.*

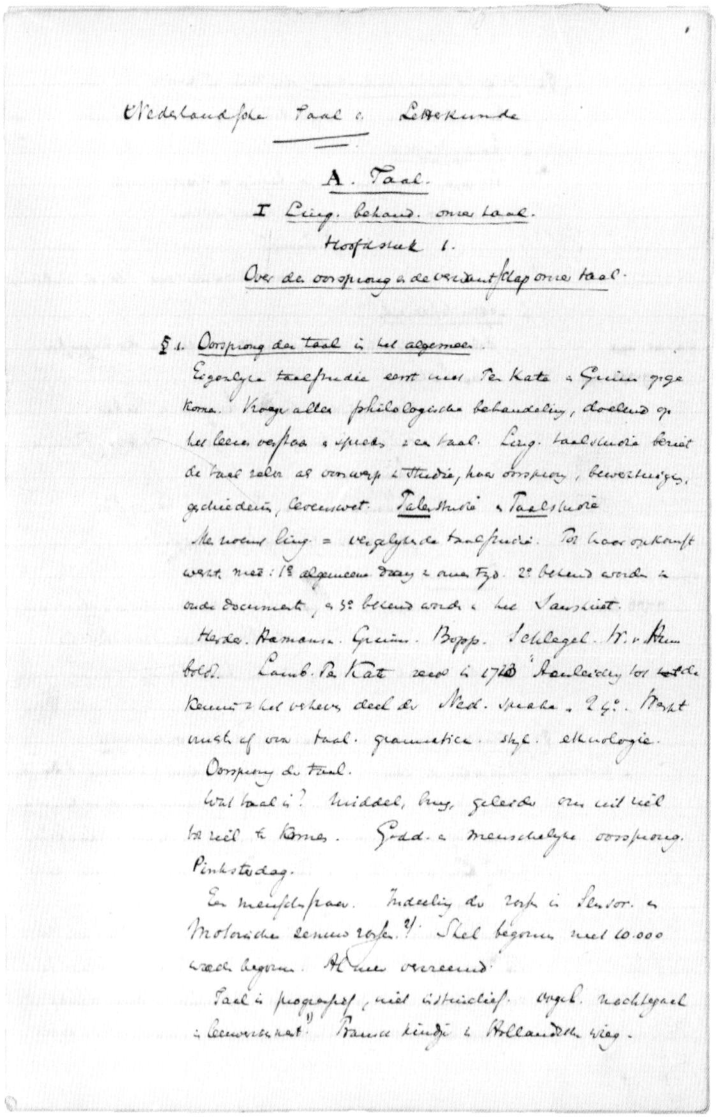

Nederlandsche Taal & Letterkunde

A. Taal.

I Leng. behand. onze taal.

Hoofdstuk 1.

Over de oorsprong & de verwantschap onze taal.

§ 1. Oorsprong der taal in het algemeen.

[handwritten lecture notes in Dutch]

Notes for a course of lectures on Dutch language and literature that Kuyper offered from 1883 until 1901.

In addition to his chair in the Theological Faculty, Kuyper was also professor in the Faculty of Arts from 1881 on. In this capacity he gave lectures on literature, linguistics, and esthetics. The latter were also attended by young ladies, including the daughters of faculty members, who were allowed to attend as auditors. Although he was not musical, Kuyper also devoted much time to music in his lectures about aesthetics. One of his students, the future president of the Supreme Court, W. H. de Savornin Lohman, commented on this: "One would truly think that Dr. Kuyper, who does not know any music, not only understands it perfectly, but is a musical genius."

Kuyper's great theological works usually first appeared in *De Heraut* as "pieces not yet published" or "a continuing series" and were subsequently published as a collection. Appearing one after another were *The Work of the Holy Spirit*, 3 volumes, 1888-1889 (previously in *De Heraut*, 1883-1886); *E Voto Dordraceno*, 4 volumes, 1892-1895 (*De Heraut*, 1886-1894); *Encyclopedia of Sacred Theology*, 3 volumes, 1893-1894; *God's Angels*, 1902 (*De Heraut*, 1894-1897); *Common Grace*, 3 volumes, 1902-1905 (*De Heraut* 1895-1901); *Our Worship*, 1911 (*De Heraut*, 1897-1901, 1911); *Pro Rege*, 3 volumes, 1911-1912 (*De Heraut* 1907-1911); and *Of the Consummation*, 4 volumes, 1929 (*De Heraut*, 1911-1918). The *Lecture Notes on Dogmatics* (5 volumes, 1891) were not published by Kuyper himself, but by his students.

Kuyper's devotional volumes, just like his other works, often had evocative titles such as *For a Thistle a Myrtle, Honey from the Rock,* and *In the Shadow of Death.* Dutch Reformed theologian K. H. Miskotte, who by no means admired the "Napoleonic" Kuyper, wrote that he had seldom seen such profound meditations as these. The strong bond between Kuyper and the Reformed in the Netherlands can be explained to a large extent by these meditations, in which he discussed religious matters in a pastoral and practical way. In the political arena this spiritual bond was of great importance.

In June 1884 A. F. de Savornin Lohman was appointed professor in the Law Faculty of the Free University and moved from 's-Hertogenbosch to Amsterdam. In addition, he remained the leader of the Anti-Revolutionary Parliamentary caucus. As a result of this move, the cooperation between Kuyper and Lohman intensified even more. That their personal relations were good during these years even though differences of opinion cropped up from time to time became apparent in a letter from Kuyper to Lohman dated 20 August 1882. Kuyper wrote the letter after he had learned that the Lohmans had lost their newborn child: "Be a support to your wife at this time. She needs it. Pregnancy and birth demand great efforts, which seek and find a natural reaction in the joy of new life. Now that that has fallen away, much love and tenderness must compensate for it. And even if there is a sense of self-sufficiency in your dear wife, do not be misled. . . . [A]nd let the little grave be a sign of life for your remaining children, something strange, but which does not leave their hearts untouched. That small being who passed through your home only briefly can still be a blessing for you all. Convey to your dear wife from us both, that in our hearts there is a kind of emptiness for her sake. God be merciful to her."

Vrije Universiteit (Keizersgracht)

Uitg. H. v. d. Linde, Amst.

Amsterdam

29-1-'85

The first building to be owned by the Free University, at Keizersgracht 162, dating back to 1615, that was purchased on 17 December 1883 for 41,000 guilders. After extensive renovations, it was officially opened on 29 January 1885. To make the building more attractive, the ground-floor façade was covered in marble. In addition to serving as a university building, it also served as a boarding house for eighteen students who each had a small living room and a bedroom. *De Standaard* of 29 January reported that the

whole building was centrally heated. The opening of the boarding house was celebrated the next day with a meal shared in a private circle.

Mrs. Kuyper to her second son, Frederik, January 1885: "Aunt Anna has now left for the boarding house for good. It was inaugurated yesterday. Thankfully everything was in order, although barely! Yesterday evening the prayer meeting was jammed full, spilling into various rooms. Aunt Anna acted most sweetly amid the surging crowd in her manageress's outfit wearing her little cap. Tomorrow there is a big dinner for sixty people. All the young people with the directors and professors. I can also come if I want to; your aunt wanted me to do so and invited me. Just imagine, if you will, how nice this will be, as we all have to bring something for the dinner: Papa and Prof. Lohman a ham each, the Rev. Van Schelven soup, Mr. Hovy beer, Prof. Rutgers cakes, Dilloo assorted nuts and raisins, Woltjer oranges, Sefat ginger, etc. etc. The Society cannot spend money on such things, of course. But it will truly be a meal lovingly prepared as in the olden days."

Kuyper was particularly fond of his eldest sister Anna, the widow of his university friend J. P. Mond, and put up with her Kohlbrüggian theological sympathies. She nursed her father in his old age, and after he died (1882) went to live with Kuyper. A few years later she became the resident director of the boarding house where students of the Free University were lodged. Kuyper's youngest daughter Cato later filled the position from 1927 to 1933.

Kuyper and his family in 1886, upon Frederik Kuyper's departure for America. Back row from left to right: Guillaume (1878-1941), Herman Huber (1864-1945), Levinus Willem Christiaan (1882-1892), Abraham Sr., Johanna, and Abraham Jr. (1872-1941). Front row, sitting, from left to right: Henriëtte Sophia Susanna (1870-1933), Catharina Maria Eunice (1876-1955), Johanna Hendrika (1875-1948), and Jan Hendrik Frederik (1866-1933), who with his hat and cane looks very much ready to leave. Frederik, Kuyper's second son, left for America in 1886, where he trained to be a dentist. Later he became a dentist in Bandung and Padang in the Dutch East Indies, where he joined the theosophical movement, much to his father's dismay.

IV. Opvoeding.
  Herma . ƒ 450. –
  Frederic . „ 675. –
  School . „ 575. –   „ 1700.00
V. Dienstpersoneel
  Bonne . 150. –
  Drijfood . 180. –
  Cadeaux . 20. –
  Tooi . 20. – ƒ 370. –
VI. Communicatie
  Reizen . ƒ 100. –
  Papier . 20. –
  Teleg. , post . 50. –
  Tram . 15. –
  Sleep . 25. – ƒ 210. –
VII. Personalia
  Zakgeld Pa . „ 52. –
  „ Ma . „ 52. –
  fooien . „ 25. –
  Receptie . „ 100. –
  Secretaris . „ 100. – „ 329. –

Transp. ƒ 8178.31

ƒ 10787.31

Kuyper's ledger. The page shows the expenses in 1885 for education, servants, communication, and personal items. The remaining entries for that year were: house (2350 guilders), household (3931.50 guilders), clothes (1160 guilders), gifts and tips (810 guilders), yearly accounts (2337 guilders), and "general" (760 guilders). Against the sum of total expenses of 14,694 guilders, his income amounted to 14,230 guilders, so a deficit had to be addressed. His income was made up of an allowance granted by the Free University (5000 guilders), De Standaard (4000 guilders), De Heraut (2400 guilders), profits from stocks (760 guilders) and royalties from his books (500 guilders).

Mrs. Kuyper, 1888.

The Dutch Reformed minister Christiaan Hunningher, who in his youth lived with the Kuyper family for a short time, testified in *Memories of the Old Guard* (1922): "I was always struck by the fact that Mrs. Kuyper, even though she was her husband's kindred spirit, was kinder towards his opponents than he was. With old family friends, for example, Beets in Utrecht and Hasebroek in Amsterdam, she was always on good terms. That is why she was so sorry that Dr. Kuyper had felt obliged to 'rake away some of those autumn leaves from my porch' in *De Heraut* after the publication of Beets's *Autumn Leaves*. I can still hear him saying to his wife: 'Yes, Jo, but it had to be done.'"

Kuyper in 1886, the year of the Doleantie.

According to Hunningher, Kuyper spoke more mildly about his opponents within the family circle than in public: "For *everyone* he used the title 'Mister': . . . Mister Gunning, Mister Beets, Mister Bronsveld, etc. And when I asked him why he judged his opponents so much more liberally and kindly in the circle of his family than in his newspapers, he answered that at home he spoke of them as often amiable and high-standing *persons*, while in the papers he had to warn 'our' nation of their pernicious *principles* and *theories*."

CHAPTER V

The Doleantie of 1886

The opening of the Free University had thrown into sharp relief the ongoing arguments over church matters, and in the years that followed, the university was a factor in the church struggle that would reach a climax in 1886. During the transfer of the rectorship of the Free University in October 1881, Kuyper, in his *Contemporary Biblical Criticism and Its Troubling Import for the Community of the Living God,* turned against Ethical theology in particular. The following year a new conflict arose when Gunning was appointed church professor at the City University of Amsterdam. The appointment was particularly painful because the Amsterdam city council had promised to fund two Dutch Reformed chairs, on the condition that the theological candidates from the Free University would not be allowed to become ministers in the Dutch Reformed Church. The Dutch Reformed synod agreed to this, although one could foresee that this pulpit ban would cause problems in the long run. In 1885 the ordination of the first Free University graduate was one of the breaking points between the synod and the *Gereformeerden.* (In Dutch there are two words for "Reformed" — *Hervormd* and *Gereformeerd.* These bore sharply different connotations in the late 1800s. *Hervormd* continued to be used for the national church, but for their opponents *Hervormd* began to mean theologically liberal or Modernist. The more theologically conservative group, such as Kuyper and his followers, began to be called *Gereformeerd.*)

It was clear that the synod did not have much liking for Kuyper's Reformed university, but given its composition, little else could be expected. Although the influence of Kuyper's group had increased significantly at the local level, for the greater part, the synod was still dominated by the Groningen movement which was able to block the reforms Kuyper wanted. It also did not hesitate to irritate those of Kuyper's movement. In January 1880 and 1883 the synod decided to liberalize the form of admission for new church members and the form of subscription for prospective pastors, which threatened to further undermine fidelity to the confessions.

Kuyper reacted to these developments with publications in which he openly discussed the possibility of a break with the "unreformed church government." He also organized the resistance against the synodical decisions, first of all in Amsterdam, where in February 1882 he had been elected as an elder and where the majority in the church council was *Gereformeerd.* Subsequently, upon the initiative of the Amsterdam church council, in April 1883 a conference took place with like-minded consistories during which it was decided to accept the Three Forms of Unity, the classical Reformed creeds dating back to 1619, as an "agreement of ecclesiastical fellowship." In May the Amsterdam consistory decided to require all elders and ministers to sign the Forms. A year later the last three Modernist ministers in Amsterdam were placed under constraint by assigning each of them two orthodox elders to monitor the acceptance of new members whom they had catechized. A result of this stricter supervision was that the catechumens of the Modernist ministers requested a certificate so that they could "make profession of faith" elsewhere. In April 1885 the consistory decided not to give out any more certificates unless the applicants signed an additional statement affirming their orthodoxy. When the conflict about the certificates escalated to such an extent that a break with the higher levels of church government threatened to take place, the consistory made an arrangement that should this indeed occur, it would retain control of church properties.

This conduct by the consistory was unacceptable to the classical [regional] authorities: on 4 January 1886 it suspended eighty members of the consistory, which formed the beginning of a dramatic break within the Dutch Reformed Church. The so-called "sawing of the panels" caused quite a stir: on 6 January, Kuyper, Rutgers, and Lohman gained access to the vestry of the Nieuwe Kerk by forcing an opening in the door. There were similar painful scenes in other parts of the country as well, and the police often had to intervene between the parties. Remarkably, while the struggle against Modernism had been the original objective, Kuyper and his Reformed supporters ended up fighting mostly against other orthodox movements. Many of the orthodox church members shared Kuyper's objections against the synod and Modernism, but were not prepared to give up the historical national church.

After a year of fierce quarrels, in which "brotherly love" seemed all too distant, some of the *Gereformeerden* left the Dutch Reformed Church under Kuyper's leadership. In 1887 they assembled to form the Nederduitsche Gereformeerde Kerken (Dutch Gereformeerde Churches) with the affix "Lamenting" [*Doleerende*], indicating their grievance that their church properties were wrongly being withheld from them. Five years later the lamenters and the greater part of the Christian Reformed, which had emerged as a result of the Secession of 1834, joined to form a new church structure: the Gereformeerde Churches in the Netherlands (1892).

In 1882 the Dutch Reformed synod decided that the theological candidates of the Free University were no longer allowed to become ministers in the Dutch Reformed Church. In his address *What Are the Prospects for the Students of the Free University?* delivered on 5 July 1882 at the Free University Day in Leeuwarden, Kuyper fiercely denounced the synod's decision, which had shown "extensive tyranny, narrow-mindedness and backwardness."

belijdenissen der Kerken zelve, en uit deze verklaring der recht-
zinnige leer, die met eendrachtige overeenstemming van allen, en
een ieder lid der geheele Synode bevestigd is.

Daarna vermaant dezelve Synode ook ernstiglijk de lasteraars,
dat zij toezien wat zwaar oordeel Gods zij op zich laden, die
tegen zoovele Kerken en zoovcler Kerken belijdenissen valsch getui-
genis spreken, de gewetens der zwakken beroeren, en bij velen de
gemeenschap der ware geloovigen zoeken verdacht te maken.

Ten laatste vermaant deze Synode alle Mede-dienaars in het
Evangelie van Christus, dat zij zich in het verhandelen van deze
leer, beide in Scholen en Kerken, godvruchtiglijk en godsdienstiglijk
gedragen; haar zoowel met de tong als met de pen tot Godes
eer, heiligheid des levens en vertroosting der verslagene gemoe-
deren richten; dat zij met de Schriftuur naar de regelmaat des
geloofs niet alleen gevoelen maar ook spreken; en eindelijk van
alle zulke wijzen van spreken zich onthouden, die de palen van
den rechten zin der H. Schriftuur, ons voorgesteld, te buiten
gaan, en die den dartelen Sophisten rechtvaardige oorzaak geven
mochten, om de leer der Gereformeerde Kerken te beschimpen of
ook te lasteren.

De Zone Gods, Jezus Christus, die, ter rechterhand zijns Va-
ders zittende, den menschen gaven geeft, heilige ons in de waarheid; brenge diegenen, die verdwaald zijn, tot de waarheid; stoppe
den lasteraars van de gezonde leer hunne monden, en begave de
getrouwe dienaars zijns woords met den Geest der wijsheid en des
onderscheids, opdat alle hunne redenen mogen gedijen ter eere
Gods en tot stichting der toehoorders. Amen.

In February 1882 Kuyper was elected as an elder in Amsterdam. By organizing the *Gereformeerde* office holders in a *"Broederkring"* ("circle of brothers"), he was able to determine the course of the Amsterdam church council and lead the resistance against the
Dutch Reformed synod, which had liberalized the rules for admittance of new members
and future pastors.

In March 1883 Kuyper published a new edition of the "Three Forms of Unity" and
the Church Order of Dort, which was meant to replace the church regulations of 1816. In
May the Amsterdam consistory decided to submit the Three Forms to the elders and the
ministers for them to sign. The photograph above shows the copy of the Three Forms
signed by Kuyper and others.

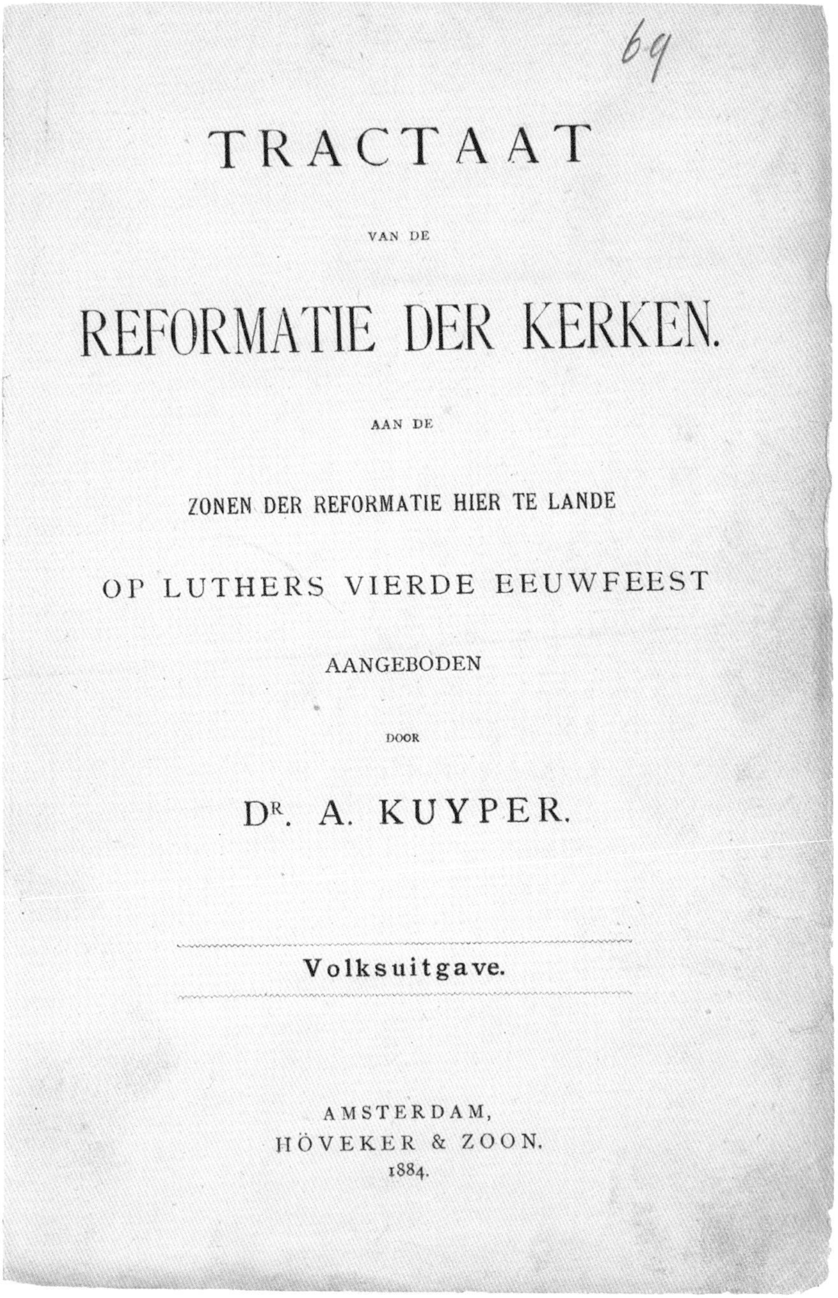

69

TRACTAAT

VAN DE

REFORMATIE DER KERKEN.

AAN DE

ZONEN DER REFORMATIE HIER TE LANDE

OP LUTHERS VIERDE EEUWFEEST

AANGEBODEN

DOOR

D^R. A. KUYPER.

Volksuitgave.

AMSTERDAM,
HÖVEKER & ZOON.
1884.

On the commemoration of Luther's 400th birthday, in November 1883, Kuyper published the *Treatise on the Reformation of the Churches*, offered to "the sons of the Reformation here in this country" and dedicated to Elout van Soeterwoude. In this work he defended the right to church reform — even "by breaking away from the ecclesiastical structure" if necessary.

Candidaat J. H. Houtzagers.

The Rev. L. Schouten, 1828-1905.

In order to emphasize once more the strictly *Gereformeerd* nature of his objectives, in *De Heraut* of February 1885 Kuyper turned against singing hymns during worship, because they were said to be of Arminian origin and were particularly popular among the Groningen school and the Modernists. The "hymn question" had been a particularly sensitive issue in church circles for many years.

Kuyper's position provoked criticism from his Free University colleague Hoedemaker and from the Utrecht minister L. Schouten, the founder of the Bijbels Museum. In a pamphlet Schouten warned that a schism in the church would certainly take place if this "pernicious hatred of hymns" were to increase any further.

J. H. Houtzagers, 1857-1940.

While the differences in Amsterdam were becoming increasingly sharp, the Dutch Reformed congregation of Kootwijk in the Veluwe region decided to defy the synodic pulpit ban of 1882. In March 1885 the consistory initiated a provisional call to J. H. Houtzagers, who was the first student to finish his theological education at the Free University.

While Kuyper followed the "Houtzagers question" with solid pieces of commentary in *De Heraut*, the Dutch Reformed consistory of The Hague refused to make available The Hague's Kloosterkerk for the prayer service preceding the fifth Free University Day that was planned for 1 July 1885. Instead, the service took place in the Waalse Kerk, where Kuyper delivered his speech *Iron and Clay*. Referring to Nebuchadnezzar's dream, he argued that it was impossible for the *Gereformeerden* (iron) and the Modernists (clay) to remain connected in one ecclesiastical structure.

STUDENT H. H. KUYPER TE KOOTWIJK

Student H. H. Kuyper on behalf of the enterprise "A. Bram and Son" on a visit to Kootwijk, caricature from *Uilenspiegel* of 13 February 1886.

On 30 December 1885 the consistory of Kootwijk followed through and issued a de-
finitive pastoral call to Houtzagers; he accepted on 8 January. The board of the classis of
Harderwijk moved to suspend the consistory on 1 February, after which, on 2 February,
Kootwijk broke all ties with the Dutch Reformed Church. On Sunday, 7 February 1886
Houtzagers was installed as a minister in the presence of twenty students of the Free
University, including Kuyper's eldest son, Herman. An attempt by the administrative
board of the classis to prevent the service with the aid of the police was foiled because
Herman Kuyper had persuaded the custodian to open the church an hour early. On
28 February the synod declared that Houtzagers was no longer a member of the Dutch
Reformed Church.

The jurist and theologian Dr. W. van den Bergh (1850-1890), curator of the Free University and a minister in Voorthuizen, played an active role in calling Houtzagers to the neighboring town of Kootwijk. On 7 February 1886, Van den Bergh and his congregation withdrew from the administrative organization of the Dutch Reformed Church.

Pamphlets by Kuyper (and Rutgers) from the year of the Doleantie, 1886.

In Amsterdam the conflict had shifted to the acceptance of new members who had been instructed by Modernist ministers. The orthodox elders refused to cooperate, after which the prospective members of the congregation requested an attestation (certificate of good moral character) so that they could be confirmed elsewhere. They would then register as members back in their own parish. In April 1885 the consistory decided not to give attestations unless the applicants signed a supplementary declaration of orthodox doctrine. When the conflict about the attestations escalated to such an extent that a rift with the higher ecclesiastical authorities threatened, the consistory decided that if such a rift occurred, each church would retain control of its own properties.

To the board of the classis the consistory's conduct was unacceptable. On 4 January 1886 it approved a motion made by its clerk, Amsterdam pastor G. J. Vos, to suspend the eighty consistory members (5 ministers, 42 elders, and 33 deacons) who had voted for the new administrative regulation. Among the elders who were suspended were Kuyper, Rutgers, Hovy, Woltjer, and Fabius, who were all associated with the Free University.

CONSISTORIE
KAMER

Uitgave van Martinus Nijhoff.　　　　　　　　　Steendruk van J.Krauss 'sHage.

„Zij schieten derwaert aen . . . .
Als tijgers, die bij nacht van honger uitgejaeght
Gebeten zijn op roof. Zij stormen onversaeght
Met boomen op de deur, om 't al voor Godt te waegen."

Vondel's Gijsbrecht van Aemstel.
iVde bedrijf.

"Church troubles in Amsterdam," caricature in *De Nederlandsche Spectator*, 9 January 1886.

Those who had been suspended did not take long to react. Because they did not acknowledge the suspension, they took it upon themselves to take control of the consistory of the Nieuwe Kerk where the church archives and the safes containing the trustees' money and church offerings were kept. On 6 January 1886, Rutgers as president and trustee, Kuyper as elder, and Lohman as legal advisor gained entry to the consistory chamber of the Nieuwe Kerk by having the door forced open, which had been locked by order of the chairman of the consistory, the Rev. A. J. Westhoff. Because the trustees kept control of church properties by virtue of the amended regulations, the group thought they had the right to do this, even after the suspension of the eighty consistory members. The Nieuwe Kerk itself remained available for Dutch Reformed church services, but the consistory remained under occupation for almost a year and only vacated in December 1886.

The door of the vestry of the Nieuwe Kerk, with the missing panel, currently in possession of the Museum Het Catharijneconvent in Utrecht. On the night of 5 January, as a precautionary measure, Rev. Westhoff had the door reinforced and fitted with a new lock.

Describing the forced entry as "sawing out a panel" is not correct, because in breaking open the door, no saw was used. The occupiers first removed the inlay frame, which exposed the right-hand panel, then removed this panel in order to unscrew the new lock, but then discovered that the inside of the door had been reinforced with steel plates. After the plates had been knocked away the lock was unscrewed and the door opened.

The expression "the sawing of the panel," which was introduced by Kuyper's opponents, was clearly meant to incriminate, because it was based on the practices of a well-known burglar of that time, Lavertu, who gained access to houses by sawing out door panels. That was the reason that a caricature entitled "sawing panels on Calvinist Principles" in *Uilenspiegel* of 16 January 1886 carried the title "Lavertu redivivus."

KIJKJES ACHTER DE SCHERMEN.

ONTHULDE GEHEIMEN

IN ZAKE HET

AMSTERDAMSCHE KERKVOOGDEN-OPROER

DOOR

D͢ˢ. A. J. WESTHOFF,

Afgetreden Voorzitter van den Amsterdamschen Kerkeraad.

Ridendo dicere verum, quid vetat?

AMSTERDAM,
A. W. BRUNA.
1886.

The Rev. A. J. Westhoff (1849-1929), in January 1886, chairman of the Amsterdam consistory, was with Dr. Vos Kuyper's foremost adversary. He wrote a pamphlet entitled *Peeks behind the Scenes: Secrets of the Amsterdam Church Warden Revolt Revealed*, pub-

K. Kater.   B. Poesiat.

lished in February 1886. Westhoff wrote that Kuyper ("our ecclesiastical Napoleon") had begun his "war of extermination" against the Dutch Reformed Church in order to save the Free University: "The Free University, Dr. Kuyper and the new administrative regulations are related to each other as *reason, cause,* and *occasion* of the current troubles."

In his pamphlet Westhoff outlined how on 8 January the entrance to the Nieuwe Kerk remained closed to the Dutch Reformed ministers and the members of the classical board, who wanted to hold a meeting in the consistory room but were left standing outside "shivering in the cold snow storm." "Just at that moment the stock exchange opened, and everyone who was anyone in Amsterdam saw us standing there. Their expressions of indignation about what had been done to us led to *public opinion* coming down on our side."

Two of Hovy's employees, K. Kater and the suspended elder B. Poesiat, chairman and secretary, respectively, of the Christian Dutch labor union Patrimonium, were involved in the occupation and supervision of the consistory room of the Nieuwe Kerk. To some degree the church struggle in Amsterdam was also social in nature, because many *Gereformeerde* believers were outsiders of lower social status.

Threatening letter addressed to Kuyper, delivered to the door of the Nieuwe Kerk in Amsterdam on 9 January 1886: "You're not going out tonight!"

The action by Kuyper, Rutgers, and Lohman was severely criticized in the conservative and liberal press alike. The liberal *Algemeen Handelsblad* suggested the possibility that the Anti-Revolutionaries would use the same methods in politics as the *Gereformeerden* in the church. On 8 January 1886 the newspaper wrote about Kuyper: "We have warned for some considerable time against the fanaticism of this constitutional-religious party leader. This ex-reverend is a far greater threat to our society, our freedoms and institutions than the other former reverend, the anarchist Domela Nieuwenhuis. The violent deed which he ordered and which he helped perform must be denounced in every way. It illustrates the kind of decision he would take if he was to stand at the head of an Anti-Revolutionary cabinet. It is to be expected that the party, which follows his orders, will at least distance itself from the now totally ridiculous name *Anti*-Revolutionary."

On 9 January 1886 the *Dagblad van Zuid-Holland en 's-Gravenhage (Newspaper of South Holland and The Hague)*, which was the main organ of the conservative movement, also used the church conflict in Amsterdam to discredit the Anti-Revolutionary Party: "Or does one not yet see how the party that calls itself Anti-Revolutionary brings about revolution in the church; how political party heads who write about the separation of church and state in their programmes are once again leaders in the church turmoil. . . . For years Dr. Kuyper has gone around with a burning torch and, like a troublemaker incarnate, swung it around, and the sparks from that torch, according to his wish and will, fell on the flammable materials that he had piled up expressly for that purpose. Indeed, the general public now says Dr. Kuyper is a disaster for our country!"

Letter by J. Kappeyne van de Coppello to Kuyper, 20 February 1886.

In addition to the ecclesiastical procedures concerning the legality of the suspension of the *Gereformeerde* members of the consistory, trials were also held in the civil courts about control of church properties. As legal advisors, Lohman and his VU colleague Fabius in particular had an important role to play in these trials. In the proceedings over the archives and the church buildings in Amsterdam, Kuyper was assisted by his one-time political opponent, Kappeyne van de Coppello, who was known as one of the best lawyers of his day. In his letter of 20 February 1886 Kappeyne offered "friendly advice," which Kuyper gratefully accepted.

Aan de vruchten kent men den boom.

D-m l- N-w nh-s. — *Wij kunnen tevreden zijn, ex-collega!... het zaad dat wij gestrooid hebben, gij en ik, begint te kiemen en hier en daar selfs reeds uit te loopen...*

K-p r. — *Ach, ik vrees, broeder, dat het nog lang duren zal, vóórdat wij oogsten kunnen. Men verstikt de kiemen met geweld!*

D-m-l- N-w-nh-s. — *Geen moedeloosheid, vriend!... Laat men doen wat men wil. Gij en ik blijven voortgaan met de zaden van onrust en beroering en van opstand tegen het gezag met volle handen uit te strooien ..*

The church conflict led to discord in Anti-Revolutionary circles and to the loss of four seats in the general elections of June 1886. In Parliament, on 29 July, Lohman questioned Heemskerk, the Minister for Home Affairs, about the "biased" way in which the police had proceeded against the Doleantie in Leiderdorp, but his party associate G. J. F. Beelaerts van Blokland made it quite clear during the exchange that he did not agree with Lohman.

This photograph shows a caricature from *Uilenspiegel* of 7 August 1886 in which Kuyper is compared to the revolutionary former pastor Ferdinand Domela Nieuwenhuis, who as chairman of the Social-Democratic Federation in his weekly paper *Justice for All* expressed his approval of the "Eel Riot," which caused serious public disturbances on 25 and 26 July 1886 in the Jordaan, a district in Amsterdam. Domela Nieuwenhuis was sentenced to prison. (The riot, mostly of poor people, was suppressed by the police and army; twenty-five people died.)

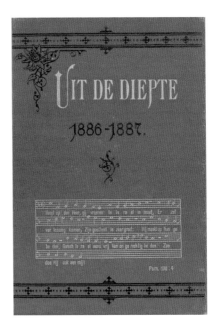

Protest against the provisional suspension of the eighty members of the Amsterdam consistory on 4 January 1886 by the board of the classis. Those who had been suspended put their case before the provincial church council of North Holland. On 1 July they (with the exception of five who had changed their minds) were permanently expelled from their offices by the provincial church government and the ministry because they had "disturbed order and peace."

A few days later, on 5 July 1886, Kuyper and Rutgers were honored in one of the halls at the Odeon for their "important services and unceasing interventions in the defence of the rights of the *Gereformeerde* Church of Amsterdam in the conflict of 1886." On behalf of the six *Gereformeerde* ministers of the capital city, each was given a Bible bound in Russian leather and adorned with silverwork. On the Bible given to Kuyper a medallion had been added depicting Jesus' clearing of the Temple, with a caption of the words from John 2:17: "Zeal for thy house has consumed me." The Bible given to Rutgers depicted Peter and John before the Jewish council.

Out of the Depths, a volume of "Scripture readings by the expelled preachers and their comrades in Amsterdam, delivered in the 'halls,'" with a cover imprint from Psalm 130:4: "Put your hope in the Lord, you who are devout." Owing to a shortage of church buildings, the worship services of the *Gereformeerden* were held in meeting rooms or concert halls.

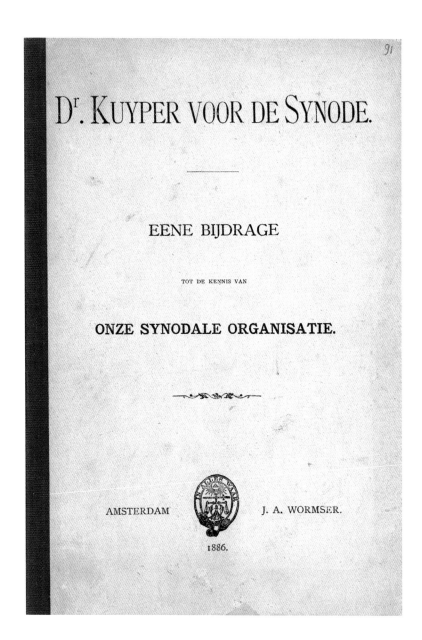

D^r. KUYPER VOOR DE SYNODE.

EENE BIJDRAGE

<small>TOT DE KENNIS VAN</small>

ONZE SYNODALE ORGANISATIE.

AMSTERDAM   J. A. WORMSER.

1886.

On behalf of all the consistory members who had been suspended, Kuyper appeared before the *synodus contracta* (smaller synod) on 16 September in the Willemskerk in The Hague. In his satirical pamphlet *Dr. Kuyper before the Synod,* Kuyper ridiculed the members of the synod: "Oh, there was something so ghost-like in this group of eleven of the Most Reverend, all children of our nineteenth century, seated there in that stuffy, somber vault around that long table, bound to something worse than the trials of the Middle Ages."

    Two months later Kuyper changed his tone in his pamphlet *Final Appeal to the Conscience of the Members of the Synod,* but to no avail.

Aan de Leden der Nederduitsche Gereformeerde Gemeente
(doleerende) te Amsterdam.

Geliefde Broeders en Zusters in onzen Heere Jezus Christus!

Op 16 December des vorigen jaars gaf de Kerkeraad ter Uwer kennisse, dat hier ter stede aan de tastbare ongerijmdheid, om een Kerk van Christus te laten regeeren door een Synode, die den Christus verwerpt, thans een einde is gemaakt.

Uw Kerkeraad heeft het juk van deze Synodale Hiërarchie afgeworpen, en de Christelijke Kerkenordening, die hier eeuwen lang gegolden had, wederom ingevoerd.

Gelijk echter te voorzien was, is door deze daad van Reformatie de bestrijding der macht-hebbenden opgewekt en gelijk de Kerkeraad in zijn *Bericht* van *Reformatie* reeds vermoeden deed, sluit men thans voor Uwe leeraars de Kerkgebouwen, onthoudt men hun de gewone tractementen en belet men Uwe Armverzorgers over de stichtingen en goederen der Gemeente te beschikken.

Hierdoor ziet derhalve Uw Kerkeraad zich voor de pijnlijke keuze geplaatst, om óf na pas de vrijheid, die in Christus is, herwonnen te hebben, weêr een voetval voor de Synode te doen, óf wel voorloopig te leven van de blijmoedige offeranden der willige liefde.

Dit zal intusschen van de zijde der Gemeente eene groote inspanning vorderen.

Geven voor onze Kerk hebben we dusver zoo goed als nooit geleerd.

Op onze groote gemeente van 175,000 werd dusver per jaar door alle collecten en in-schrijvingen saâm hoogstens een *f* 90,000 saâmgebracht.

Men gaf dus met inbegrip van Turf-collecten en alle extra's, slechts even één cent per hoofd en per week voor Kerk en *voor Armen* saâm.

Vergelijk nu hiermede eens, wat ieder aan den Staat in belasting betaalt, of ook op allerlei manieren voor Vereenigingen en voor vermaak in den loop van een geheel jaar uitgeeft, dan springt het op beschamende wijze in het oog, hoe schraal dusver voor uwe Kerken gezorgd is.

In heel Amerika onderhouden alle Kerken zich zelven en bijna zonder uitzondering bloeien ze en hebben ze zulk een overvloed van goed, dat ze buitendien nog tienmaal meer voor de zending doen kunnen, dan wij.

In Engeland en Schotland winnen alle vrije Kerken het van de Staatskerken in gelde-lijken welstand. En ook hier te lande hebben de Kerken, die het vrijwilligheidsbeginsel aandorsten nooit gebrek gehad aan eenig goed.

On 1 December 1886 the Dutch Reformed synod permanently discharged from office the suspended members of the consistory. On 16 December the discharged consistory members severed their bonds with the synodical organization and took the name Dutch *Gereformeerde* Church, with the affix *"Doleerende"* (Lamenting), because they were wrongly being denied their church properties. In a "Declaration of Reformation" they explained that "casting off the yoke of the synodical hierarchy" was not an act of seces-sion or of independence, but a return to the old, historic church structure.

This photograph shows a plea to the members of the Dutch *Gereformeerde* congre-gation (Lamenting) of Amsterdam to contribute to church funds, 1 January 1887.

Plechtige inwijding van de doleerende kerk in 1887

Caricature in *Uilenspiegel* of 1 January 1887 about the upcoming congress of the *Gereformeerden,* entitled "The solemn consecration of the lamenting church."

From 11 until 14 January 1887, the *Gereformeerde* church congress was held in the Frascati building in Amsterdam, which gave the impetus for the exodus of more local churches out of the Dutch Reformed Church. By 1889, 200 congregations consisting of 180,000 members and 70 ministers had joined the Dutch *Gereformeerde* Churches. Its administrative center was the office of the congress, housed in the Free University and run by the secretary of that university, J. van Oversteeg.

Kuyper's university colleague Philip Hoedemaker, who had initially supported the Doleantie, decided not to take part in the congress because it was open only to those who believed that "casting off the yoke of the synodical hierarchy was a duty." "The congress," according to Hoedemaker, "means to organize *kindred spirits.* This is the essence of sectarianism. I intend *the preservation of the church.*" On 1 January 1888 he resigned as professor of the Free University.

Dr. G. J. Vos (1836-1912), minister in Amsterdam (1875-1912), was Kuyper's greatest opponent in Amsterdam. Like Westhoff he was one of the Confessional-orthodox ministers who remained loyal to the Dutch Reformed Church. Other orthodox groups, such as the Kohlbrüggians, Hoedemaker's followers, the Ethical-orthodox, and the Pietistic Reformed, also disapproved of the Doleantie. The fact that Vos was an orthodox minister working against the Doleantie may explain the fierceness with which Kuyper attacked him.

The consistory of the Nieuwe Kerk in Amsterdam had been returned to the members of the national church with the help of the police on 21 December 1886. On 7 January 1887 Dr. Vos received a sum of money from his colleagues as a token of appreciation for everything he had done for the "church of the fatherland," so that he could buy a fur coat. In a biting satire in *De Heraut* of 30 January 1887 Kuyper wrote that Vos had certainly earned a reward. He continued: "Have they given him *a Bible*? No, of course not. One does not honor someone with a Bible who has just opposed those who fight for God's Word. No, apparently they wanted to make a *symbolic* gesture. They did not give him an honorary title, or higher wages. No, they had to give him a *symbolic* tribute. So falling back on the most improper symbolism, on Dam Square, in the place next to the Nieuwe Kerk that was so widely discussed, they hung around Vos's neck *the skin of a carnivorous animal*.

"And so the man, whose own name of Vos (Fox) had been such a sad symbol throughout the whole year; and who is now known throughout the land as someone who has silenced his brotherly heart and his human feeling in order to attack his brothers on behalf of the Synodical Hierarchy, . . . around that man's shoulders one symbolically places a skin to which still clings the smell of the wild animal. Of course they did not mean *that* symbolism. On the contrary, those who gave it to him could only have meant to add *some warmth to a heart that had grown cold*, that had quenched so much of its radiating love."

The Rev. H. A. J. Lütge, 1850-1923.

A week later Kuyper retracted his article, because the case was too serious "for the scourge of satire." What did continue to "disgust and irritate" him was that Kohlbrügge's supporters had taken part in the tribute for Vos. The Kohlbruggian minister H. A. J. Lütge made him particularly angry. Lütge had once given Kuyper a portrait of Kohlbrügge as a present, but on 24 January 1887 Kuyper sent it back with the words: "After the way in which you used your office to help save the synodical hierarchy which ecclesiastically killed the late Dr. Kohlbrügge, the image of his loyal witness *given by you* as a gift no longer has a place under my roof. What was sent to me at the time, I hereby return to you. *It has much to say to you!*" For his part years later Vos again felt the effects of Kuyper's wrath. When in 1902 Vos celebrated his 25th anniverary as a pastor, the customary royal honor was not granted because Kuyper, as Minister for Home Affairs, refused to cooperate. Only after Kuyper had resigned did Vos receive his much-coveted decoration.

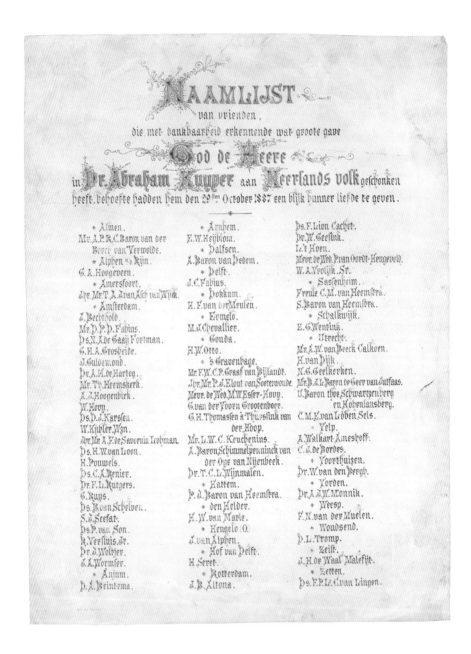

On the occasion of his fiftieth birthday on 29 October 1887 Kuyper was honored by friends and sympathizers, who gratefully acknowledged "what a great gift in Dr. Abraham Kuyper the Lord God had given the Dutch people."

De Rector der Vrije Universiteit en Mevrouw Kuyper—Schaay, zouden zeer prijs stellen op Uwe tegenwoordigheid bij de AVOND-RECEPTIE, die zij a. s. Vrijdag 20 Januari 1888, te half negen ure, bij de heropening der lessen aan de Vrije Universiteit, te hunnen huize wenschen te houden.

Amsterdam, 16 Januari 1888.

Invitation for a reception given by Kuyper and his wife on the occasion of the resumption of lectures at the Free University, 16 January 1888.

The schism of 1886 also meant that from then on the theology students of the Free University could be trained for the ministry in the *Gereformeerde* churches. The Free University as such became exclusively Kuyperian-*Gereformeerd* in nature, because men who remained loyal to the Dutch Reformed Church such as Hoedemaker, the directors G. H. L. Baron van Boetzelaer and J. C. Fabius, as well as the president-curator, the Rev. J. W. Felix, resigned their positions at the Free University. The number of students rose from 56 in 1885 to 87 in 1891.

A marriage in the circle of the Free University: Witius Hendrik de Savornin Lohman (1864-1932) and his wife, Emelia Pauline Hovy.

On 27 April 1888 Lohman's eldest son, W. H. de Savornin Lohman, was awarded his doctoral degree at the Free University in jurisprudence. It was the first dissertation to be defended at the Free University and discussed a current subject: *The Church Buildings of the Gereformeerde (Reformed) Church in the Netherlands*. The doctoral student defended the viewpoint of the Doleantie that the church buildings were the property of the local congregations. Lohman had earlier defended his dissertation at the City University because promotions at the Free University were not yet legally acknowledged. The following year he wrote a first, short biography of Kuyper, which appeared in the series "Men of Significance in Our Day" from the publishing house of Tjeenk Willink in Haarlem.

On Wednesday, 4 June 1888 Kuyper and his wife celebrated their silver wedding anniversary with a "quiet country party" at the tavern Oud-Valkeveen near Naarden. The menu of the celebratory dinner made a lavish impression, but the dinner was probably served "à la Française," meaning that the guests were not served individually, but were able to choose from dishes that were set on the table for each course.

Shortly after this family party in the countryside, bad news arrived. On 15 June 1888 the Supreme Court of the Netherlands ruled that those who had been suspended could not lay claim to the church properties of the Dutch Reformed Church. This important ruling was celebrated on 26 August with prayers and a service of thanksgiving in the Nieuwe Kerk, conducted by Vos. In his sermon he commemorated the destruction of Spanish (1588), French (1688), and Kuyperian (1888) power in the same breath.

The ruling by the Supreme Court meant that the Doleantie had to build new churches. This photograph shows the Keizersgrachtkerk in Amsterdam, the first building of the *Gereformeerde* churches, which was opened in 1888. The church, with its distinct neo-gothic architecture, was designed by the architects G. B. and A. Salm and could seat 1600 churchgoers. Kuyper was the chairman of the building committee. When criticism was expressed about the architects not being *Gereformeerd*, he referred to King Solomon, whose temple had been erected by non-Jewish builders.

CONCEPT-ACTE.

De Gereformeerde Kerken dezer landen, saamvergaderd in de beide Synodale vergaderingen, die dit jaar in de maanden Juni en Augustus te Utrecht en te Assen zitting hielden: de éene bekend als „de Algemeene Synode der Christelijke Gereformeerde Kerk", en die te Utrecht als „voorloopige Synode van Nederduitsche Gereformeerde Kerken";

over en weder de verzekering gegeven en ontvangen hebbende, dat zij niet anders bedoelen, dan te blijven bij de Formulieren van Eenigheid, de Liturgie en de Kerkenordening, gelijk die door de Gereformeerde Kerken dezer landen het laatst op hare Synode van Dordrecht, gehouden in de jaren 1618/19, zijn vastgesteld;

staande in de overtuiging dat kerken, die alzoo in Belijdenis, Liturgie en Kerkenordening en ook in taal overeenkomen, van 's Heerenwege geroepen zijn tot openbaring van hare eenheid die in Christus Jezus, haar heerlijk Hoofd, is, door een gezamenlijk optreden tegenover de wereld, door betooning van Christelijke liefde in het toezien op elkander, en door het dragen van elkanders lasten;

zijn te rade geworden met Gods hulpe aan haar gescheiden leven een einde te maken, door een saamkomen in gemeenschappelijke meerdere vergaderingen voor te bereiden.

Te dien einde verklaren zij:

1°. elk voor zich geen andere bedoeling te hebben dan om de Gereformeerde Kerk dezer landen, die van haar glans beroofd en verbasterd was, wederom tot zuiver openbaring te brengen als de omstandigheden dit toelaten;

2°. over en weder te erkennen, dat in het herstel der Gereformeerde Kerk, in zooverre zulks een vrucht was van de bekende gebeurtenissen uit de jaren 1834 en 1886 (ondanks eigen schuld en zonde en in weerwil van veel gebrekkigs dat menschenhand er in mengde) eeniglijk te verheerlijken is de ont-

In 1892 the Dutch *Gereformeerde* Churches and the greater part of the Christian *Gereformeerde* Churches (which had emerged from the Secession of 1834) joined to form the *Gereformeerde* Churches in the Netherlands. The new denomination had two seminaries: the Theological Faculty at the Free University and the seminary at Kampen, which had been founded by the Christian *Gereformeerden* in 1854. The relations between the two institutions would be strained, in part because Kampen was not permitted the right to grant doctoral degrees.

The photograph shows the "draft of the act of union" of the two *Gereformeerde* groups, with Kuyper's additions and corrections.

Herman Bavinck (1854-1921), the leading theologian of the Christian *Gereformeerde* Churches, which in 1892 had united with Kuyper's *Gereformeerden*. Bavinck had been a professor at the Theological Seminary in Kampen since 1883, but succeeded Kuyper as a professor of dogmatics at the Free University in 1902. He was also politically active, serving as chairman of the central committee (1905-1907) and as a member of the first chamber of Parliament (1911-1921). In 1915 he would turn against Kuyper's political leadership.

CHAPTER VI

The Anti-Revolutionary Party, 1880-1894

After *Ons Program* (1879) Kuyper continued to work on the elaboration and expansion of Anti-Revolutionary political principles, which were in part based on his theological works. Against the individualism of Liberalism and the collectivism of Socialism, Kuyper set his organic vision for society, to which the conception of sphere sovereignty was central. The antithesis, or the opposition on principle between believers and non-believers, already formulated by Groen van Prinsterer, was used by Kuyper as an effective instrument for the mobilization of the Anti-Revolutionary movement, not only in the field of politics but in "all fields of life." Moreover, with his creed of sphere sovereignty, Kuyper prevented his followers from falling into the trap of "world avoidance," to which many orthodox Protestants were traditionally inclined, and he encouraged them to accept their political and social responsibility.

In the 1880s the influence of the Anti-Revolutionaries steadily increased, including in the second chamber of Parliament, where Lohman led the party representatives. Besides expanding, the party was also growing in influence as a result of ever-closer cooperation with the Roman Catholics under the leadership of H. J. A. M. Schaepman. The increasing power of the two confessional factions found its expression in the politics of "non-possumus," whereby they made the fulfillment of their demands regarding religious schools a condition for their support of broadening the franchise, which in these years of social turmoil was championed by the Liberals in particular. Eventually a compromise was reached, after which the number of voters was greatly increased by the constitutional revision of 1887. In the elections of 1888 the coalition of Anti-Revolutionaries and Roman Catholics gained a majority, and the first confessional cabinet (1888-1891) was formed under the leadership of the Anti-Revolutionary Aeneas Mackay.

Kuyper himself did not join the cabinet, but tried as party leader to bend the agenda to his will. Although the Mackay cabinet Factory Act passed and made a start on the equalization of state and religiously affiliated education by way of a School Law, Kuyper was not happy with the cabinet's general cast, which he thought to be insufficiently principled. His critical comments in *De Standaard* led to tensions with his closest supporter, Lohman, who as leader of the party representatives in the second chamber and later as a cabinet minister felt that he did not get enough support. This was the beginning of a rift between the two Anti-Revolutionary leaders, which led to a break within the Anti-Revolutionary Party a few years later.

With Mackay's education bill, the school issue faded into the background for the time being. In the 1890s suffrage and labor relations were of central importance, while the rise of social democracy also quickened social and political unrest. The differences within the Anti-Revolutionary Party intensified when Kuyper began to pay more attention to the social question. At the Christian Social Congress of 1891 in Amsterdam he denounced the "criminal" state of affairs regarding social issues, while he also made radical statements about the extension of suffrage. The tensions between the conservative and the progressive Anti-Revolutionaries (the "droite" and the "gauche"), which did not surface during the school struggle, now began to increase. In the end the progressive franchise bill that was submitted by the Liberal J. P. R. Tak van Poortvliet in 1894 led to a break between Kuyper and Lohman. After the party convention of March 1894 had chosen for Kuyper's side, the more conservative Anti-Revolutionaries under Lohman broke away. In the newly elected chamber they formed a separate parliamentary party of Free-Anti-Revolutionaries, which would later be incorporated into the Christian-Historical Union. Kuyper himself was also elected to the chamber, where he would lead the Anti-Revolutionary parliamentary coalition until 1901.

	Liberals	Conservatives	Roman Catholics	Anti Revolutionaries	Socialists	Radicals	Total members
1869	40	18	16	6	-	-	80
1871	44	15	16	5	-	-	80
1873	42	14	16	8	-	-	80
1875	43	9	16	12	-	-	80
1877	49	6	16	9	-	-	80
1879	51	6	17	12	-	-	86
1881	49	5	17	15	-	-	86
1883	45	4	18	19	-	-	86
1884	42	3	18	23	-	-	86
1886	47	1	19	19	-	-	86
1887	48	-	19	19	-	-	86
1888	45	1	25	26	1	-	100
1891	53	-	25	21	-	1	100

Composition of the second chamber, 1869-1891.

During this period the number of Conservatives steadily declined; after 1891 they were no longer represented in the second chamber. The number of Anti-Revolutionary seats increased from 12 (1879) to 26 (1888). The decline in 1886 can be explained in part by the Doleantie church split, which brought dissension to the ARP.

In the Constitutional revision of 1887, the electorate was increased from approximately 12 to 24 percent of the adult male population. The biennial elections for half of the second chamber seats were abolished. The number of members of the second chamber was established at one hundred, with all the members up for re-election simultaneously every four years.

P. C. Mondriaan, 1839-1921.

In the 1880s Kuyper worked on expanding the Anti-Revolutionary Party organization, which was a close-knit combination of the nationwide networks of *De Standaard*, the "School with the Bible" Union, and the Free University. The fifth convention of the ARP took place on 2 July 1885 in The Hague, more or less coupled to the Free University Day which had taken place in the same city on 1 July.

Kuyper maintained many contacts with local party men. They kept him informed about what was happening in the electoral districts and gave him material for his "three-stars" in *De Standaard*, particularly during election campaigns. One of these confidants was Piet Mondriaan, the father of the artist of the same name (1872-1944). As a teacher in Amersfoort and Winterswijk, Mondriaan regularly corresponded with Kuyper about political issues. As a graphic artist he illustrated Christian books and crafted festive historical and commemorative plaques.

For the Anti-Revolutionaries the Eighty Years War (1568-1648) was a source of inspiration. Kuyper liked to compare his followers to the brave Calvinists who, for the sake of their religion, had rebelled against Spain. The photograph shows a colored lithograph by Mondriaan (1884) depicting the murder of the leader of the Protestant rebellion, Prince William of Orange, on 15 July 1584. In his youth Piet Mondriaan Jr. also made etchings and drawings of edifying and historical scenes.

C. Th. Baron (after 1882, Count) van Lynden van Sandenburg, 1826-1885.

Despite their weak electoral position, during the 1880s the Conservatives remained in power. The Conservative cabinets of van Lynden van Sandenburg (1879-1883) and J. Heemskerk (1883-1888) were tolerated by the Liberal majority, which was not homogenous enough to form a cabinet itself. The Roman Catholics and the Anti-Revolutionaries were disappointed that the religiously orthodox Van Lynden, whom they had initially regarded as a sympathizer, obliged the Liberals by implementing Kappeyne's Education Act.

H. J. A. M. Schaepman (1844-1903), Roman Catholic clergyman, poet, and flamboy-
ant orator, in his study at the major seminary Rijsenburg near Driebergen, where he
was professor of church history. From 1880 on Schaepman was a member of the second chamber and encouraged cooperation with the Anti-Revolutionaries, although he
had to overcome the predictable opposition to this in his own circle. The elections of
1883 were the first time that organized cooperation between Roman Catholics and Anti-
Revolutionaries took place, whereby both parties supported the favorite to win in local districts. The Anti-Revolutionaries gained the most from this cooperation, because
they often needed the support of the Roman Catholics to gain a majority in the districts
to the north of the great rivers, while they themselves were of little importance elector-
ally in the south of the country, which voted for the Roman Catholics en masse.

Because of the school struggle, the Anti-Revolutionaries and the Roman Catholics grew closer together. This caricature in *De Lantaarn* from 1885 depicts MPs Keuchenius and Schaepman as "Knights Templars abroad" in the fight for "special schools."

In the mid-1880s a stalemate developed in the second chamber with regard to the burning issues of those days, suffrage and education. Startled by the social unrest that was fueled by an economic depression, the majority of the Liberals were prepared to expand the franchise. The confessional parties were also in favor of this. However, they would cooperate on the necessary constitutional reform only if the obstacles that prevented the subsidization of religiously oriented education were removed. With such politics of "non possumus" ("we cannot do otherwise") the confessional parties blocked constitutional reforms, which had to be passed with a two-thirds majority.

Uitgave van Martinus Nijhoff.   Steendruk van J.Krauss. s'Hage

„Och Heer! Och Heer!
Wie zet ons op het droge weer!"

In order to break the political deadlock, the Heemskerk cabinet had the second chamber dissolved in May 1886. The moment was well chosen, because the Anti-Revolutionaries had been weakened by the conflict within the national church. The Liberals won some seats in the elections, but the ensuing parliamentary debates proved that they were willing to make concessions on the school issue in order to make the extension of suffrage possible. The breakthrough came when they gave up their position that the current constitution forbade subsidies for Christian education. This meant that the constitutional article concerning education could remain unchanged and that confessional wishes could be dealt with through laws rather than constitutional reforms. This paved the way for constitutional reform on suffrage. In the end the amended constitution was proclaimed in November 1887.

Because of the extension of suffrage in 1887, the parliamentary elections of 1888 resulted in a victory for the coalition of Anti-Revolutionaries and Roman Catholics. Once again Kuyper led his party's campaign using his daily articles in *De Standaard*. On the left side of the photograph is the "Register of Sins of the Liberal Coterie" in twenty points; on the right the electoral "three-stars" in which Kuyper offered specific voting suggestions for local contests. From the "three-stars" it appears that he was fully informed about the situation in each electoral district.

F. DOMELA NIEUWENHUIS
(omstreeks 1886).

F. Domela Nieuwenhuis, 1846-1919.

The election contest between the Liberals and the Confessionals was bitterly fought. Characteristic of the polarized relations was that the Anti-Revolutionaries in the district of Schoterland preferred the revolutionary Social Democrat Domela Nieuwenhuis to the Liberal candidate. Domela Nieuwenhuis was subsequently elected as the first Socialist in the second chamber, where he was avoided like a leper by his fellow members. Only the stubborn Anti-Revolutionary Keuchenius welcomed him upon his arrival in the chamber by shaking his hand. Overall, Domela Nieuwenhuis was condemned to barren isolation as a loner whose word had no influence whatsoever, but who did provoke sharply-worded objections. After his resignation as a member of the chamber in 1891 he ended up in anarchist waters.

After the elections of April 1888, the first coalition cabinet of Anti-Revolutionaries and Roman Catholics was formed under the leadership of Aeneas Mackay, a moderate Anti-Revolutionary. Because the first chamber still had a Liberal majority, the cabinet had to operate carefully. Lohman remained a member of the second chamber for the time being, but became a cabinet minister after Keuchenius resigned in February 1890.

Mackay (1839-1909) came from an old Scottish family that had settled in the Netherlands at the end of the seventeenth century. His uncle Æneas Mackay (1806-1876), a supporter of Groen van Prinsterer, had been vice-president of the Council of State. Mackay was a conciliatory man who brought people together. About his chairmanship of the cabinet Lohman later wrote, "In meetings he seldom offered his advice first. His power lay in listening and judging well. After everyone had put forward his opinion, he expressed what he felt with great clarity and frankness every time. As I remember, it was only very seldom that others did not agree with what he said. And in cases where there were differences of opinion, there was never any unpleasantness with his political colleagues."

On 21 April 1888 the Roman Catholic Justice Minister G. L. M. H. Ruijs van Beerenbrouck (1842-1926) was characterized by the liberal *Algemeen Handelsblad* as a "convinced conservative man." And yet in May 1889 his Factory Act was passed, which improved the working hours of women and young people in factories and other workplaces. The Act resulted from the work done by the parliamentary investigative committee of 1886-87, which in its report had brought to light a wide range of social wrongs in agriculture and industry. Ruijs had been a member of the committee.

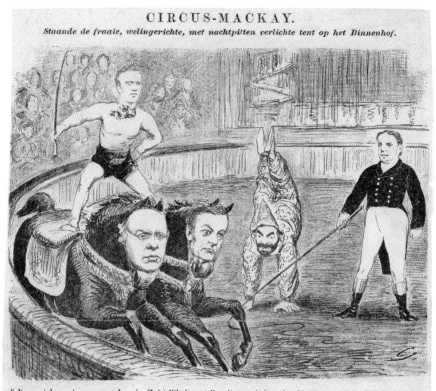

CIRCUS-MACKAY.

Staande de fraaie, welingerichte, met nachtpitten verlichte tent op het Binnenhof.

Salto mortale op twee raspaarden, in Christelijk bewustzijn uitgevoerd door den Directeur, nooit in Nederland vertoond.

Mackay as a circus artist, riding on the horses Schaepman (Catholic) and Lohman (Anti-revolutionary), with Kuyper acting as the animal trainer. This is how the satirical paper *Uilenspiegel* of 24 August 1889 saw the relations within the coalition.

Kuyper was unfavorably disposed towards the cabinet's policies, which he thought lacked principle. In his opinion, Lohman's Anti-Revolutionary Parliamentary Club also failed in this regard. Kuyper's critical commentaries in *De Standaard* led to tensions with Lohman in particular, who felt that he was not getting enough support for the often thankless parliamentary work he did.

The greatest achievement of the Mackay cabinet was to pass a School Act which made the partial subsidization of "special schools" possible. Although Kuyper thought the bill did not go far enough, in *De Standaard* he did advise in favor of its acceptance because the Act was a first step towards equal rights for state and "special" Reformed (and Catholic) education.

The caricature from *De Nederlandsche Spectator* of 28 September 1889 shows Mackay with the School Act on his way to the first chamber after it had been passed by the second chamber. He is preceded by Lohman and Schaepman and followed by the Liberal J. G. Gleichman, a representative of the seventeen Liberal members of the second chamber who had voted to pass the bill. The first chamber passed the bill on 6 December, 31-18.

ELEKTRQS IN DE TWEEDE KAMER.

Uitgave van Martinus Nijhoff

Steendruk van J.Krauss's Hage.

Vrij hanteere de drom van obscurantisten den domper. . . . .
Nooit dompt een menschlijke kracht 't licht van de negentiend' eeuw.
't Straalt onverwinbaar en rijst zegevierend in 't hart van het menschdom,
Niet aan den domper verwant als dat van Rome en van Dordt.

In the autumn of 1889 the second chamber was fitted with electric lighting. This inspired *De Nederlandsche Spectator* of 23 November 1889 to attack obscurantists such as
Schaepman and Lohman, whom it depicted going around with a light extinguisher in
order to work against the progress and enlightenment of the modern age.

Mr. Keuchenius als hervormer.

Vrede op aarde!

Caricature by Johan Braakensiek in the weekly paper *De Amsterdammer* of 29 December 1889, commenting on Minister Keuchenius's colonial policy in the Dutch East Indies (i.e., Indonesia), which had come under attack from the opposition from the very start. When he was sworn in as a cabinet minister, the Liberal *NRC* characterized Keuchenius, who was as pious as he was hard-headed, as "the man who with his endless sermons drives the chamber to distraction . . . a source of gall and venom that wells up without end. . . . The most impossible man who ever had a seat in our chamber."

Keuchenius was indeed fierce, and often offended his opponents unnecessarily. Even a like-minded man like A. W. Idenburg had to admit that he "used the Name of the Lord in both a timely and an untimely manner." Despite all his competence in colonial matters, he was more suited to the chamber than to the cabinet. On 31 January 1890 the Liberal majority in the first chamber rejected his budget, because the reforms they wanted were not forthcoming, but in particular in protest against the way in which the cabinet minister let "his peculiar religious concepts" affect his policies.

„Lohman!... in 's hemels naam wat ga je beginnen?!..."
— Ik?... Och Heer hoe kom ik zoo verstrooid?... Ik dacht zoo waar, dat 'k in de Nieuwe Kerk was!...

Against the wishes of Kuyper, who in *De Standaard* had written that Keuchenius would not be able to fall "without taking the whole cabinet with him," the cabinet decided that only Keuchenius should tender his resignation. On 24 February 1890, Mackay succeeded him as minister of colonies, while Lohman entered the cabinet as home secretary.

Lohman's appointment aroused the indignation of the Liberal press, because the Liberals felt that it was improper that the "head of the church rebellion" of 1886 was now responsible for the enforcement of public order. The caricature in *Uilenspiegel* of 1 March 1890 refers to Lohman's breaking into the Nieuwe Kerk. On 19 February 1890 the *Algemeen Handelsblad* wrote, "Mr. De Savornin Lohman — minister for home affairs! Who would have dared to predict this two years ago, when the attack on the Nieuwe Kerk in Amsterdam, in which he cooperated with Dr. Kuyper, was still fresh in our minds!" The *Handelsblad* acknowledged that Lohman was one of the "most hardworking and capable" Anti-Revolutionaries, but believed that this was also the reason that "strict control" of the new minister was necessary.

The Anti-Revolutionary rank and file deeply regretted Keuchenius's resignation. That was why Kuyper took the initiative to raise funds to buy a present, which was presented to Keuchenius on 20 May 1890 "on behalf of about three thousand of his friends" in the great hall of the Hotel de Indes in The Hague. In his speech Kuyper said that the meeting was not meant as a political demonstration, but as "proof of brotherly sympathy for the courageous and firm way in which Mr. Keuchenius, both as a member of the chamber and as a king's minister, had defended the confession of Christ." The present consisted of a bronze bust of Groen van Prinsterer as well as a nicely carved bookcase adorned on either side with Protestant heroes, containing works "that profess the Lord from every century and every country," excluding writers still living. A catalogue and an album with the names of the donors completed the present. The "Keuchenius case" is now owned by the library of the Free University.

Het Huygensplein te Gravenhage tijdens het voorbijtrekken van den Koninklijken rouwtrein op 4 December 1890.
Teekening van P. DE JOSSELIN DE JONG.

The royal funeral procession at the Huygensplein in the Hague, 4 December 1890, taken from a drawing by P. de Josselin de Jong in *Eigen Haard*, 1891, no. 3.

On 23 November 1890 King William III died at Het Loo Palace near Apeldoorn. As minister for home affairs, Lohman was closely involved with the question of his succession. Because of the young age of the successor to the throne, the ten-year-old princess Wilhelmina, her mother Queen Emma, Princess of Waldeck-Pyrmont, served as regent until 1898. The condolence speech that the second chamber passed on 27 November was opposed only by Domela Nieuwenhuis, the only republican in the chamber. The funeral service in the chapel at Het Loo on 2 December was led by Kuyper's old opponent, Nicolaas Beets. Kuyper himself did not think much of the king (a man who could, as he wrote to Lohman, barely handle "a short complete sentence") and was disappointed about his attitude in 1878 after he had signed Kappeyne's School Act.

Uitgave van Martinus Nijhoff   Steendruk van J Krauss's Hage

Om dezer dingen wille ween ik; . . . . . mijne kinderen zijn verwoest, omdat de vijand de overhand heeft.
Klaagliederen van Jeremia. I. 16.

Kuyper on the remains of the Dutch Zion, with the names of the lost electoral districts. Caricature in *De Nederlandsche Spectator* of 13 June 1891, after the defeat of the religious coalition parties in the general elections. (The biblical text is Lamentations 1:16.)

After passing the Factory Act and the School Act, the Anti-Revolutionary/Catholic coalition started to fracture. The Army Bill submitted by the Roman Catholic Minister Bergansius in particular created much dissension. At the elections of June 1891, the Roman Catholics and the Anti-Revolutionaries lost their majority in the second chamber to the Liberals. It would take ten years before another coalition cabinet was formed.

The relationship between Kuyper and De Savornin Lohman had deteriorated during the Mackay cabinet. Lohman's principal grievance was that Kuyper had asked too much of the cabinet and the parliamentary caucus, and had raised the expectations of Anti-Revolutionary supporters too high. On 17 November 1891 Lohman wrote to Kuyper, "I told you as far back as 1888 that I thought *no government could* possibly bring about the principles as laid down in the program of action without being in power for at least *eight* years; you answered that the voters would not want to believe this anyway, and instead of convincing them that they *must* believe, you have nourished the opinion that the responsibility for the disappointment lies with *the cabinet*." After his resignation as a minister, Lohman once more resumed his work as a professor at the Free University and became a member of the first chamber. In February 1894, after the death of Keuchenius, who in May 1890 had succeeded him as a member of the second chamber, Lohman was again elected as a member of the second chamber.

An important occasion during this period was the Christian Social Congress, which took place in Amsterdam from 9 to 12 November 1891. The congress had been convened by the central committee of the ARP upon the request of the Christian Dutch Labour Union Patrimonium. Kuyper played an important role in the preparatory work for the congress, as appears from the prospectus that he drew up.

Already as a city pastor in the 1870s, Kuyper had become acquainted with the plight of the working population and had written about it in 1871-72. Since then the situation had hardly improved, because traditional poor relief and philanthropy continued to fall short. Thanks in part to the increase in the number of factory workers and the emergence of the labor movement, it became clear to Christian leaders that the social question had to be dealt with in a fundamental way.

Opening van het Sociaal Congres op Gereformeerden grondslag.

„Mannen-broeders, vrouwen-zusters! Wij hebben ons Christelijk Kabinet gehad, en nu hebben wij ons Christelijk sociaal congres. De Heere heeft groote dingen aan ons gedaan, en dies zijn wij verblijd. Als ik den blik laat weiden over deze talrijke vergadering, en vooral als ik de tevreden gezichten zie der mannen van Patrimonium, een jaar geleden nog zoo grimmig, dan vouw ik de handen en sluit de oogen, en ik roep den Heere-Heere aan, om Hem te danken, dat Hij op zoo wonderbaarlijke wijze onze wegen leidt en ons telkens de middelen in de hand geeft, om ons groot te maken te midden van de kleinheid diergenen, die den Heere niet zoeken..."

"Opening of the Social Congress on Reformed Principles," caricature in *Uilenspiegel* of 14 November 1891.

At the opening of the social congress in Amsterdam, Kuyper delivered a radical speech, *The Social Question and the Christian Religion*. He rejected the remedies that Socialism and Liberalism proposed, but also believed that Christian philanthropy could no longer offer a solution by itself. Kuyper argued for an "architectonic," structural social criticism that was founded on God's Word: "Only one thing is necessary if the social question is to be real for you: you must realize the untenability of the present state of affairs, and you must account for this untenability not by incidental causes but by a fault in the very foundation of our society's organization. If you do not acknowledge this and think that social evil can be exorcised through an increase in piety, or through friendlier treatment or more generous charity, then you may believe that we face a religious question or possibly a philanthropic question, but you will not recognize the *social* question. This question does not exist for you until you exercise an architectonic critique of human society itself, which leads to the desire for a different arrangement of the social order."[1]

1. Translation adapted from: James W. Skillen (ed.), *The Problem of Poverty* (Grand Rapids: Baker Book House, 1991), 50-51, 72, 75.

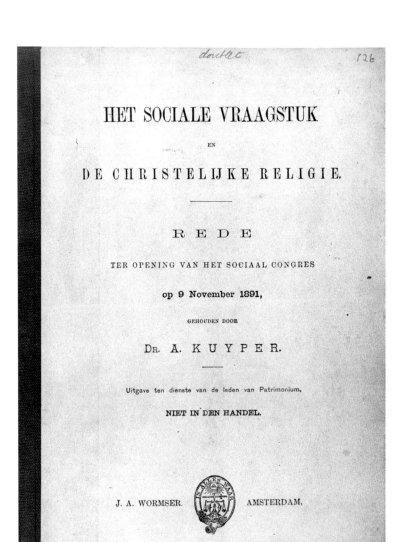

HET SOCIALE VRAAGSTUK

EN

DE CHRISTELIJKE RELIGIE.

REDE

TER OPENING VAN HET SOCIAAL CONGRES

op 9 November 1891,

GEHOUDEN DOOR

Dʀ. A. KUYPER.

Uitgave ten dienste van de leden van Patrimonium,

NIET IN DEN HANDEL.

J. A. WORMSER.   AMSTERDAM,

Title page of Kuyper's speech in a free edition for the members of Patrimonium, who also had free access to the congress. A later edition was published containing thirty pages of notes and further references to promote the study of the social question.

It was to Kuyper's credit that he addressed the social question in Christian circles in a fundamental way, but differences of opinion arose about how much state influence was necessary and desirable. To put it in Kuyper's own words: where does the "duty of the state that creates laws and protects" stop and where does the "regulatory mania of the over-meddling state" begin? This dilemma would continue to play a role in Anti-Revolutionary circles and was one of the issues over which Kuyper and Lohman (who also took part in the congress) parted company.

Dr. H. Pierson (1834-1923), a Dutch Reformed minister and philanthropist, was one of the chairmen of the Social Congress, as was Kuyper. The dividing line in church affairs that had been caused by the Doleantie between members of the Dutch national church and the *Gereformeerden* did not (yet) play a significant role socially or politically.

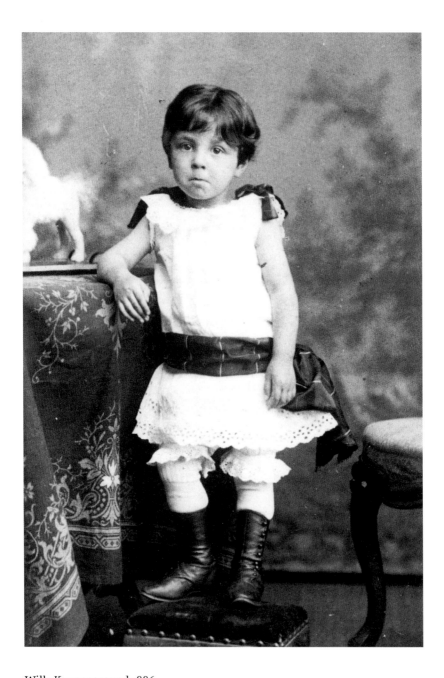

Willy Kuyper around 1886.

On 27 July 1892, the youngest son of the Kuyper family, nine-year-old Levinus Willem Christiaan (Willy) Kuyper, named after Keuchenius, died at the seaside resort of Zandvoort. At the time of his death Kuyper was in Innsbruck. Before he departed for the Netherlands, on 31 July he sent his wife the following telegram (in French) from Innsbruck: "Arrived too late to leave/will be back on Tuesday at the latest/ tomorrow more at length/I feel stunned/my poor William/God reigns. Kuyper."

Telegram from Kuyper to his wife upon his arrival in Brussels on 1 August 1892, after Willy's death: "Arrived in time. Wonderful to see Herman. 7:45 we will be with you, and then at eleven o'clock we will carry our small sweet darling to Zandvoort to his little grave. Kuyper."

In November 1893 Kuyper published a collection of meditations, *In the Shadow of Death*, which also included the meditation "Like a Flower of the Field" that had been published in *De Heraut* of 14 August 1892 shortly after the death of his youngest son. In his preface, Kuyper wrote that he had completed the collection from the "experience of his own soul" after he "had cried at the grave of an unforgettable child."

Friedrich Nietzsche, 1844-1900.

On 20 October 1892, Kuyper passed on the rectorship of the Free University to Lohman with the rectorial address *The Blurring of Boundaries*. In it he warned against the dangers of pantheism, which he found particularly in the views of Darwin and Nietzsche. Kuyper was one of the first people in the Netherlands who drew attention to the German philosopher Friedrich Nietzsche. From his correspondence it also appears that while preparing for his oration he inquired about Nietzsche's state of health.

Earlier, in *De Heraut* of 15 May 1892, Kuyper reviewed Nietzsche's *Thus Spoke Zarathustra*. In his review he characterized Nietzsche as "rather like a Multatuli for the Germans. A great writer. A hero of the word who is not sparing in prejudices. And simultaneously the perfect disbeliever." The tragic contrast between Nietzsche's "übermensch" and his own madness gave rise to the exclamation: "What a priceless gift to be *allowed* and to be *able* to believe!"

J. P. R. Tak van Poortvliet (1839-1904), minister for internal affairs in Van Tienhoven's Liberal cabinet (1891-1894).

In addition to the social question, the question of suffrage continued to stir up great political differences in the Netherlands. The pivotal question was how to legally define suffrage as laid down in the new constitution of 1887. Article 80 of the constitution granted the vote to adult males who possessed (yet to be determined) characteristics of suitability and social prosperity. In September 1892, the Liberal minister Tak van Poortvliet submitted a bill that offered a very generous application of Article 80. It would grant suffrage to all men who could read and write and who were not dependent on charity.

After a parliamentary debate about the amended bill in February 1894, Tak withdrew his proposal. On 17 March the government dissolved the second chamber, after which early elections were held on 10 and 24 April. The fierce struggle about the bill had great political repercussions and split all the parties into "Takkians" and "anti-Takkians."

Uitgave van Martinus Nijhoff.

Wir stiften keinen neuen Bund.....
Wisset Brüder!
Ob uns der Glaub', ob uns die Kirche scheiden,
Sind wir in anderer Hinsicht auch nicht einig,
Jetzt sind wir eines Sinnes, eines Strebens;
Denn ein Gesetz nur ist's, zu dem wir wollen.

Naar Schiller, Wilhelm Tell.

Steendr.van J.Krauss 's Hage.

"A New Triumvirate," political caricature in *De Nederlandsche Spectator* of March 1894 about the unusual alliance between Schaepman, Tak van Poortvliet, and Kuyper as leaders of the "Takkians." Among the Anti-Revolutionaries the discord about Tak's bill led to an open struggle between Kuyper and Lohman, who in February 1894 had been reelected as a member of the chamber. It highlighted the opposition between the conservative and the progressive wings within the ARP. As leader of the conservatives, Lohman put forward mainly constitutional arguments against Tak van Poortvliet's bill. Kuyper argued that Tak's (individualistic) electoral system did differ on principle from the Anti-Revolutionary ideal of "householder franchise" (franchise for heads of families), but in effect boiled down to the same thing.

After the dissolution of the chamber and with an eye to the elections, the meeting of deputies of the ARP was convened in Utrecht on 30 March 1894. In order to influence the deputies in advance, Lohman and nine other Anti-Revolutionary members of the chamber (with only one exception, all members of the aristocracy) sent out a manifesto to all the electoral associations on 24 March in which they denounced Tak's plans. This "fatal manifest," as *De Standaard* called it, was a direct challenge to Kuyper as party leader.

A public invitation to the meeting of deputies of the ARP on Friday, 30 March 1894 in the Hall of Arts and Sciences in Utrecht, advertisement in *De Standaard* of 23 March 1894. Owing to the lack of time before the elections, there had been no opportunity to send personal invitations.

The meeting of deputies was held in the same building where the ARP had been founded twenty-five years earlier. The convention made use of this fact to express its loyalty to Kuyper at the start. In a motion it spoke of its "humble gratitude to the Lord God for the expression of his compassion given to our Anti-Revolutionary party now for almost a quarter of a century in its leader given by Him." Kuyper himself furnished Lohman and his supporters with a reply to their manifesto. In his speech to the delegates he argued that his support of Tak's proposals was in accordance with the democratic tradition of the ARP. He had argued, with Groen van Prinsterer's approval, for the extension of suffrage as early as 1869 and 1873. He would not be able to justify it to God if the Anti-Revolutionary Party now came down on the side of reaction: "Calvinism has never, in any country, lagged behind, but has always led the way. That is how it ought to be now and that is why I now cry: Say to Israel that it goes forward." This was language that the Anti-Revolutionaries understood.

After a lengthy debate, the meeting of delegates came down on Kuyper's side and stated in a resolution that the forthcoming elections had to be regarded as a "struggle between the *Conservatism* that is to everyone's liking on the one hand and on the other hand those who defended the *people behind the voters*; a struggle in which the Anti-Revolutionary Party, true to its principles and to its past, from its own point of view, has to offer resistance *against* Conservatism in unexpected ways." Only those candidates could be supported who were prepared to cooperate in "a final extension of suffrage." This meant that "all pro-Conservative candidates, from *whatever wing*, must be *contested as opponents* both in the first and in the second rounds of balloting."

Caricature by Johan Braakensiek in *De Amsterdammer* of 20 May 1894 about the "civil war" between Kuyper and Lohman. Lohman fires a cannon at the Anti-Revolutionary stronghold above which *De Standaard* flies. The cannon bears the name of Lohman's new daily paper *De Nederlander*. Lohman's first article written as editor in chief was published in *De Nederlander* on 16 May 1894.

With the deputies' statement, the break between the "Takkians" and the "anti-Takkians" within the ARP was a fact. Lohman and his supporters entered the elections independently and formed in the newly elected chamber a separate parliamentary group of Free-Anti-Revolutionaries that counted eight members. The party representatives of the ARP claimed seven seats and were led by Kuyper himself, who had been elected to the chamber as the representative of the Sliedrecht district. Although he had only become a member in order to participate in the discussions concerning the electoral bill, Kuyper would remain a member of the chamber until 1901.

	Union Liberals	Free or Old Liberals	Radical Liberals/Liberal Democrats	Roman Catholics	Anti-Revolutionaries	Free Anti-Revolutionaries/Christian-Historicals	Social Democrats	Free Socialists
1894	29	28	3	25	7	8	-	-
1897	35	13	4	22	16	7	2	1
1901	18	8	9	25	23	10	6	1
1905	24	10	11	25	15	8	6	1
1909	20	4	9	25	23	12	7	-
1913	19	10	8	25	11	9	18	-

Composition of the second chamber, 1894-1913. In 1913 the last regular elections according to the constituency voting system were held. In 1918 proportional representation was introduced.

Not only the Anti-Revolutionaries but, after 1894, the Liberals as well were split into separate parliamentary factions: conservative Free or Old Liberals, moderate Union Liberals, and Radical Liberals (as of 1901 Liberal Democrats). Lohman's Free-Anti-Revolutionaries merged with the small Christelijk-Historische Kiezersbond (Christian-Historical Electoral Union) of Kuyper's old rival Bronsveld, and in 1908 with the Friese Christelijk-Historischen (Frisian Christian-Historicals), who had been influenced by Hoedemaker's Netherlands Reformed theocratic views. From this the Christian Historical Union emerged, which with its looser party organization would, to a great extent, bear the hallmark of Lohman's love of freedom.

Samuel van Houten, 1837-1930.

At the general elections of 1894 the "Takkians" received a majority in the second chamber, while all the Liberals together won more seats than in 1891. Given this result, the formation of an anti-Takkian Liberal cabinet was the most obvious choice, one that could also count on the support of the conservative Confessionals. J. Röell, a moderate conservative Liberal who was also responsible for Foreign Affairs, was appointed prime minister. However, the most striking figure was Minister for Internal Affairs Samuel van Houten (1837-1930), whose task it was to draw up a new franchise law. Van Houten was an independent-minded Liberal who had held a seat in the second chamber since 1869. Kuyper had crossed swords with him in 1874, when Van Houten defended his bill against child labor. Having started out as a left-wing Liberal, over time he had become more conservative.

Van Houten's franchise law, which he drew up in 1896, did not go as far as Tak van Poortvliet's proposal but did lead to a doubling of the electorate. During the deliberations about the bill in the second chamber in May 1896, Kuyper argued in vain for the implementation of householder suffrage. Kuyper's Anti-Revolutionaries did not take part in the final vote on the bill; Lohman voted in favor.

Alexander F. de Savornin Lohman, a drawing by J. H. Isings, 1903.

From the very start and during the many years that Kuyper and Lohman worked together there had been tensions and conflicts, which in part sprang from differences in character and personality, but also in part from differences of opinion about church and political affairs. In spiritual matters one could say that as a follower of the *Réveil*, Lohman was averse to adhering too closely to dogmas and programs, while Kuyper, as a follower of Calvin, set stricter boundaries and wanted to enforce them. Although Lohman had taken part in the Doleantie (mainly for ecclesiological reasons), he felt akin to the Ethicals and was averse to churchism and dogmatics. In politics too, he was opposed to the strict party discipline that Kuyper tried to impose upon his followers, and emphasized the freedom to form different opinions. Socially, the aristocratic Lohman was more conservative than the "man of the people" Kuyper, while Lohman's wariness of government interference in socio-economic matters was tied to his individualist and libertarian views.

CHAPTER VII

Days of Jubilation and Mourning, 1894-1901

The political rift between Kuyper and de Savornin Lohman was confirmed two years later by a personal break when Lohman, in part through Kuyper's doing, had to resign his professorship at the Free University. It was alleged that the education he provided did not accord with Reformed principles. Lohman was so hurt about the way in which he had been removed that he avoided meeting Kuyper in person for a year in Parliament. Upon Lohman's suggestion, in April 1897 the business side of the relationship was restored so that they could continue their political collaboration, albeit on a different footing. In cooperation with Schaepman, Kuyper and Lohman led the Confessional opposition in the chamber against the Pierson Cabinet (1897-1901), which would bring a dignified end to the era of Liberal domination.

Intellectually for Kuyper these were fruitful years, during which he published a great number of works. In addition to his great theological works *Encyclopedia of Sacred Theology* (1894) and *E voto Dordraceno* (1893-1895), he also published a short biography of Keuchenius (1895), the collected articles *Women of the Bible* (1897) and *For When You Are at Home: Devotionals for Home Life* (1899), the *Lectures on Calvinism* (1899), the travel report *Varia Americana* (1899), the rectorial address *Evolution* (1899), a pamphlet on *The South African Crisis* about the origins of the Boer War (1900), and as the fruit of his political work *The Kuyper Amendment to the Industrial Injuries Act* (1899) and the ARP convention keynote address *Full Hearted for the Ideal* (1901). Indeed, during these years Kuyper's productivity as a many-sided author knew almost no bounds.

On 1 April 1897, in the large concert hall of the Palace of People's Industry, the twenty-fifth anniversary of *De Standaard* was celebrated, and Kuyper as editor-in-chief was enthusiastically honored. The celebration also served to confirm him as the undisputed leader of the ARP, which after the events of 1894 had regained its unity. A tribute of a very different nature was the honorary doctorate in jurisprudence from Princeton University, which Kuyper was able to receive in person on 22 October 1898. At Princeton he also delivered his famous Stone Lectures, in which he offered his vision of the historical and current importance of Calvinism. His visit to the United States concluded with a lecture tour that attracted much attention.

In June 1899 Kuyper and his wife saw their third son, Abraham Kuyper Jr., obtain his doctorate and their eldest son, Herman Kuyper, appointed as a professor at the Free University. Just two months later Kuyper was struck by the unexpected death of his wife. She died on 25 August in the Swiss town of Meyringen at the age of fifty-seven, and was buried there. From then on Kuyper would be taken care of by his three unmarried daughters, of whom the eldest, the writer Henriëtte Kuyper, occasionally assisted him in publishing his works.

J. A. Wormser, 1845-1916.

Despite all the political developments, 1894 was a fruitful year for Kuyper as a theologian. In January and July, J. A. Wormser of Amsterdam published the three-volume *Encyclopedia of Sacred Theology*, which elaborated theology as a scientific discipline. The work of 1700 pages contained the substance of the lectures he had given at the Free University since 1880. According to Rullmann the *Encyclopedia* ought to be regarded as Kuyper's "life's work." In July 1894 Wormser also published the third volume of *E Voto Dordraceno*. The first two volumes of this comprehensive commentary on the Heidelberg Catechism had already been published in June 1892 and July 1893; the fourth volume was published in July 1895.

For twenty years J. A. Wormser was Kuyper's foremost publisher. In 1886 he replaced H. J. Kruijt, who until then had also published *De Standaard*, because Kruijt refused to join the Doleantie.

In the summer of 1894 Kuyper contracted a serious lung disease, which forced him to suspend all activities for nearly six months. At first there were even fears for his life. The illness was diagnosed in Brussels on the return journey from his ususal vacation. In October he travelled to the Pyrenees to recuperate further, and from there journeyed to Tunisia for a few weeks. On 31 December 1894 Kuyper returned to Amsterdam.

The photograph shows the Grand Hotel Gassion in Pau in the Pyrenees where Kuyper stayed for quite some time. On 27 October he wrote to his children who still lived at home: "Yes, it is true my darlings, I could have been gone for good. Looking back on it now, I first felt, owing to my fearful weakness, how close I had come to the gates of death, and what a great favor and grace it was of my God that I did not sink away into the pit, but have now already recovered somewhat."

Before his illness, Kuyper had already hinted in *De Standaard* of 2 June 1894 that Lohman's political views would have consequences for his position at the Free University. Although his stay abroad meant a reprieve, Kuyper was determined not to let the matter rest. After his return to the Netherlands, he purposefully went to work. Under his direction Lohman's position was further undermined despite protests by Hovy, who as president-director feared that the Free University would come to ruin as a result of these divisions. In a letter of 6 February 1895 Hovy criticized Kuyper for the insinuations he had levelled against Lohman in the press: "May one write in that way without any proof whatsoever? Is that not a sin before God?"

Hovy (portrayed above) was also personally involved in the matter because his daughter Emelia was married to Lohman's eldest son, W. H. de Savornin Lohman, who in 1890 had been appointed as a special professor at the Free University. Under pressure of the college of directors, on 22 March 1896 the seven professors of the VU signed a joint declaration in which they stated that the education given "ought completely and exclusively to rest on the foundations of Reformed principles." During the further elaboration of this statement, Lohman and his son ended up on opposite sides from the others.

On 27 June 1895, at the Hotel Seinpost in Scheveningen, the annual meeting of the Society for the Free University was convened under Kuyper's chairmanship. The meeting was attended by about 2000 persons — more than usual, because Kuyper and Rutgers had mobilized their supporters. At their instigation, thirty-five members submitted a protest against Lohman's teaching, which supposedly ran contrary to Reformed principles as formulated in Article 2 of the statutes. After a lengthy debate an overall majority in the meeting decided to set up an investigative committee that would scrutinize the objections.

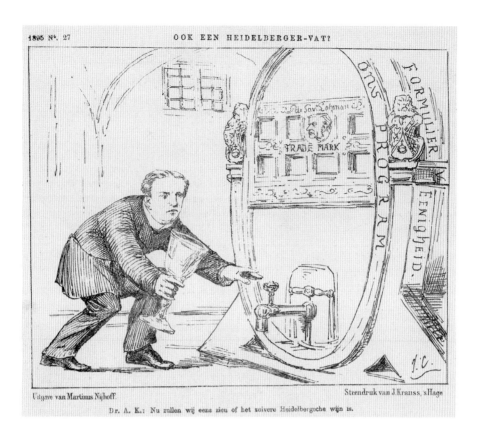

Uitgave van Martinus Nijhoff.   Steendruk van J. Krauss, 'sHage

Dr. A. K.: Nu zullen wij eens zien of het zuivere Heidelbergsche wijn is.

"Is it a Heidelberg barrel?," caricature in *De Nederlandsche Spectator* of 6 July 1895 about the conflict at the Free University: Kuyper tests whether Lohman is serving pure Calvinistic wine. Shortly before, the fourth volume of Kuyper's commentary on the Heidelberg Catechism, *E voto Dordraceno*, had appeared.

In the same month Kuyper published a short biography of Keuchenius, which put further pressure on his relationship with Lohman. In this booklet, Kuyper strongly emphasized the difference between Keuchenius and Lohman. He was sorry that he had not previously supported Keuchenius enough. Keuchenius, being a democrat and a Calvinist, had struck the pure Anti-Revolutionary note, while Lohman had listened to the Roman Catholics too much, and had dampened the fire in the party with his conservatism. Clearly, Kuyper used his Keuchenius biography (according to Schaepman "a narrow-minded and ugly booklet") to attack Lohman.

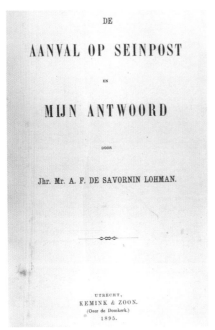

Lohman's pamphlet against the criticism of his teaching at the Free University.

At the foundation day of the Free University on 20 October 1895 it became known that Kuyper and Rutgers were behind what had occurred in the Hotel Seinpost. In a statement, the two pointed out that there existed a deep-seated difference with regard to principle. They had advised in favor of an investigative committee in the hopes that the Free University would be spared a prolonged conflict: "Already memberships had been resigned and contributions had decreased significantly. In this way the university was being *threatened in its existence.*" Hovy, who was well-versed in the Scriptures, and who was disillusioned about the "most sorry demonstration at Seinpost," reacted in a letter to Kuyper dated 11 November 1895 with the words: "The members walked away! I read in my Bible that Saul too could not wait (1 Samuel 13 vv. 7-12) and that he then went on to help himself. His members (soldiers) also walked away."

Theo Heemskerk (1852-1932), son of the Conservative statesman Jan Heemskerk, Anti-Revolutionary member of the chamber and alderman of Amsterdam, was the only lawyer on the nine-member investigative committee. Chairing the committee was Kampen professor Herman Bavinck, who had already been asked by Kuyper to do this before the Seinpost meeting.

On 2 July 1896 the annual meeting of the Society in Leeuwarden agreed with the conclusion of the investigating committee that the education Lohman had provided did not do justice to Reformed principles. On 12 September Lohman tendered his resignation as a professor. His son also resigned his position. Hovy resigned as president-director of the Free University, but did continue to support the university financially.

Lohman was so aggrieved by his dismissal from the Free University that he avoided all personal contact with Kuyper for a year and even refused to shake his hand. As they saw each other in Parliament every day, in the long run this situation became untenable. That was why Lohman restored the official side of their relationship a year later in a letter of 19 April 1897, which would form the basis of their future political cooperation. "That I want to retain the freedom to express myself and air my opinions in public," he wrote, "freedoms for which I have sacrificed much, goes without saying."

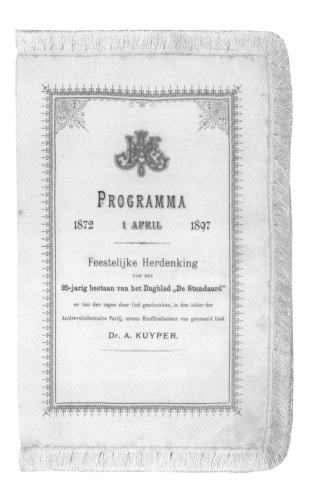

On 1 April 1897, the twenty-fifth anniversary of *De Standaard* was celebrated in the large concert hall of the Palace of People's Industry, and Kuyper as editor-in-chief was enthusiastically honored. The initiative for the meeting had begun in September 1896 (the month of Lohman's resignation) with the Amsterdam electoral association "Nederland en Oranje" (The Netherlands and Orange) "to express the sincere love, the high honour and the heartfelt appreciation that it bears its leader, the learned gentleman Prof. Dr. A. Kuyper." With parliamentary elections planned for June, the homage was also meant as a manifestation of Anti-Revolutionary ardor. The meeting was attended by "more than 5,000 men and women from every walk of life, bound together by a holy principle, and by their very presence declaring a powerful testimony supporting this principle." On this occasion Kuyper was addressed by Heemskerk in his capacity as the jubilee committee's chairman and by Bavinck, who acted as the official speaker.

The above photograph shows the "deluxe edition" of that evening's program, offered to the guest of honor, bound in a cover of plain bronze-colored calf's leather, printed on white satin, bordered on all sides by a narrow white satin fringe. The monogram was embroidered in orange and consisted of the interwoven letters "Dr. A. K."

The principal speaker was Kuyper himself, who, looking back on his life, placed it in a broader perspective: "All that I am . . . what is it finally but His talent and His work? He who created me, He who predestined me, He who led me since my youth, He who without my presuming it in the least, brought me to this position without my knowing it, to defend His holy Name, it was He alone who also gave me access to your hearts. And even if you ask me whether behind all the gifts and talent there is not also an 'I' to be found in my person, and whether that 'I' is not the person who makes all gifts to glow and be inspired, then still my answer is: 'even that "I," even that person does not come from me, but is only given by God to me.'" Kuyper ended his speech with a poem he had written in which he summed up his life's aim, "singing in the style of Da Costa in his own tone." The poem was later put to music by P. Anders.

> For me, just *one* longing rules my life,
> *One* higher urge drives will and soul.
> And rather let my breathing fail me
> Than this holy force lets me go.
> 'Tis to restore God's holy ordinations,
> In home and church, in state and school,
> Regardless of the world's protestations,
> For the good of all the nation.[1]

1. Translation adapted from that in *Creating a Christian World View: Abraham Kuyper's Lectures on Calvinism* by Peter S. Heslam (Grand Rapids: Eerdmans, 1998), pp. 54-55.

The Anti-Revolutionary Party gave Kuyper a statue of the Dutch Maiden (personifying the Netherlands) holding a banner engraved with the words, "Our help is in the name of the Lord, who created heaven and earth." The two other female figures represent history and religion and hold *Our Program* and the Bible respectively.

During the anniversary celebrations, nearly all the attention went to Kuyper, but R. C. Verweijck (1859-1937) also played an important role at *De Standaard*. As editor and editor-in-chief (1883-1931) he was in charge of the paper day-to-day. Kuyper himself was "the political editor in chief" and limited himself to writing lead articles and three-stars. Using the pseudonym "Bijltje" (Little Axe), Verweijck wrote a well-known weekly column in *De Standaard*. He was also Kuyper's right-hand man in the political arena; for many years he acted as the central committee's deputy secretary (1901-1925).

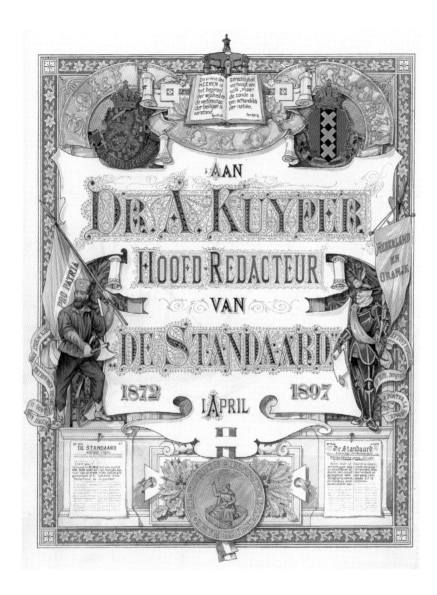

Title page of the album with the names of all those who had contributed to the jubilee celebrations.

A *Gedenkboek (Memorial Book)* was also published on the occasion, including a large number of newspaper commentaries.

Dr. P. H. Ritter in the *Nieuws van den Dag:* "Dr. Kuyper has more than one style at his disposal. He uses a different style in a learned work, such as his *Encyclopedia,* than in an edifying article in *De Heraut;* the style in his oration differs from that in *Our Program* and is different in a sermon than in an article in one of the daily papers, and those newspaper articles in turn vary in style according to the demands of the subject matter. But whatever words flow from his pen, his style is always clear like Multatuli's and as distinguished as that of Busken Huet."

Kuyper as a writer, a charcoal drawing by Jan Veth, circa 1892.

In an edition of the *Standaard* published exclusively by the family on 1 April 1897 in a printing of one copy, Kuyper's daughter Henriëtte described her father as a writer: "Dr. Kuyper *writes*, and for him writing is the immediate outpouring of his thoughts into visible signs. No outline, no points jotted in advance to show him the way. He puts down the paper in front of him, and from the thoughts crowded together, all interrelated, the ones that are called upon group themselves in such a way so as to spin out a thread that must lead to the foreseen goal. Immediately, as the stream of thought begins, the pen ticks on the paper. At first slowly with round lettering; then, as the activity in the circle of thoughts increases, the more quickly and with smaller points and more little figures made up of dashes."

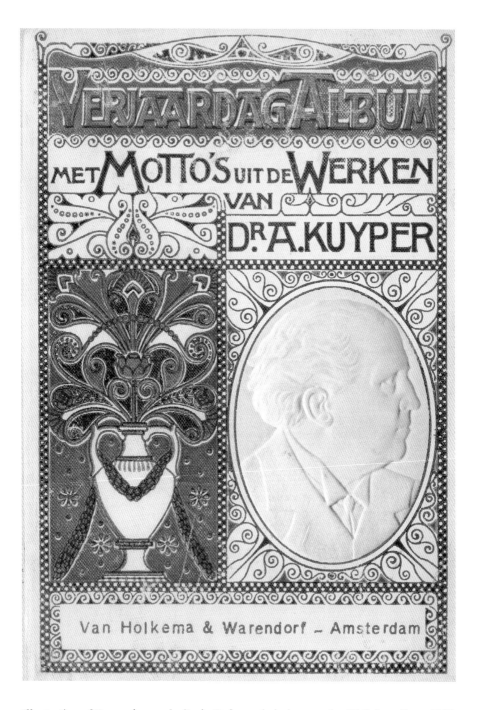

Illustrative of Kuyper's popularity in Reformed circles was the *Birthday-album: With Sayings from the Works of Dr. A. Kuyper,* which the booksellers Höveker & Wormser brought onto the market in December 1897. It featured one citation from Kuyper's work for each day, as selected by his daughter Henriëtte.

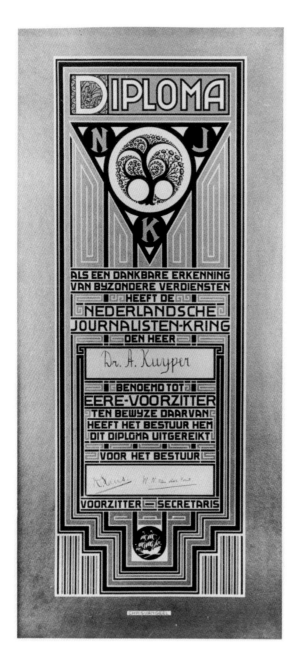

Despite all their political differences, as a journalist Kuyper enjoyed a great reputation among his colleagues of the daily press. He had an eye for the importance of the press, which in his speech at the opening of the Free University he called "a power within the nation." From 1898 until 1901 Kuyper was the chairman of the Dutch Association of Journalists, in which he worked together amicably with Liberals such as Charles Boissevain and Jacques Deen. When he resigned as chairman in 1901, the Dutch Association of Journalists appointed him as an honorary chairman (see above).

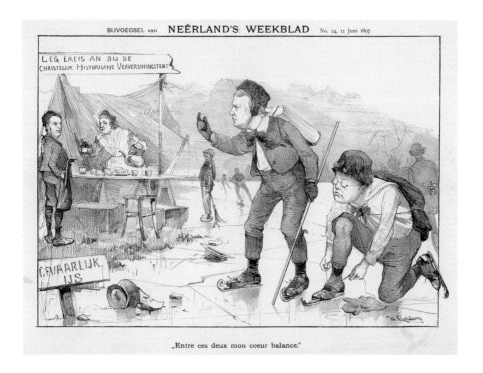

LEG EREIS AN BIJ DE
CHRISTELIJK HISTORISCHE VERVERSCHINGSTENT

C.N.AARLIJK,
IJS

„Entre ces deux mon coeur balance."

Shortly after the *Standaard* party, the campaign for the parliamentary elections of June 1897 commenced. For these elections the Anti-Revolutionaries and the Roman Catholics again worked together, but Lohman's Free Anti-Revolutionaries and Bronsveld's Christian-Historicals entered into the elections independently. Many *Hervormde* voters were not in favor of cooperating with the Roman Catholics and were afraid moreover that an election victory by the ARP, whose foreman Kuyper had also led the Doleantie, would damage the position of the Dutch Reformed Church.

The drawing by P. J. van Geldorp in *Neerland's Weekblad* of 12 June 1897 shows Lohman standing in front of Bronsveld's stall refusing to come along with Kuyper and Schaepman.

CHARLES BOISSEVAIN op zijn bureau aan het Alg. Handelsblad.

The editor-in-chief of the *Algemeen Handelsblad* Charles Boissevain (1842-1927) played on the feelings of *Hervormde* voters by reminding them of Kuyper's "illegal" action during the "sawing of the panels" in 1886. Upon Boissevain's suggestion, the polemic that ensued between Kuyper and Boissevain in the *Handelsblad* was published in March 1898 in the pamphlet *Correspondence between Dr. A. Kuyper and Charles Boissevain*. Despite this political quarrel, the personal relations between the two remained good.

Kuyper as deputy for the electoral district of Sliedrecht, 1894-1901.

In a commemorative issue of *De Standaard* devoted to Kuyper on 29 October 1937, MP A. Zijlstra recalled memories of the election campaign of 1897 when Kuyper delivered a speech in Noordhorn: "It was a beautiful July evening when Dr. Kuyper arrived and was led to the meeting hall by the chairman, Rev. Scholten. He had sought out the biggest hall. But what a scene met our eyes! The hall was packed to the rafters, the speaker could not get to the platform, and hundreds crowded outside trying to get in — men, women, and children from all walks of life, who held many different political beliefs. What was one to do?

"Then there was a Liberal landowner who said: go to my plot of land and hold the meeting in the open air. The order to do so was given, and there the crowd went. Whoever was able to lay his hands on a chair took one with him. It was as if the hall was about to be demolished. Later, the electoral association had to compensate quite a bit for damages. In this way a large crowd gathered on that field. An improvised platform was set up and Dr. Kuyper began his speech. It was interesting, informative, entertaining.

"However, the high point was the debate. At this moment a registrar, a Liberal man, raised objections to the Anti-Revolutionary Party because of the death penalty in its programme. Have you forgotten, he called out to Dr. Kuyper, that the Lord Jesus was condemned by the authorities and underwent the death penalty? Without that statute, this would not have happened.

"Then Dr. Kuyper spoke. Meanwhile, it had grown quite dark. A sumptuous evening. It was as quiet as it can be in the wide-open fields. Across the countryside there hung a light summer's haze, so that the soft shades of sunset glowed in the sky. The chairman held up a match for Dr. Kuyper whenever he wanted to consult his notes for the debate. How quiet it was amongst that great crowd as it listened with bated breath, just as in the past, during field preaching, the eager crowd absorbed what was said.

"Dr. Kuyper had put on his hat because it was getting chilly. When it came to the debater's question about the death sentence, his voice became most solemn. Our Saviour was, he said, brought to death. Condemned by the authorities, He died on the cross. And now, he continued, now that I must speak of these things, I will bare my head. And then . . . all hats and caps were removed. There we all stood, believers and atheists, all of us most apprehensive.

"And there the voice sounded full of heartfelt emotion: 'Now I believe with all of God's people, that if the death penalty had not been the right of the authorities, who rule by the grace of God, and our King and Lord had not been condemned to death on the cross, there would have been no salvation and mercy for you or me for all time and eternity.' And raising his voice, he called out, 'And whoever believes this as I do, say "amen."' Then from the multitude of mouths there arose 'amen,' as it had never been said before.

"For a moment there fell a wondrous silence. There were those for whom it all became too much. They wanted to leave. . . . However, Dr. Kuyper gave thanks and then we left. Never have I experienced such a moment as this in the political fray.

"I had seen Kuyper at the height of his powers."

Dr. N. G. Pierson, 1839-1909.

Because many *Hervormde* voters voted for the Liberals in the second round of balloting, the Confessional parties remained in the minority, despite a substantial gain of eleven seats for the Anti-Revolutionaries. The Liberals lost eight seats, but retained a small majority in the second chamber. Again a Liberal cabinet was formed, led by the finance minister, the economist N. G. Pierson (1839-1909), a younger brother of Allard and Hendrik Pierson; like them, he sported remarkable sideburns. Unlike the Röell cabinet, the Pierson cabinet pursued an energetic and progressive set of policies that brought to a close the long period of Liberal supremacy in a dignified way. Although the Confessional parliamentary groups were at full strength with Kuyper, Lohman, and Schaepman in the second chamber, the Pierson cabinet excelled because it had among its ranks strong cabinet members such as P. W. A. Cort van der Linden (Justice), W. H. de Beaufort (Foreign Affairs), H. Goeman Borgesius (Home Affairs), C. Lely (Transport and Communications, Trade and Industry), and J. T. Cremer (Colonial Affairs). This ministry passed a number of important social laws and also introduced compulsory education and military service.

Queen Wilhelmina at her inauguration in the Nieuwe Kerk, Amsterdam, 6 September 1898, next to Queen Emma.

On 31 August Queen Wilhelmina reached the age of eighteen, which ended the regency of her mother, Queen Emma. On 6 September the traditional inauguration of the new Queen took place in the Nieuwe Kerk. Although Kuyper as a Member of Parliament was expected to attend this ceremony, he had excused himself owing to his American trip. He was also unable to attend as chairman of the committee that received the foreign press covering the inaugural celebrations.

THE CUNARD LINE R.M.S. ''CAMPANIA'' & ''LUCANIA '' 12,950 TONS.

On 11 August 1898 Kuyper left Amsterdam for the United States in order to receive an honorary doctorate in jurisprudence in Princeton, New Jersey, which Princeton University had already awarded him on its 150th anniversary in 1896. In addition, he had been invited to give the famous Stone Lectures there. This annual series of lectures, financed by the L. P. Stone Foundation, took place under the auspices of the Princeton Theological Seminary. In those years the seminary had an unmistakably orthodox slant. Through the many contacts that existed between Dutch and American Calvinists (some of whom were descendents of the secession of 1834), Kuyper's work had become known in America.

After a stay in London, on 20 August Kuyper embarked on the Cunard steamship *Lucania*. On 27 August he arrived in New York.

Geerhardus Vos (1862-1949), professor of biblical theology at Princeton Theological Seminary (1893-1932), played an important part in disseminating Kuyper's work in the United States. Vos was a Dutchman by birth and had attended the Amsterdam gymnasium with Kuyper's eldest son. In 1881 he had emigrated to America with his parents. In 1886 he turned down an appointment at the Free University. Together with his colleague B. B. Warfield, Vos saw to it that Kuyper's *Encyclopedia of Sacred Theology* was translated into English.

B. B. Warfield (1851-1921), professor in dogmatics (1887-1921) and head (1887-1902) of Princeton Theological Seminary. Warfield was a leading theologian and a convicted supporter of neo-Calvinism. He was known as an opponent of Modernism and "revivalism" in the American churches. Warfield also worked hard for the translation of the *Encyclopedia* and wrote a preface for the English edition.

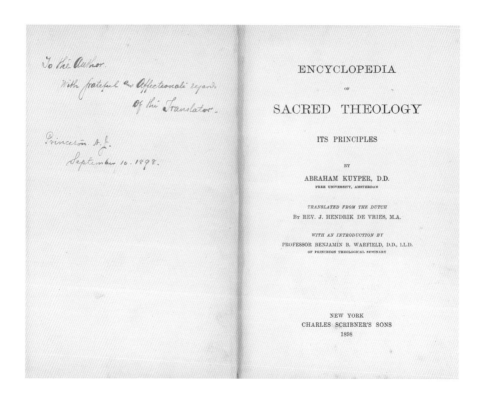

In New York Kuyper was presented with a copy of the *Encyclopedia of Sacred Theology: Its Principles*, the English translation of the second, general volume of his *Encyclopedia*, to which the beginning of the first, introductory volume had been added. The book was published by Charles Scribner's Sons in New York. Kuyper received the copy from the translator J. H. de Vries (1859-1939), a Dutch immigrant and Presbyterian minister in Princeton who as of 1892 had translated much of Kuyper's work.

On 8 October 1898 Kuyper wrote to his wife, "The book [the *Encyclopedia*] has now been published, and is beautiful. However, I only received one copy and must buy all the others at a rate of 25 guilders apiece. Just imagine that." The *Encyclopedia* did not sell well at first, but after 1954 the book was reprinted seven times in the United States.

:ede & Son,
ietors.
'HTON, Manager.

Kuyper used the weeks prior to his stay in Princeton to rest and to shorten his Stone Lectures. The English translation he had brought with him from the Netherlands was replaced at the very last moment by a translation that had been made in Princeton. From New York Kuyper also visited Albany, Saratoga Springs, Keene Valley, and Boston. The photograph shows St. Hubert's Inn in Keene Valley, as depicted on the hotel stationery; here he spent fourteen days in the mountains.

Miller Chapel of Princeton Theological Seminary, where the Stone Lectures were given.

On 10, 11, 14, 19, 20, and 21 October 1898 Kuyper delivered his Stone Lectures on Calvinism to an enthusiastic audience in Miller Chapel, with the central theme being the superiority of Calvinism as a worldview for all fields of life. In six lectures he successively discussed Calvinism as it pertained to history, religion, politics, science, art, and the future. According to the British historian Peter Heslam, the Stone Lectures offered "the most complete, cogent, and visionary expression of Kuyperian thought."

As a condensed vision of the historical and current significance of Calvinism, the Stone Lectures are Kuyper's most widespread and translated work. Dutch and English editions were published as soon as 1899. Since then it has often been republished, and it has appeared in print in countries such as Germany, Hungary, India, Japan, South Korea, and Russia.

On 22 October 1898 Kuyper was awarded an honorary doctorate in law by the president of Princeton University, F. L. Patton. When he was awarded the honorary doctorate in 1896, he had been offered the choice between a doctorate in theology or in law. Kuyper opted for the latter as an acknowledgment for all he had done in the political field. In his word of thanks he revealed that Utrecht philosopher C. W. Opzoomer ("not at all a Calvinist") had already suggested giving him an honorary doctorate in law in 1879 for the publication of *Ons Program*, but the Utrecht theologians had opposed this. It was for this reason that he now appreciated the Princeton award so much. Moreover, the honorary doctorate in law was a confirmation of his opinion that Calvinism was not only a theological system, but one that had a much broader significance in the political and social fields.

In his word of gratitude Kuyper again pointed out the importance of Calvinism as a source of political freedoms, both in the Netherlands and in the United States. In doing so he compared the historical struggle of the Dutch Calvinists against Spain with that of the Spanish-American War (1898), which had just recently been won by the United States: "Calvinism is not limited to theology, but unfurled its banner on the whole field of human life, more especially in politics; and in your country as well as mine, the political liberties we so freely enjoy are due to the valiant spirit instilled by Calvin in the heart of our *sea beggars* [Dutch sailors fighting against Spain] and of your *pilgrim fathers*."

Kuyper as honorary doctor of Princeton, 22 October 1898.

On 22 October Kuyper wrote to his wife that his speech "succeeded so excellently that it ended in continuous applause, and the professor of oratory said to me that he was grateful for that specimen of English eloquence. God trained me, I myself do not know how . . . it was a perfect day."

His co-laureate, the British professor of English law in Oxford, Albert Venn Dicey (1835-1922), was also impressed with Kuyper's performance, as appears from a letter to his wife: "We were each asked to say a few words. This led to the most remarkable speech I have heard in a long time. Kuyper . . . looked like a Dutchman of the seventeenth century. He spoke slowly and solemnly. His English was impressive, with here and there a Dutch idiom. He told us he was a Calvinist; that he had been persecuted by anti-Calvinists — this itself sounded like the language of another age. All the good in America had its root in Calvinism, which was as much a legal and an ethical as a religious creed. The Continental States had sympathized with Spain. Not so the Dutch Calvinists. 'We have not forgotten our contest with Spanish tyranny; we fought it for a hundred years. In six weeks you have given Spanish power its *coup de grace,* but neither England nor the United States would have been free but for Dutch heroism. Spain has in all countries and in all ages been a curse to the world.' . . . This was the tone of the whole speech. There was not a word of flattery to America. One felt as if the seventeenth century had visibly risen upon us to give the last curse to Spain. After that I spoke, said nothing very remarkable."

BANQUET...

IN HONOR OF DR. A. KUYPER,
Amsterdam, Netherlands.

...At New City Hotel, Holland, Mich.
October 23, 1898.

NEWS PRESSES.

After his stay in Princeton, Kuyper made a tour through the United States that became a veritable triumphal procession. He gave lectures in many places, which were attended by thousands of people, largely descendents of Dutch immigrants. His tour included stops in Grand Rapids, Holland, Chicago, Pella, Des Moines, Orange City, Cleveland, Rochester, New Brunswick, and Hartford.

The photograph shows the menu of the banquet that was given in Kuyper's honor on 28 October in the New City Hotel in Holland, Michigan, for which more than one hundred tickets were sold. Among the dishes the guests were served were "Saragota Chips à la Kleine Luyden" and "Coquilles of Sweet Breads à la Free University."

One of the many newspaper reports of Kuyper's tour, in *The Holland Daily Sentinel* of 28 October 1898, about his lecture in the Third Reformed Church at Holland. After a few introductory remarks, Kuyper gave the same lecture as in Princeton about "Calvinism and the Future." The reporter was afraid that the topic was too advanced for the average listener: "The subject was handled in a masterly way, and the lecture proved to be extremely learned. It was a broad survey of the history of the civilized world with a look into the future. To thoroughly grasp the subject as discussed, it was necessary for one to be versed in history — profane and ecclesiastical — in science in nearly all of its branches, and in theology. One listening to the broad survey of men and matter and the deep insight into the principles underlying human affairs today knew at once that here was a master mind. To those who could understand the lecture it was a rare treat and it will leave its impression." In this lecture Kuyper once more emphasized the meaning of Calvinism for American society: "America has a grand future to look forward to, but it needs the principles of Calvinism to strengthen its backbone." He called upon the Dutch in his audience to become true Americans and learn the English language. Only as English-speaking people could they enable Dutch traditions (including Calvinism) to fully permeate the social life of America.

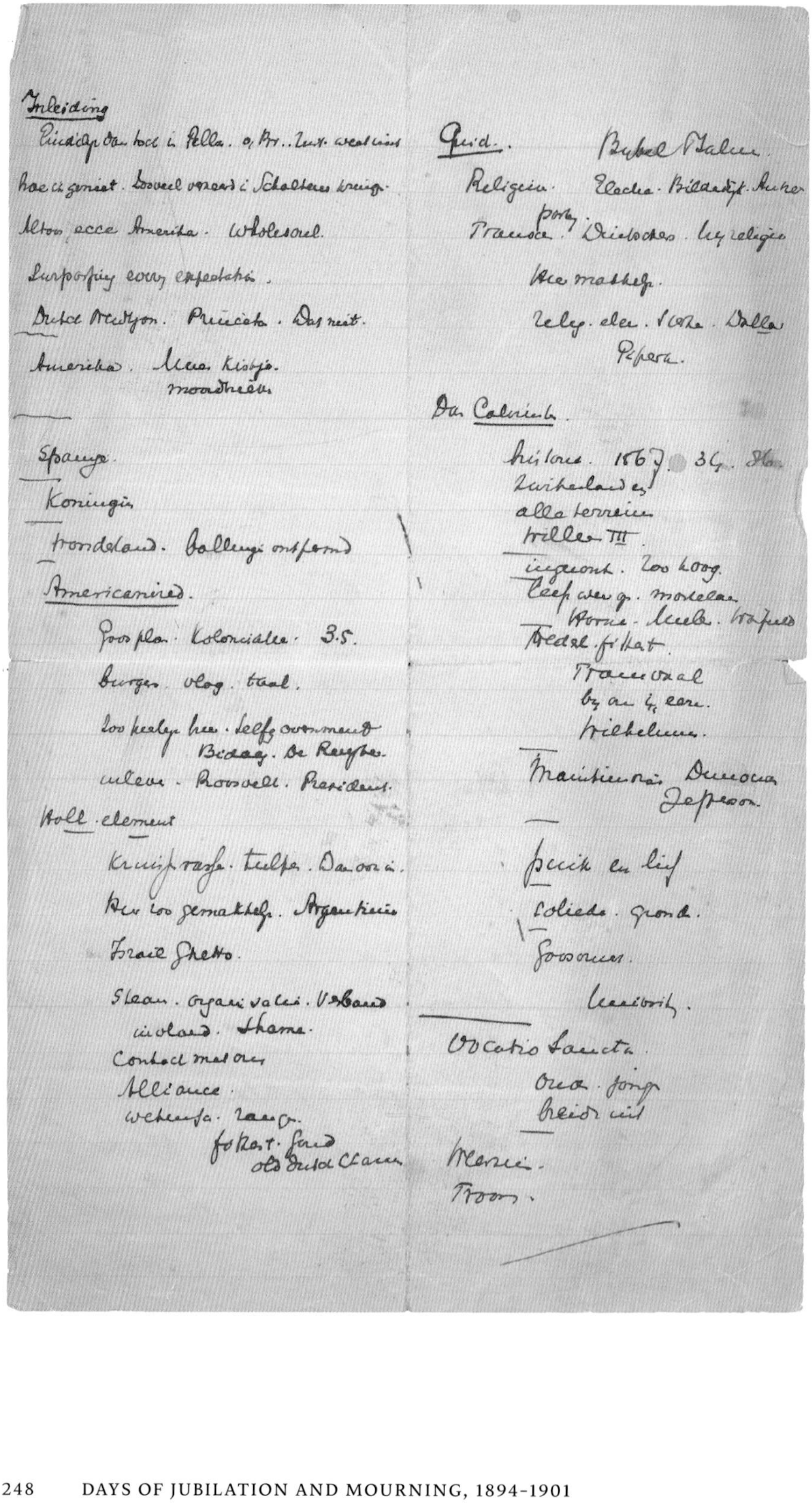

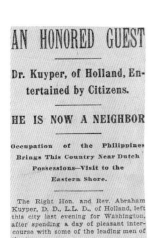

AN HONORED GUEST

Dr. Kuyper, of Holland, Entertained by Citizens.

HE IS NOW A NEIGHBOR

Occupation of the Philippines
Brings This Country Near Dutch
Possessions—Visit to the
Eastern Shore.

The Right Hon. and Rev. Abraham Kuyper, D. D., L.L. D., of Holland, left this city last evening for Washington, after spending a day of pleasant intercourse with some of the leading men of the town.

He met Governor Lowndes in the morning at the Hotel Rennert, and in the afternoon lunched at the Merchants' Club, where the geniality of the member of the States-General impressed all who met him with his ability as a statesman and diplomat.

Governor Lowndes had a long conversation with Dr. Kuyper about his journeys in this country. On Dr. Kuyper stating that he intended visiting various places in Maryland where colonists from Holland have settled, Governor Lowndes said he would place the State steamer Governor McLane at his service. Dr. Kuyper will return from Washington tomorrow, and will take the McLane for a trip of several days. One of the places he will visit will be Wilhelmina.

While Governor Lowndes was convers-

DR. KUYPER AT THE MERCHANTS' CLUB.

On his lecture tour Kuyper did not allow his audience to sing the official Dutch national anthem by Hendrik Tollens, because he did not think the opening lines ("Let him in whom true Dutch blood flows untainted, pure, and free") were appropriate in a diverse society such as the United States. He preferred the Luther hymn "A Mighty Fortress Is Our God" and the old "Wilhelmus van Nassauwe," which dated back to the time of the Eighty Years' War, the "heroic anthem that fits well with our colonists, most from Calvinist stock." This song had also been played at Queen Wilhelmina's inauguration and in 1932 became the official Dutch national anthem. Kuyper to his wife, Chicago, 11 November 1898: "On Monday I had a big speech in Marlowe Hall, an opera house that was packed full, and where I spoke for two hours amid thunderous applause and the singing of the 'Wilhelmus.' All the Dutch people here still relied on 'Wien Neerlands bloed,' but I soon put a stop to that and had the 'Wilhelmus' replace it. Two thousand copies with sheet music were printed and handed out at the entrance. And honestly, the singing went better than I had expected."

Kuyper during a reception in the Merchants Club in Baltimore, "where the geniality of the member of the States-General impressed all who met him with his ability as a statesman and a diplomat" (*The Morning Herald*, 30 November 1898). When Kuyper mentioned that he had plans to visit a number of Dutch colonies in Maryland, Governor Lowndes placed the state yacht *Governor Maclane* at his disposal.

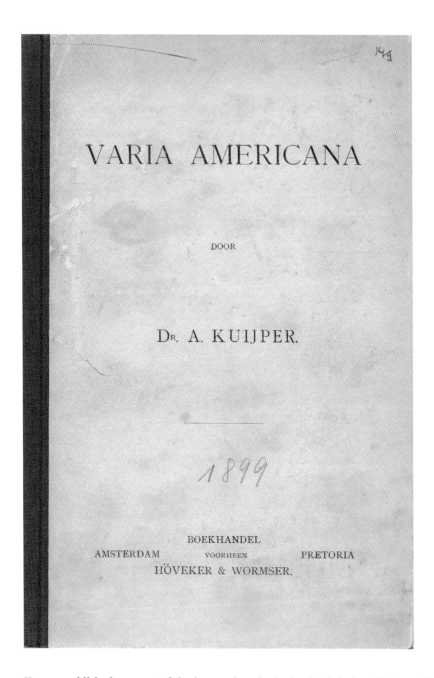

VARIA AMERICANA

DOOR

DR. A. KUIJPER.

1899

BOEKHANDEL
AMSTERDAM   VOORHEEN   PRETORIA
HÖVEKER & WORMSER.

Kuyper published a report of the impressions he had gained during his travels in his book *Varia Americana* (June 1899), in which he wrote about "our kinfolk," church life, and the political system in the United States. In New York he witnessed up close the struggle for the governorship between the Republican Theodore Roosevelt and the Democrat Augustus van Wijk, "both from old Dutch stock" as he happily noted. Roosevelt led his campaign from the Fifth Avenue Hotel on Madison Square, where Kuyper was also staying, while the headquarters of the Democrats was nearby.

On 30 November Kuyper made a short visit to President William McKinley (1843-1901), about whom he remarked in *Varia Americana:* "McKinley is not a statesman of the highest order, but he is a man of prayer." Kuyper lobbied in favor of the interests of the South African Boer Transvaal Republic, which was being threatened by British imperialism. A year later the "Second War of Liberation" (1899-1902) between England and the Boer Republics would break out.

McKinley (see illustration above) died on 14 September 1901 as a result of an anarchist attack. He was succeeded by Vice-President Theodore Roosevelt.

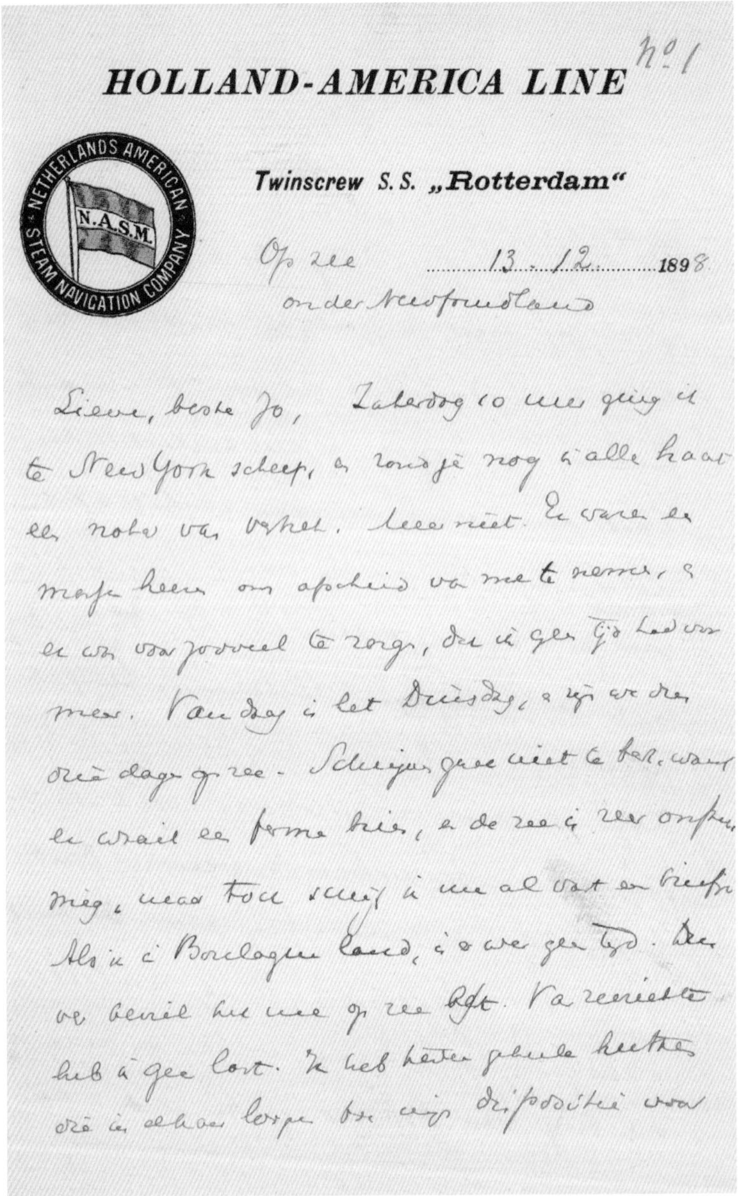
HOLLAND-AMERICA LINE No 1

Twinscrew S.S. „Rotterdam"

Op zee 13. 12. 1898
onder Newfoundland

Lieve, beste Jo,

Letter by Kuyper to his wife, written on his return trip to Europe, 13 December 1898. The 22 letters that Kuyper wrote during his travels in America were published in 2004 in the book *More and More I Feel That This Is Where I Had to Be,* which can be regarded as a personal counterpart to *Varia Americana.*

On 10 December in New York Kuyper boarded the steamship *Rotterdam* of the Holland-America Line, on which he made the crossing to Europe. He arrived in Boulogne on the night of 19 December, after which he travelled back to Amsterdam by way of London, Paris, and Brussels. On 30 December he was reunited with his family.

De briefwisseling tusschen Jhr. Wttewaal v. Stoetwegen
en Dr. Kuyper.

In Parliament after his return, Kuyper was kept busy with foreign affairs. From 18 May until 29 July 1899, upon the initiative of the Russian Tsar Nicholas II, the first International Peace Conference was held in The Hague. Because the South African Boer Republics had not been invited to the conference, early in May Kuyper used question time in the second chamber to demand that Minister for Foreign Affairs W. H. De Beaufort explain the exclusion of the Transvaal and the Orange Free State.

Although no results issued from Kuyper's intervention, the parliamentary questions did have an unexpected aftermath when the Dutch envoy in St. Petersburg, E. W. F. Wttewaal van Stoetwegen, responded in the *NRC* of 11 May 1899 to a critical remark Kuyper had made about him in the chamber. The envoy's letter to the editor contained confidential statements about the negotiations that had taken place, and the tone in which it was written was rude and personal. He addressed it directly to Kuyper: "The incense of admiration that wafts towards you from lower spheres has gone to your head, has suffocated your sense of piety, has led to the germination of pride and has brought you to the brink of the dreaded and incurable disease one calls 'megalomania.'"

In the same newspaper Kuyper put Wttewaal in his place in such a devastating way that the Queen put him on non-active service without pay. Braakensiek's caricature in *De Amsterdammer* of 21 May 1899 shows Kuyper giving the young uncouth Wttewaal a good tongue-lashing.

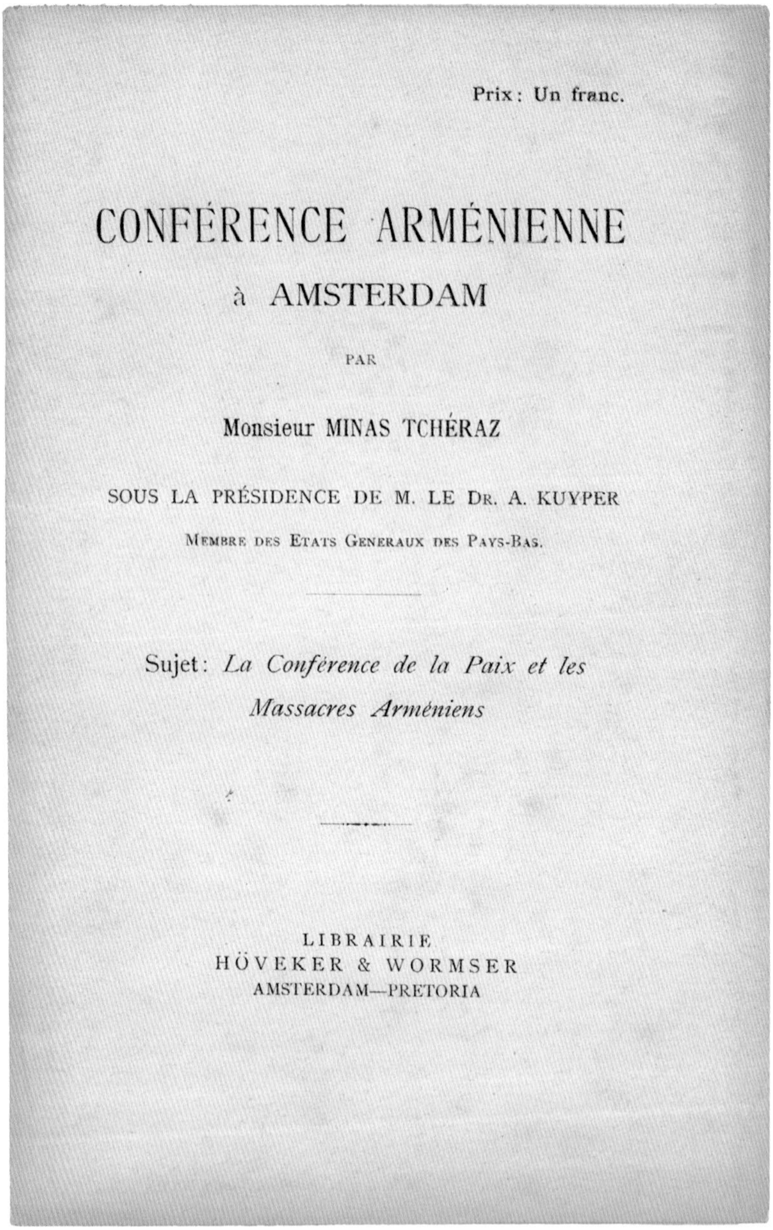

CONFÉRENCE ARMÉNIENNE

à AMSTERDAM

PAR

Monsieur MINAS TCHÉRAZ

SOUS LA PRÉSIDENCE DE M. LE Dr. A. KUYPER

MEMBRE DES ETATS GENERAUX DES PAYS-BAS.

Sujet: *La Conférence de la Paix et les Massacres Arméniens*

LIBRAIRIE
HÖVEKER & WORMSER
AMSTERDAM—PRETORIA

Kuyper supported the Christian Armenians who were being oppressed in Turkey. In 1895-96 pogroms in various Turkish cities had killed an estimated 100,000 Armenians. When on 30 May 1899 the Armenian exile Minas Tcheraz wanted to deliver a speech in The Hague about the fate of the Armenians, it was forbidden by the police. The appeal that he submitted to the Peace Conference was rejected. On 7 July a protest meeting was held under Kuyper's leadership in Amsterdam on the theme of "The Peace Conference and the Armenian Massacres."

Kuyper with his sons Herman (left) and Abraham during a holiday in South Tyrol.

Shortly before the summer holidays of 1899, Kuyper and his wife celebrated two feast days. On 23 June their third son, Abraham Kuyper Jr., obtained his doctorate in theology at the Free University with a dissertation on the Polish theologian Johannes Maccovius (1588-1644), professor at Franeker and a brother-in-law of Rembrandt. F. L. Rutgers was his supervisor. On 29 June 1899 their eldest son, Herman, was recommended as a professor of theology at the Free University. On 6 January 1891 Herman Kuyper had also obtained his doctorate under the supervision of Rutgers, becoming the first Doctor of Theology of the Free University.

During the summer vacation of that year, on 25 August 1899, Johanna Kuyper-Schaay died unexpectedly in Meyringen in the Berner Oberland region of Switzerland at the age of fifty-seven. She had fallen ill during a stay in the Grimsel Hospiz (see photograph) on Grimselsee, and with a temperature of 104, lying on a camp-bed, had been taken from there to Meyringen, where she died shortly afterwards. Kuyper was not present when she died. She was buried in the churchyard of Meyringen in the presence of Hovy and Rutgers, who delivered a eulogy in German. On the Sunday after her death, on 27 August, Kuyper preached in Meyringen on Hosea 14:9: "Those who are wise understand these things; those who are discerning know them. For the ways of the Lord are right, and the upright walk in them, but transgressors stumble in them."

The church in Meyringen, with Mrs. Kuyper's grave to the left of the path leading up to the church door.

On 27 August Lohman wrote to Kuyper: "*Amice!* Yesterday evening I read the newspaper reports that your wife has died of her illness. At the deathbed everything that separates us may be forgotten and I can fulfill the desire of my heart by expressing my heartfelt condolences upon this most painful loss. One of the sad consequences of everything that has occurred between us these past years was that I so seldom had the opportunity to see your wife. For you, she was a support; for her children, a loyal mother; for everyone whom she could help or comfort, a dear sister. To my mind, a true Christian. She went through life quietly, doing good. Many, very many, even though they could see her only from afar, will miss her; they will continue to remember her with love. May He who is our only comfort in life and in death support you and enable you to find peace with this hard blow, in His ordaining order. Let me, even though we must

keep fighting about principles, and although we differ in our views, shake your hand in silence. May you be commended to God."

Also on behalf of his children, Kuyper replied on 30 August with a short thank-you letter to Lohman: "*Amice.* I cannot bear to answer all the friendly words that I have been receiving these days. I am still too much in shock. But to your letter, a reply of melancholy gratitude must immediately be sent back. Not everything is comforting, but your sincere word and unfeigned pity enlivened me and my children in such a special way that I must tell you how highly we value this expression of Christian love. My daughter hopes to write back to Mrs. [Lohman] herself. I cannot postpone my words of gratitude. May the Lord reward your love, expressed in such a friendly way to your intensely sad brother Kuyper."

In *De Heraut* of 3 September 1899 Kuyper published the first of a series of meditations in which he placed grief over the death of a loved one in a biblical perspective: "Before the eye that peers from your soul into eternity lies a dead corpse, not as a sign that Death has triumphed, but as a *sign of the triumph of life.*" The fifty-two meditations that he wrote on this subject between 1899 and 1900 were published as *Asleep in Jesus* in December 1902.

The oldest daughter, Henriëtte, publicist and assistant to her father, led Kuyper's household after her mother's death. His other daughters, Johanna and Cato, usually lived with their father as well. Both periodically worked in the nursing profession. Although Henriëtte had not been able to receive a university education, she was a gifted woman who made a name for herself as a translator and a writer of literary sketches, poems, and in particular travel accounts. As fond of traveling as her father, she published books about her sojourns in America, Russia, France, England, Belgium, Italy, and Hungary. About America she wrote two books: *Half a Year in America* (1907) and *Second Journey to America* (1921). She was a member of the Nederlandsche Maatschappij van Letterkunde (Dutch Literary Society) (1913), and founder (1918) and honorary president of the Bond van Meisjesvereenigingen op Gereformeerden Grondslag (Federation of Girls Associations on Reformed Principles).

Influenced by her first trip to America, where she had witnessed the freer position of women in social life, Henriëtte Kuyper started to give lectures, one of the first women in orthodox Protestant circles to do so. At first Kuyper forbade this, but ultimately he gave in to her insistence. When a few years later she gave a lecture in The Hague with slides about Rome, Kuyper, to her great pleasure, was seated in the audience. She was even more satisfied when he complimented her when she got home.

In October 1900, a year after his wife's death, Kuyper moved into the house at Keizersgracht 164, which had been purchased by the Free University in 1899 and was situated next to the university building. He would live there for only a year. After his appointment as prime minister he moved to The Hague in October 1901.

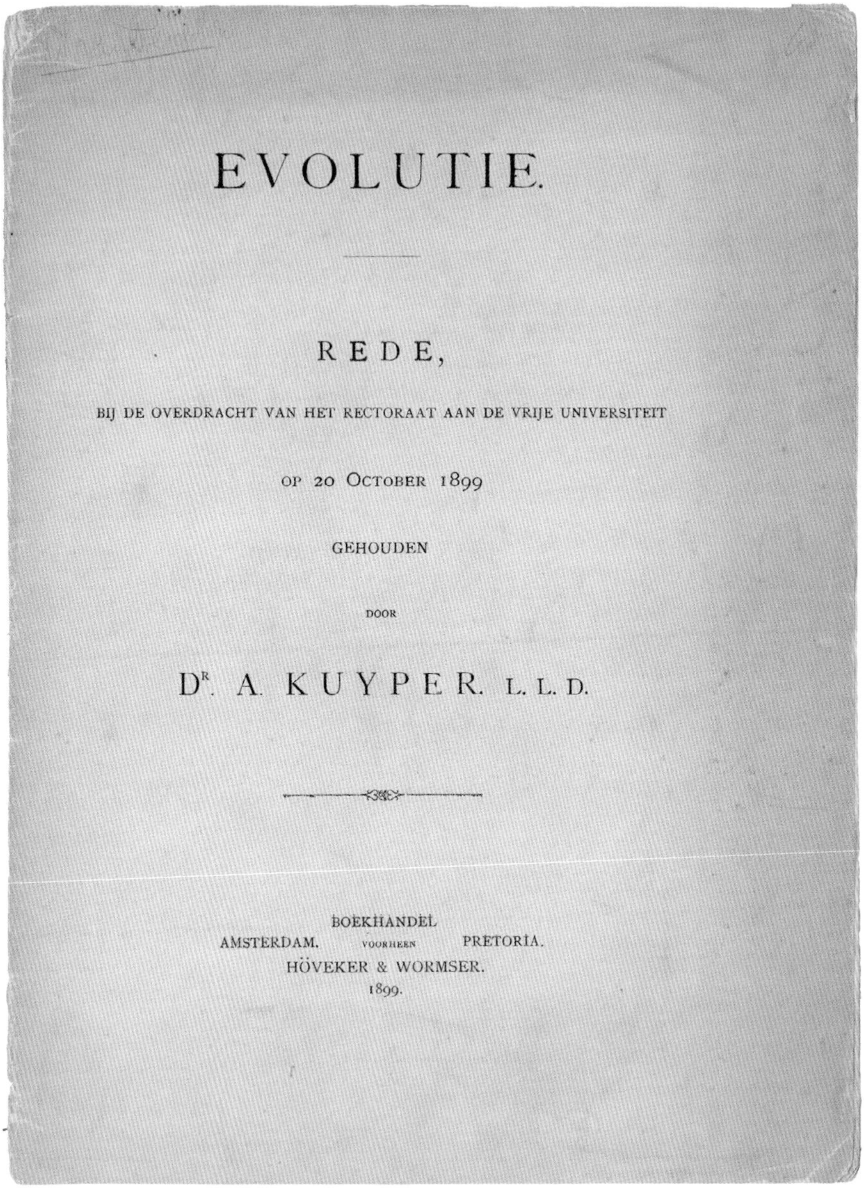

EVOLUTIE.

REDE,

BIJ DE OVERDRACHT VAN HET RECTORAAT AAN DE VRIJE UNIVERSITEIT

OP 20 OCTOBER 1899

GEHOUDEN

DOOR

D#R# A. KUYPER. L. L. D.

————❀————

BOEKHANDEL
AMSTERDAM.   VOORHEEN   PRETORIA.
HÖVEKER & WORMSER.
1899.

Upon the transfer of the rectorship of the Free University on 20 October 1899, Kuyper delivered the last of his great academic orations, *Evolution*. After the death of his wife he had stayed on in Switzerland for quite a long time, preparing his speech, and did not return to the Netherlands until October. During this academic ceremony Kuyper wore the doctor's cape from Princeton over his robe. On the title page of the printed edition of *Evolution* he added the initials L.L.D. (Doctor of Law) to his name. In the foreword Kuyper wrote that he had not been able to add explanatory notes to the text this time: "Sad circumstances forced me to write this speech, far away from my literary aids."

UIT DEN OORLOG IN ZUID-AFRIKA: De terugtocht der Engelschen over de Toegela na de nederlaag bij den Spioenkop.

Retreat of the British troops after the defeat at Spionkop.

On 11 October 1899 the long-expected war broke out between Great Britain and the Boer Republics of the Transvaal and the Orange Free State. Public opinion in the Netherlands supported the Dutch kinsmen, the Boers, against "perfidious Albion." The Boers' initial successes, such as at the Battle for Spionkop in January 1900 (see above), were greeted with enthusiasm.

KUOPIO
OSAKEYHTIÖ KUOPION UUSI KIRJAPAINO

1 mk. 25 p.

In a lengthy article entitled "The South African Crisis" in the famous French magazine *Revue des Deux Mondes* of February 1900, Kuyper defended the Boers' case. The article was published as a pamphlet under the same title in French, English, German, Dutch, Finnish, and Swedish. Kuyper's plea made a significant impression on international public opinion. The English edition even saw sixteen editions, the first (May 1900) in a run of 20,000 copies. The photograph shows the Finnish translation of 1901.

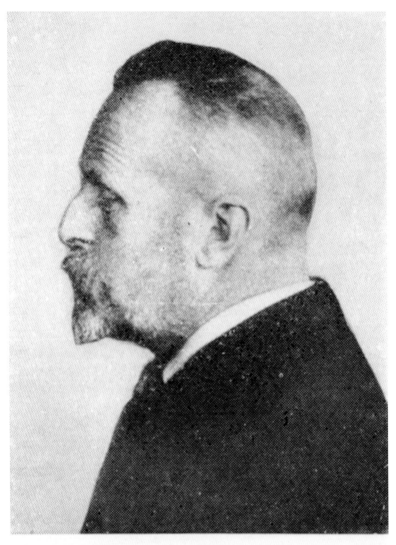

C. K. ELOUT

C. K. Elout, 1870-1947.

Queen Wilhelmina personally expressed her heartfelt agreement with Kuyper's pamphlet in her audience with the board of the Dutch Association of Journalists at the end of April 1900. She added that she hoped the pamphlet would also be disseminated in the United States. When the *Algemeen Handelsblad* reported this on 27 April 1900, Minister De Beaufort was forced to deny the accuracy of the article. The Dutch edition, *De crisis in Zuid-Afrika*, had been published in March in a translation made by the Liberal journalist C. K. Elout, parliamentary editor of the *Handelsblad* and a critical admirer of Kuyper. His parliamentary sketches about "The Gentlemen in The Hague" (with illustrations by Louis Raemaekers) are still famous.

CHAPTER VIII

Prime Minister, 1901-1905

In the parliamentary elections of June 1901, the Confessional parties gained a clear victory, so that after ten years they returned to power. As the principal opposition leader, Kuyper was charged with forming the new government. Although he found the process an ordeal ("a delivery by forceps with heavy contractions"), he succeeded in forming the cabinet within three weeks, which he himself went on to lead. Kuyper was a domineering prime minister who was not afraid to tackle his colleagues on their own ground. He had a particular interest in foreign affairs, as the weak minister for foreign affairs, Robert Melvil baron van Lynden, discovered. Characteristic of Kuyper's dominant position was that the cabinet chairmanship, which up until then had rotated, was changed into a permanent post.

It was to be expected that a man with Kuyper's temperament and character would also make his presence felt in Parliament. Unlike his predecessors, who avoided political conflicts as much as possible, Kuyper as prime minister could not let go of the habits of a party leader. In the second chamber he did not avoid confronting his opponents and entered into debates, particularly on questions of principle and the cabinet's Christian foundations. In defending his policies, Kuyper easily stood his ground with his great rhetorical talent. He was superior and elusive, but also provocative and polarizing, so that he often aroused resistance from the opposition unnecessarily.

In getting legislation passed, Kuyper was not very successful, and his ministership did not bring what many — not least himself — had expected of it. True, the financial position of religiously affiliated schools was improved, but not a complete equalization with state education. A proposal to amend the Higher Education Act, which included state accreditation for degrees from the Free University, led in 1904 to a conflict between Kuyper and the Liberal first chamber, which rejected the bill, whereupon, at the recommendation of the cabinet, it was dissolved by the queen. This dissolution — certainly permitted constitutionally, but from a political perspective astonishing — created bad blood with the Liberals, who lost their majority in the first chamber. In the social domain, the amendment of the liquor law in 1904 was not without significance, but to his disappointment, Kuyper did not manage to institute the Labor Code for which he had already argued in 1878 and which would have made his name as a social legislator. His bills concerning social legislation were submitted too late and were too extensive to be dealt with in time by the States-General.

The most important event during his ministry was undoubtedly the railway strike of 1903, which attracted attention from well beyond the country's borders. Supported by Lohman, who insisted on the forceful maintenance of authority, Kuyper acted firmly against this "criminal agitation" that threatened to cripple public life. That in doing so he brought the hatred of the Socialists on himself was understandable, although their grievance that he had betrayed his earlier social opinions is not supported by the facts, given the various social reforms he tried to pass as a minister.

The aversion that Kuyper had aroused through his policies found an outlet in the elections of June 1905. After a particularly fierce campaign in the spring of 1905, in which the Liberals and the Socialists cooperated to bring down the hated prime minister, the confessional coalition lost its majority. Deeply disappointed at this unexpected defeat, which to his mind caused an undeserved and premature end to his ministership, Kuyper did not wait around for the installation of the new Liberal government. On 7 August 1905 he left for a long trip around the Mediterranean, which (not counting a short break) would take nine months. He did not return to the Netherlands until June 1906.

"The Christian Part of the Nation on Its Way to Power," caricature by Johan Braakensiek after the first round of parliamentary elections of 1901, in *De Amsterdammer* of 23 June 1901. Kuyper is on top of the box with Schaepman as assistant coachman, while Lohman encourages them from behind.

Despite the successful policies of the Pierson cabinet, in the elections of June 1901 the Liberals lost their majority in the second chamber. They also suffered significant losses in the elections for the provincial councils that were held at the same time, which in the long run threatened their majority in the first chamber. The defeat was due in part to disunity in Liberal circles, where the progressive Liberals had formed a new party, the Liberal Democratic Federation. In the election contest the Confessional parties took the initiative by making the antithesis a central issue. As tangible grievances against ten years of Liberal rule, they cited in particular the school issue, which had still not been successfully resolved, and the biased appointments policy of the Liberal cabinets. In addition, Kuyper skillfully capitalized on nationalist feelings that existed in the country over the Boer War.

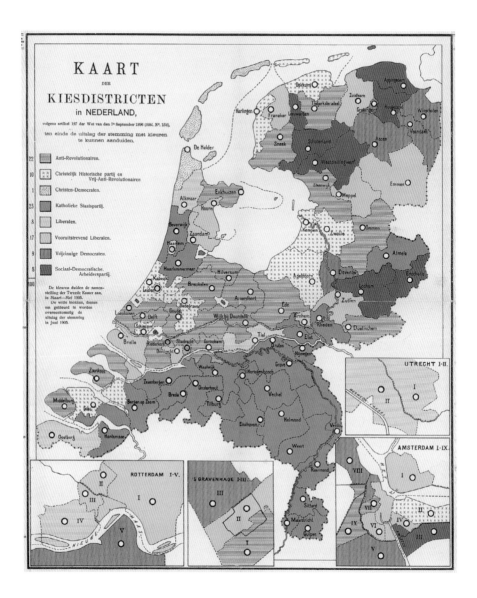

Map of the electoral districts in the Netherlands showing the distribution among the parties. The map dates from the spring of 1905, after a number of bi-elections, but it gives a good overview of the balance of power that existed after the parliamentary elections of 1901. The Confessional parties won 58 seats (Catholics 25, Anti-Revolutionaries 24, Free-Anti-Revolutionaries 7, Frisian Christian-Historicals 1, Christian-Historicals 1), the Liberals 34 seats (Union Liberals 18, Free Liberals 8, Liberal-Democrats 8), and the Social Democrats 7 seats.

Buitenl. Zaken : Melvill van Lynden, Alex Schimmelpennin, ×Beelaertz kell
          Mackay de Stuers. ×. Bylandt. Modderi

Binnenl. Zaken : Mackay, Kuyper, Barte, Ruys etc., Colÿn
          Van Swinderen.

Koloniën : ×. Idenburg × Heyck , van d Bergh.

Financiën : Meuser Kolkman Rovers and Bispÿ Godin.

Justitie   Ruyse Loeff Meuser Lotma.

Waterstaat   de Marez Oyens. Raveloo. Tula Waterman.
          Colÿn Sel.

Arbeid. Bedrÿven : Kuyper

Oorlog   Bergansius, Kool, Schimmelpennin.

Marine :   Kruys. van Heweden.

Although Kuyper was the obvious person to be in charge of forming the new government, he was reluctant to become the prime minister for personal and financial reasons. Not only would he have to move from the familiar setting of Amsterdam to The Hague shortly after the death of his wife, which in itself entailed significant expense, but he would also lose his income from his professorship at the Free University (5000 guilders), as chief editor of *De Standaard* (5000 guilders) and *De Heraut* (4000 guilders), and his compensation as member of the second chamber (2000 guilders). A minister's annual salary in 1901 was only 12,000 guilders.

While the queen conferred with her advisors, Kuyper stayed in Brussels from 5 to 10 July to recover from the strenuous electoral contest. In the meantime he took seriously the possibility that the queen would appoint him to form the new government, as appears from the list of possible ministers that he drafted on the stationery of the renowned Métropole hotel.

Like her father King Willem III, Queen Wilhelmina was not particularly fond of Kuyper, but as the election results favored the confessional parties, she had no other choice than to entrust him with forming the government. In notes written in 1903, she wrote the following: "This crisis was not difficult to solve as the victorious party had 'a working majority,' as Kuyper himself called it in his paper in those days. . . . The majority was made up of Anti-Revolutionaries and Catholics. Kuyper with his loyal supporters (a herd of voters), Lohman with his small group of party representatives, the progressive and more conservative Catholics, a wide variegation with whom Kuyper had to remain on good terms. . . . It was clear what I had to do, I had no choice. I had to entrust Kuyper with the formation of the cabinet." For Queen Wilhelmina it was her first cabinet formation, not an easy task for a young sovereign who was just going on twenty-one, although she could turn to her mother, Queen Emma, for advice. Despite her lack of experience and inner uncertainty, she managed to play her royal role with decisiveness and style.

On Thursday, 11 July 1901, Kuyper was received in audience by the queen at Het Loo Palace and entrusted with forming the new cabinet. Before Kuyper was given the assignment, he had to pledge the queen his word on four points, one being that the Netherlands would stay neutral in the conflict between England and the South African republics.

Letter from Schaepman to Kuyper about forming the cabinet, 15 July 1901.

Although initially Lohman and Schaepman had a preference for Mackay as the person to form the new cabinet, they loyally cooperated with Kuyper. Lohman, however, refused to join a cabinet under Kuyper's leadership. As early as 17 June 1901, he wrote to Mackay in terms that left no room for doubt: "Everyone regards Kuyper as the man for the job. If he takes upon himself the leadership and can form a new government, then I will not work against him; instead, disregarding all my grievances against him, I will support him. But I will not work *under* him. First and foremost, one must be able to trust the person charged with forming the new government, in particular his personal character. However, Kuyper leaves his best friends when *he* thinks it is necessary; he leads us to where *he* wants to go, but hides his plans, lies if it suits him, *uses* people, and always sees to it that *he* always ends up on top. I have witnessed this too often to be able to put myself at his command."

Lydia von Zaremba, 1869-1955.

Although Kuyper was able to complete the formation of the new government within three weeks, he had to deal with a major setback. To his great disappointment, Theo
Heemskerk, as an alderman of Amsterdam and a member of Parliament, one of the
most promising young Anti-Revolutionaries, refused to join his cabinet. This rejection
was the first difficulty in their relationship, compounded by the fact that Kuyper was
not told the real reason for the refusal. What was the matter? Heemskerk's wife, Lydia
von Zaremba, a temperamental woman of Polish-Russian nobility, had a great aversion to Kuyper, whom she knew from the social circle of the Free University. When she
heard that Kuyper had offered her husband a minister's portfolio, she intervened. From
Interlaken in Switzerland where she was on vacation, she sent her husband a telegram
with the following ultimatum: "Kuyper is a liar. The best men won't have anything to do
with him, and you want to associate yourself with him. It is madness. I will not return
to The Hague under these circumstances. Lydia." After this message, Heemskerk had no
choice but to refuse.

Kuyper in 1901.

Kuyper was appointed minister for internal affairs on 31 July 1901. The other ministers were appointed a day later. Internal Affairs was a very extensive department, including not only internal politics but also education, the arts, science, agriculture, and
social affairs. Kuyper's dominant position within the cabinet was formalized shortly afterwards by his appointment as permanent chairman of the council of ministers. Before
this the cabinet had only had temporary chairmen, to which position the members were
appointed in turn.

The Kuyper cabinet in the Trêveszaal at the Binnenhof in The Hague, summer 1903. By this point the cabinet had already undergone two changes as a result of the deaths of T. A. J. van Asch van Wijck (minister for colonial affairs) and G. Kruys (Navy). The cabinet counted three Catholic members: Bergansius, Harte, and Loeff. Lohman's Free Anti-Revolutionaries had not provided any ministers, but remained willing to support the cabinet as much as possible.

From left to right A. W. F. Idenburg (Colonial Affairs, as of 25 September 1902), J. W. Bergansius (War), J. C. de Marez Oyens (Public Works, Trade, and Industry), A. G. Ellis (Navy as of 16 March 1903), R. Melvil baron van Lynden (Foreign Affairs, until 9 March 1905), Kuyper (Internal Affairs), J. A. Loeff (Justice), and J. J. I. Harte van Tecklenburg (Finance).

The house on Kanaalstraat (on the left in the photograph, now Dr. Kuyperstraat 5) in The Hague, where Kuyper lived from 1 October 1901 until his death. Kuyper rented the house from the famous art historian Abraham Bredius (1855-1946). In 1921 the building was purchased for 50,000 guilders by Kuyper's successor, Hendrik Colijn, who donated it to the ARP, after which, furnished in part with the original items, it was put to use as the party office.

Survey showing how mayoral posts were divided among the parties, drawn up upon Kuyper's request in 1901.

With his policy of appointments as internal affairs minister, Kuyper tried to push back the influence of the Liberals, who were greatly overrepresented in official and political posts. In 1900 there were 539 Liberal and 67 Confessional mayors in the counties above the Moerdijk (thus not including the Catholic south). Thus, Kuyper's policy to appoint more sympathizers was no more than a correction to the appointment policies of previous cabinets.

The Christian-Historical politician D. J. de Geer later commented, "This was surely Dr. Kuyper's greatest achievement: he introduced another spirit into the administration of our country. He mercilessly attacked Liberal sacred cows. . . . He flung Liberalism from the pedestal on which it had placed itself. He pulverized the liberal Monroe doctrine: Holland for the Liberals. Only those who know the audacity with which they tried to put theory into practice can understand the bitterness that would arise against the man who mercilessly put an end to the glory of the 'liberalistic' empire."

"The Minister for Internal Affairs at Work," caricature by Johan Braakensiek in *De Amsterdammer* of 13 April 1902 about Kuyper's frequent interference with foreign policy.

Kuyper had a particular interest in foreign affairs and made grateful use of the opportunities left to him by weak Foreign Minister R. Melvil Baron van Lynden to visit the European capitals on a regular basis. The Social Democrats in particular criticized Kuyper, saying that his interest in international politics came at the expense of the social reforms that he had promised to institute.

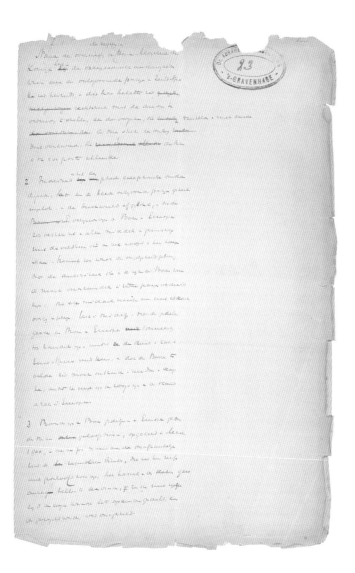

In January 1902 Kuyper tried to put an end to the war in South Africa, which was not going well for the Boers. From 11 to 15 January he stayed in London while the Dutch proposal to serve as intermediary was informally put before the British minister for foreign affairs by Lord Reay. Reay was a British aristocrat of Dutch descent, by birth D. J. Baron Mackay van Ophemert (a nephew of the former Dutch Prime Minister Mackay), who in 1877 had inherited the Scottish title Reay of Reay and had as such become head of the Mackay clan. Although the semi-official offer of intermediary was rejected, as was the official Dutch offer that followed, Kuyper's initiative gave an indirect impetus to the warring parties to start making contact, which led to the "Vrede van Vereeniging" peace treaty of 31 May 1902.

The photograph shows the opening lines of the draft that Kuyper himself drew up for the note to the English government, with the offer of intermediary.

Dr. Kuyper.

Dr. Kuyper, der Ministerpräsident der Niederlande, während seines Besuches in Berlin.
Spezialaufnahme für die „Woche" von Zander und Labisch, Berlin.

Kuyper at the entrance of the Hotel Bristol in Berlin, a photograph in the German weekly paper *Die Woche (The Week)* of April 1902, which also appeared in the Dutch press.

  After Kuyper had successively visited Berlin, Vienna, and Rome, foreign newspapers wrote about a possible rapprochement between the Netherlands and Germany, or an entry by the Netherlands into the Triple Alliance consisting of Germany, Austria-Hungary, and Italy, which would mean a break with the traditional Dutch policy of neutrality. Kuyper and his foreign minister had to deny these rumors.

Minister for Foreign Affairs Melvil van Lynden (1843-1910) was no match for Kuyper's imperious tendencies and was bypassed more than once by his prime minister. Repeatedly, as in the case of the Dutch proposal of intermediary in January 1902, Kuyper would confront him with settled plans. On 9 March 1905 Van Lynden had to retire from office early, after already having been placed under legal restraint by the cabinet.

ZONDAGSBLAD.   6 JULI 1902.

HET VOLK

DE BRANDKAST, BESCHERMD MET BIJBEL EN WIEROOKVAT.

On 6 July 1902 the first issue of the Sunday paper *Het Volk (The People)* was published as the organ of the Social-Democratic Workers' Party. It contained a drawing by Albert Hahn with a caption that read, "The safe protected by Bible and incense barrel," by which the Confessional leaders Kuyper and Schaepman were portrayed as the protectors of capitalism. Hahn (1877-1918), a confirmed socialist and one of the most gifted Dutch political caricaturists of his day, went on to draw hundreds of political cartoons attacking Kuyper.

On 25 September 1902, Alexander W. F. Idenburg (1861-1935), a former officer of the Engineering Corps in the Dutch East Indies and after 1901 an ARP member of Parliament, became minister for colonial affairs, succeeding T. A. J. van Asch van Wijck upon his death. Unlike Keuchenius, Idenburg was a capable member of the cabinet. He held on to his Anti-Revolutionary views, but because of his balanced approach, he also gained respect among his political rivals. A firm friendship arose between Idenburg and Kuyper which would last until Kuyper's death.

As the minister for colonial affairs in three cabinets (1902-1905, 1908-1909, 1918-1919), as governor of Surinam (1905-1908), and as governor-general of the Dutch East Indies (1909-1916), Idenburg made a mark on the colonial politics of the period. He was a supporter of "ethical politics" as formulated by Kuyper in *Our Program* of 1878, which focused on the spiritual and material development of the native population. To this end Protestant and Roman Catholic missionaries had an important part to play. The amendment of the Indian Compatibility Law (1903) that was introduced during his ministry brought a definite end to the exploitative politics of *batig slot*, in which the "surplus" of the colony was transferred to the Dutch treasury. However, Idenburg would not hear of restitution for such surpluses that the Netherlands had previously received. In 1905, however, he did make available 40 million guilders for the economic development of the Dutch East Indies.

J. B. van Heutsz, 1851-1924.

During Idenburg's ministry, General J. B. van Heutsz was appointed governor-general of the Dutch East Indies (1904). As governor of Atjeh (1898-1904) he had, with a hard hand and firm policies, managed to bring the rebellious province of Atjeh under control, which brought the lingering colonial war to an end. Idenburg supported strong Dutch rule to facilitate the development of the Dutch East Indies, and he supported the politics of pacification implemented by Van Heutsz as governor-general. Idenburg also firmly rejected the criticism expressed in Parliament against the way the Dutch East Indian army had operated.

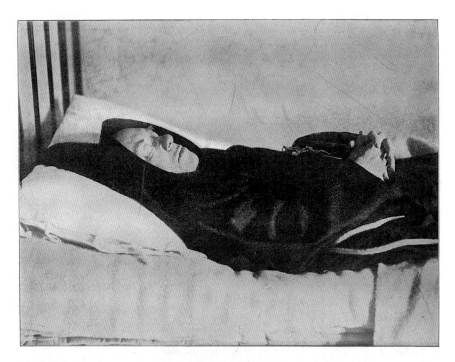

MGR. DR. H. J. A. M. SCHAEPMAN † St. Agnes 1908.
Naar een photographie van E. Orlay de Karwa, te Rome.

Schaepman on his deathbed.

Kuyper lost a prominent ally on 21 January 1903, when the Roman Catholic leader H. J. A. M. Schaepman died in Rome. Shortly before, when Schaepman was feeling a bit better, Kuyper had written him: "For all those in my circle, but especially for me, you would leave such a great emptiness behind if you were called home to heaven." Schaepman answered (in Latin): "Deo gratias quod in bono certamine cum boni certaminis socio renovatis viribus ingredi possim. Mors pia accepta, vitam renovat." ["I thank God that in the good fight I can stand together with you and continue with renewed energy. A death accepted in faith renews life."] After Schaepman's death, Kuyper expressed his condolences in a telegram, with the words from the Stabat Mater: "Quis non fleret?" ["Who would not weep?"]

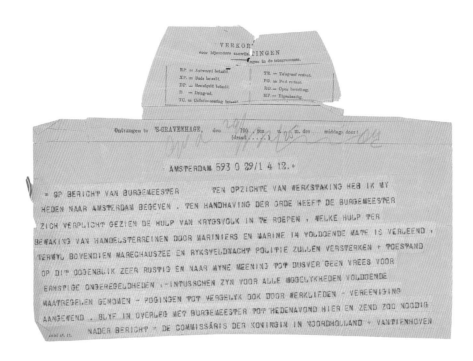

Telegram sent on 29 January 1903 to the cabinet by the royal commissioner of the queen for the province of North Holland, G. van Tienhoven, about the riots in Amsterdam, which initiated one of the most serious labor disputes in Dutch history.

On 28 January 1903 a strike broke out in the port of Amsterdam, where for years there had been unrest among the employees of the shipping companies and warehouses. On 30 January the railway workers in Amsterdam also stopped their work in solidarity with the dock workers, who had gone on strike after the dismissal of an engineer who had refused to shunt "contaminated goods." The railway strike spread across large parts of the country as those workers themselves also had serious complaints and seized the opportunity to force concessions from management.

The effects of the strike were great. Both the boards of the railway companies and the government were caught off guard by the strike, which threatened to isolate Amsterdam and disrupt train services in other parts of the country as well. The postal services had to be maintained by using automobiles. The transportation of soldiers from Amersfoort to Amsterdam was made difficult because engineers and boilermen refused to let the trains run. Everyone was on strike — shunters, brakemen, signalmen, crossing guards — and the strike was successful. On 31 January railway management gave in to the demands of the strikers.

The quick and unexpected end to the strike led to a euphoric mood on the political left wing, as typified by Albert Hahn's well-known drawing and motto, "The whole mechanism stands still, if it's your mighty arm's will." The socialist daily paper *Het Volk* wrote on 8 February 1903: "The Amsterdam, the Dutch, the international proletariat has unfurled a wonderful image of its power. The transport workers, they live!" In the bourgeois camp, however, there was serious concern because the establishment was under threat.

In his book *The Railway Strikes of 1903*, historian A J. C. Rüter captured the mood of excitement: "The Socialists believe they are in heaven, conservatives of every hue at hell's gate. In the recent struggle, Domela Nieuwenhuis celebrates the first of a series of work strikes, Troelstra recommends the transport workers' strike as a means of forcing through universal suffrage. De Savornin Lohman speaks of anarchy, Kuyper of a coup d'etat. Nothing is lacking to fan the flame."

Secret code, drafted on 13 February 1903 by the Department of Internal Affairs, for contact between the cabinet and the royal commissioners.

Although the cabinet had adopted a reserved attitude during the strike, it now decided to take measures to prevent a repetition of what had happened. Not only had the legal authorities been challenged and the country exposed to a "situation of annoying anarchy," as Foreign Minister Van Lynden wrote to the Dutch envoys abroad, but it had also become clear how easily the economy could be paralyzed in a country like the Netherlands that was dependent on international trade.

First of all, the militias were called up to ensure the maintenance of public order, which, as tensions continued, remained under continuous pressure. In addition, on 25 February, Kuyper submitted three bills on behalf of the cabinet, making civil servants' and railway workers' strikes punishable. This elicited a strong response from the Socialists and Anarchists. They formed a committee of defense and threatened new strikes to prevent these "strangulation" or "compulsion laws" from being passed.

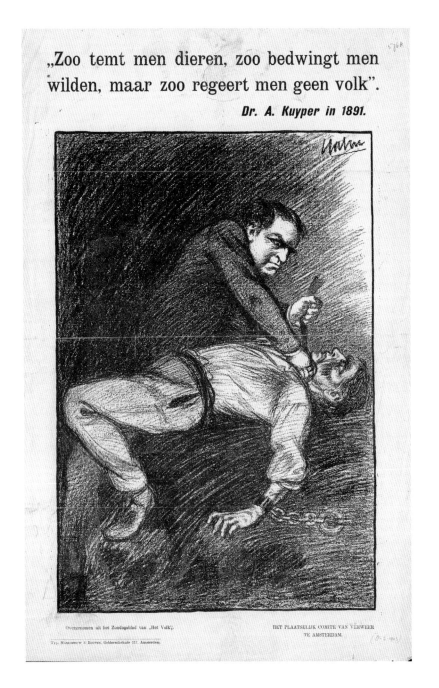

„Zoo temt men dieren, zoo bedwingt men wilden, maar zoo regeert men geen volk".

Dr. A. Kuyper in 1891.

The Socialists' and Anarchists' bitterness about Kuyper's actions against the strikers is apparent from the well-known caricature by Albert Hahn regarding the "strangulation laws" (*Het Volk*, 8 March 1903). It quoted Kuyper's speech to the Christian-Social Congress in 1891: "This is how one tames animals, this is how one breaks the wild, but this is not how one rules a nation." A year later, during legal proceedings instituted against the exhibition of the caricature, Kuyper himself said, "I felt insulted by that picture in the most grievous way."

Letter by Lohman to Kuyper, 10 February 1903, with draft articles.

In his handling of the railway strike and in preparing the bills, Kuyper was advised by Lohman, who unreservedly supported the cabinet in Parliament. Lohman argued for the strict maintenance of law and order, but also for an inquiry into the legitimacy of the strikers' grievances.

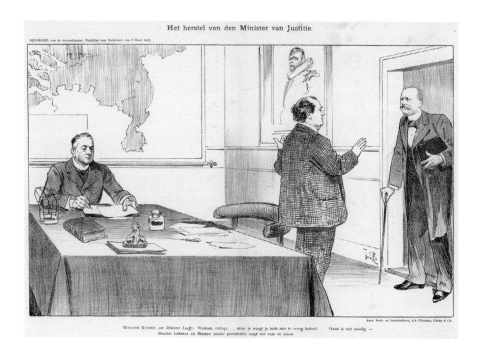

Het herstel van den Minister van Justitie.

BIJVOEGSEL van de Amsterdammer, Weekblad voor Nederland van 8 Maart 1903

MINISTER KUYPER (tot Minister Loeff): Welkom, collega... maar je waagt je toch niet te vroeg buiten!... Haast is niet noodig. —
Broeder Lohman als Minister zonder portefeuille zorgt wel voor de zaken.

Caricature by Johan Braakensiek (*De Amsterdammer*, 8 March 1903) about Lohman's role in suppressing the strikes. Kuyper is depicted brushing off Justice Minister Loeff, who had just recovered from an illness, because Lohman can take care of business more effectively.

During the discussion of the bills in the second chamber at the beginning of April 1903, a strike again broke out to put pressure on Parliament. This political action by Socialists and Anarchists met with less success. While the army and the navy were mobilized to maintain order, the bills submitted by the Kuyper Cabinet were passed with large majorities. Only the Social Democrats and a number of Liberal Democrats in the second chamber voted against them on 9 April. On 11 April the bills were passed unanimously in the first chamber. The strike had actually already ended a day earlier, because the Socialists and Anarchists had become deeply divided.

"The Man with Two Mouths," drawing by P. J. van Geldorp in *De Amsterdamsche Courant*, March 1903, of the Social Democrat leader P. J. Troelstra, who had taken a different line about the strike in his daily paper *Het Volk* than in the second chamber.

Although the Social Democrats had worked together with the Anarchist-Socialists of Domela Nieuwenhuis in the struggle against the "strangulation laws," the failure of the railway strikes led to a permanent rift between the two movements. In the words of union leader Henri Polak at the Social Democratic congress in Enschede, held during Pentecost 1903, "Much will have to change before we step forward together with those anarchist crooks and traitors again."

After 1903 the moderate, parliamentary wing of social democracy gained the upper hand.

The strikes in the Netherlands attracted attention far beyond its borders. On 7 April 1903 a *New York Times* story (left) called attention to the crisis. On 12 April the *New York Sun* reported that the German emperor Wilhelm II had offered to help the Dutch government in their efforts to maintain order. "Good for Holland!" was the headline in the *New York Tribune* of 14 April above a report about the end of the conflict, which added, "Well, the Dutch know how to manage such things." An American admirer placed the articles about the strike in a beautifully bound album and gave it to Kuyper; it is now kept in his archive.

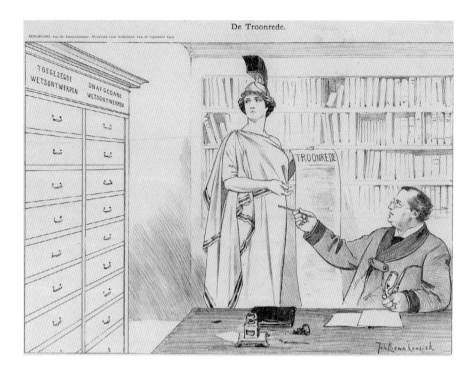

Drawing by Johan Braakensiek in *De Amsterdammer* of 20 September 1903 about the ambitious plans in the queen's speech.

The queen's speech (drafted by the prime minister) at the state opening of Parliament in September 1903 deemed the railway strike a "criminal disturbance." This description led to a verbal dispute in the second chamber between Kuyper and the Social Democrat Troelstra about the meaning of the word "criminal." According to an additional explanation by Kuyper, the word had not been used in a legal but only in an ethical sense.

The Marxist historian Jan Romein describes Kuyper's role in 1903: "To blame Kuyper on the basis of the 'strangulation laws' is not fair. After all — not only a Liberal, but also a Catholic and even a Social Democrat minister would have acted in much the same way, although he may have put things differently. History has borne that out sufficiently since then. However, there remains an unbridgeable gap between these laws and the expectations everyone had of Kuyper as a social politician when he came to office."

EEN WINDEI.

Caricature by Albert Hahn about Kuyper's draft labor bill, *Het Volk*, 7 February 1904. The title, "A Wind Egg," suggests that the labor bill was big, but empty.

In early 1904 Kuyper submitted to Parliament an ambitious proposal for a "labor statute book," which contained no less than 444 articles concerning labor protection. This bill was so extensive, however, that it did not get beyond its initial reporting. Kuyper was disappointed; he had hoped the bill would restore his reputation as a social reformer, which had been tarnished by the railway strike. The parliamentary historian Vermeulen believes that with this bill Kuyper was far ahead of his time, in particular with regard to the principle of social decentralization, but also points out his failings as a legislator.

Idenburg accurately described these failings in 1907: "The events of 1901 took the great man from his normal work and placed him in an entirely new job. In his circle he was, one could say, everything. As a member of Parliament he was great. He could criticize, point out the bigger picture, develop brilliant ideas — all in a vacuum. But then, in 1901, he was called out of the vacuum and had to try to create what he had proclaimed as his desires and principles. He has done so to the best of his ability, in a brilliant way. But in doing so he had to experience: first, that the practice of life forces one to make concessions; that it is one thing to utter exciting slogans as leader of the people and to enthuse the masses, but quite another as a statesman to add to a cord that has already existed for years and ages; and second, that brilliance and erudition — in short, skill — are not everything. Legislative work simply does not function in the same way as the press does. . . . As a theologian-minister, one cannot get things done without the help of others who may have read fewer books but are more thoroughly trained [in politics]."

IK ZEG MAAR: ZOO'N „KUIPERTJE" SMAAKT!

TRIUMPH DER DRANKWET.

The Alcohol Licensing Act of 12 October 1904 was the principal social act that the Kuyper cabinet got through Parliament. The act, passed after difficult and lengthy discussions in Parliament, also attracted popular attention, as is apparent from a series of postcards that came into circulation. The second chamber alone dedicated twenty-five parliamentary sessions to discussing the bill, which strengthened the rules against alcohol abuse.

Likewise, the bill to amend the Higher Education Act that Kuyper submitted to Parliament in March 1903 became law only after two years of heated political struggles. The bill contained provisions that were not very controversial, such as the implementation of special professorial chairs and the upgrading of the Polytechnic School in Delft to the status of Technical University. However, resistance arose against the proposal to grant official status to the degrees awarded by the Free University and other (future)

DeMan
MET DE
REUZEN-
BICEPS
KAMPIOEN
VAN
NEDERLAND
ZWAAR
GEWICHT

DE WARE
JACOB

WORSTEL
NUMMER

N°40

DE
OVER-
WINNAAR
VAN DEN
ANTI-CHRIST

religiously oriented universities. As a result of this opposition, fierce agitation arose against this proposal in the press and in Parliament. After a debate that lasted for days, the bill was passed by the second chamber on 24 March 1904, but it was rejected on 14 July by the first chamber, which had a Liberal majority.

Kuyper did not let the matter rest there. Upon the proposal of the cabinet, on 19 July 1904 the first chamber was dissolved by the Queen in the expectation that a new first chamber would gain a majority for the bill. This expectation was based on the fact that the Provincial Councils, which elected the first chamber, had had a Confessional majority since 1901. The dismissal created bad blood with the Liberals, who were side-lined by Kuyper's unexpected maneuver and lost their majority in the first chamber as expected. Ultimately the bill, again after lengthy parliamentary debates, was passed by the first chamber in May 1905.

Because of the powerful way in which he had acted, Kuyper was depicted by Albert Hahn as a champion wrestler in "The True Jacob" on 2 July 1904. This was Hahn's hundredth political cartoon against Kuyper since his debut as an illustrator for *Het Volk* in July 1902. The caption reads: "The Man with the Giant Biceps. Champion of the Netherlands Heavyweights. The Victor over the Antichrist."

In September 1904 the opening of the States-General took place for the first time in the Ridderzaal (the Knights' Hall) in The Hague. On the dais sat Queen Wilhelmina reading her speech to Parliament, in which the policy intentions of the government for the new parliamentary year were revealed. She was flanked by Queen Emma and her husband, Prince Hendrik. The ministers sat on either side of the podium.

During the general deliberations in November 1904, Kuyper strongly emphasized the differences in principle between the religious coalition parties and the opposition of Liberals and Socialists. In his parliamentary speech delivered on 10 November, he argued that the antithesis between the "Christian and [the] modern way of life," which used to exist on a small scale, had now penetrated "continually deeper, to the root of life," and also dominated relations in the political field.

Drawing by Soranus (W. H. van der Nat) in the *Groene Amsterdammer* of 15 April 1905.

The bill for more subsidies for special primary (Christian) education met with fierce resistance from the Liberal opposition, who called it "a party law of the worst and most irritating kind." Again the parliamentary debates took much time (almost 800 pages in the *Proceedings*), but ultimately the bill was passed by both chambers with support from the coalition parties. This was a new step toward equal financing for state education and Christian schools.

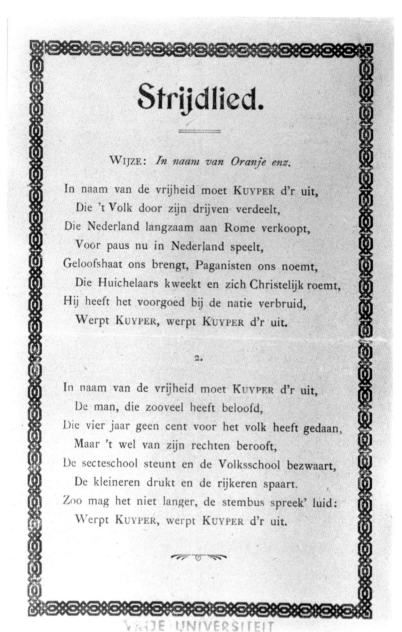

Strijdlied.

WIJZE: *In naam van Oranje enz.*

In naam van de vrijheid moet KUYPER d'r uit,
 Die 't Volk door zijn drijven verdeelt,
Die Nederland langzaam aan Rome verkoopt,
 Voor paus nu in Nederland speelt,
Geloofshaat ons brengt, Paganisten ons noemt,
 Die Huichelaars kweekt en zich Christelijk roemt,
Hij heeft het voorgoed bij de natie verbruid,
 Werpt KUYPER, werpt KUYPER d'r uit.

2.

In naam van de vrijheid moet KUYPER d'r uit,
 De man, die zooveel heeft beloofd,
Die vier jaar geen cent voor het volk heeft gedaan,
 Maar 't wel van zijn rechten berooft,
De secteschool steunt en de Volksschool bezwaart,
 De kleineren drukt en de rijkeren spaart.
Zoo mag het niet langer, de stembus spreek' luid:
 Werpt KUYPER, werpt KUYPER d'r uit.

The elections of June 1905 were dominated by the choice for or against Kuyper. Liberals and Socialists worked together as one to bring about his downfall; as the socialist daily *Het Volk* wrote, "to keep Kuyper out we'll vote for the devil if necessary."

The above photograph shows a "battle song" against Kuyper, whose final line read, "Throw Kuyper, throw Kuyper out." The rest of the song listed his sundry sins: he was said to have sold the Netherlands to Rome, introduced religious hatred and hypocrisy, destroyed state education, and defended the rich instead of the poor.

In 1905 Albert Hahn also contributed to the election contest with this cartoon about Kuyper and the class struggle. The drawing is part of a portfolio of twelve caricatures, with the title "Under Dark Regime," in which "the Dutch chancellor, Kuyper I" was criticized. Next to the caricature the following lines were printed:

> When Bram was promoted in state as its head,
> The angel of mercy should hover o'er the land,
> But the ghost of class hatred has fearsomely spread:
> Flames of discord stoked by Abe's very own hand.

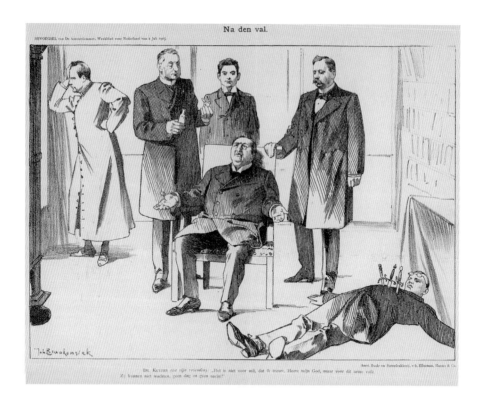

"After the Fall," caricature by Johan Braakensiek commenting on Kuyper's electoral defeat in 1905, *De Amsterdammer*, 2 July 1905. Again the caption comments on his 1891 speech about the social issue: "Dr. Kuyper (to his friends): 'It is not for myself that I am sad, Lord my God, but for these poor people. They cannot wait a day or a night longer!'"

The "monster alliance" of Liberals and Socialists, which had come about in part as a response to Kuyper's antithetical sloganeering, achieved its aim. The Confessional coalition fell from 58 to 48 seats and so lost its majority.

Kuyper as Prime Minister in official dress, April 1905. The photograph, taken by the sculptor Toon Dupuis, was used as a pattern for the controversial bust (see p. 372) that he made of Kuyper.

When he resigned his ministerial post, Kuyper wrote Lohman a letter thanking him for his loyal support in the chamber. On 13 August 1909 Lohman answered in his characteristic way: "As far as my cooperation is concerned, I always did so with pleasure. However disappointing past incidents may have been for me, under no circumstance was our country or our party to suffer any more consequences than necessary. I was sure that as soon as you stood at the helm, you would see some things differently than before and that you had misjudged my views. That is why I was *able* to cooperate. But you too made it easy for me; in my view you surpassed yourself more than once. Sometimes you pursued debates that were started by the opposite side of the chamber too much. . . . No one can accuse you of having done anything to thwart spiritual freedoms, but some have incited others, not because of what you did, but for what you believed in and professed."

Prof. J. Kraus (1861-1951) had worked closely with Kuyper to found the Technical University in Delft. In 1905 he became the first *rector magnificus* of Delft, but was appointed minister for transport in the new cabinet shortly afterwards.

On 10 July 1905 the Technical University at Delft was officially opened by Queen Wilhelmina. Kuyper did not attend the ceremony, excused on the grounds that he had tendered his resignation. On 1 July 1905 he wrote to Kraus, at that time still the *rector magnificus* of the university: "After a month of having been abused by every ragtag and bobtail . . . I, as a Minister, cannot appear in public at a ceremony *that does not allow me to put these hired assassins in their place.* However much I appreciate your insistence, the opposition has, by the way in which it has fought, made it impossible for me to appear. I explained this to Her Majesty; the queen appreciated it."

Four years later in the speech to the ARP convention (22 April 1909) entitled *We, Calvinists . . .* , Kuyper indicated that he was still hurt by the way in which he had been brought down in 1905: "Nothing was off limits, nothing bothered anyone anymore. Every weapon was good, as long as it could inflict a wound. What at first appeared to be popular enthusiasm flared up, even before the day of reckoning had dawned, into popular fury, particularly among young people; after the triumph, that fury increased to political rage. Even on the *Hochstrasse* in Cologne I was jeered at in public by a 'party of compatriots.' . . . What had started as a political struggle ended up as nothing more than a personal attack."

CHAPTER IX

Ambitions and Decline, 1905-1910

Disappointed about the "iniquitous victory of the Liberals," Kuyper at first disappeared from the political arena. He did not appear in the first or second chamber, but went abroad before the inauguration of the new Liberal cabinet of De Meester for a trip around the Mediterranean Sea, which, despite an interruption of a few weeks, would take almost nine months. In his two-volume work *Around the Old-World Sea* (1907-1908) Kuyper not only recounted his travels, but also discussed at length the political and religious developments of the day in the region. In chapters such as "Het Aziatisch gevaar" (The Asiatic Danger) about the rise of Japan and Asia's newly emerging nationalism, "Het Joodsche probleem" (The Jewish Problem) about Zionism and assimilation, "Het raadsel van den Islam" (The Riddle of Islam) about the expansion of Islam and pan-Islamism, he gave an analysis of issues that he believed were also important to the future of Europe.

It is interesting to compare Kuyper's travels around the Mediterranean with his visit to the United States. Then, in 1898, it was a journey to the new world, which as the "appendix of Europe" lay wedged between the Atlantic and the Pacific Oceans, which Kuyper called "new world seas." Now, in 1905, he embarked on a journey around the sea of antiquity, the birthplace of European civilization, where a "struggle over centuries for world power" between Europe and Asia had been fought. Kuyper was convinced that this struggle would not be over for a long time. Europe (including America) and Asia remained "the principal complex of life on our planet," and therein the contrasts between Christianity and Islam would play a decisive role. In this spiritual struggle, religiously tired and skeptical Europe would not be able to do without the vital and religious America, where Christian civilization, in part thanks to Calvinism, was more firmly anchored.

After his return to the Netherlands in the summer of 1906, Kuyper again appeared on the political stage. Despite the disappointment of 1905, he had not given up his political ambitions. Hoping to become prime minister once again, he geared his tactics toward letting the weak De Meester government fulfill its four-year term, after which the time would be ripe for a second Kuyper cabinet. In the meantime he tried to strengthen his political position by leading Anti-Revolutionary action by way of *De Standaard* just as he had always done. In October 1907 he once more took over the chairmanship of the ARP from Bavinck, who since 1905 had acted as interim chairman. At public events he also worked on his political comeback. His speech at the Bilderdijk commemoration of 1906, the honors that were bestowed upon him on the occasion of his seventieth birthday in October 1907, and the publication in the same month of the first volume of *Around the Old-World Sea* were in part meant to mark his firm position as the Anti-Revolutionary leader.

His disappointment was all the greater when not long afterwards these plans were thwarted by the early resignation of the De Meester cabinet, after which not Kuyper but his political associate Heemskerk was called to form the new government. The government had been forced to resign by Heemskerk's actions as leader of the Anti-Revolutionary parliamentary caucus in the second chamber, so his appointment as the person to form the new government made good sense, as even Kuyper had to admit in his advice to the queen. Also, as a moderate and less controversial Anti-Revolutionary, Heemskerk was better equipped than Kuyper to lead a Confessional emergency cabinet, which could not rely on a fixed majority in the chamber. However, Kuyper was not able to let go of the idea that Heemskerk had forced the government crisis to thwart his (Kuyper's) progress. Heemskerk was hurt by this suspicion, and the result was that the relationship between the two Anti-Revolutionary leaders was permanently damaged. It is true that upon the proposal of the cabinet Kuyper was appointed as minister of state in August 1908, and that same autumn he was reelected as a member of the second chamber, but in reality he was shunted to the side. Although he played an important role in the great Confessional electoral victory of June 1909, on 24 June the Heemskerk cabinet decided to continue with the same members — thus without Kuyper.

The cabinet decision was taken shortly before reports emerged about the so-called "decorations affair," which seriously discredited Kuyper and brought a definite end to his political aspirations. The affair was made public on 27 June 1909 by a lawyer from Haarlem in an interview with the socialist daily paper *Het Volk*. It was alleged that Kuyper as prime minister had recommended a number of businessmen from Amsterdam for a royal decoration in return for donations to the ARP. A racy touch was added to the affair when it emerged that an adventurous lady of rather dubious virtue had acted as a mediator.

The decorations affair was to dominate public opinion for over a year and divided the country into two camps. It was all the more painful for Kuyper because the trivial and tragicomic aspects of the case contrasted strongly with the exalted pretensions of his political leadership. Only with the verdict of an investigative committee or "honorary council" exonerating Kuyper of corruption in August 1910 did the affair come to an end. Many of his political rivals, however, remained rightly convinced that the committee had not gotten to the bottom of the matter, because the honorary council had not been able to question witnesses under oath. The decorations affair cast a lasting stain on Kuyper's reputation and constituted the low point of his political career.

A free man once again. Kuyper, seen from behind, strolling through Bad Kissingen, August 1905.

On 7 August Kuyper left the Netherlands for Bad Kissingen, a spa in Bavaria, in order to take his annual cure. From there he went on a journey lasting nine months around the Mediterranean Sea, a "long cherished intention" which he could now at last fulfill "as a citizen suddenly without office as I had not been in fifty years." He successively visited Austria-Hungary, Romania, and southern Russia. To his disappointment, he had to abandon plans to travel on to Moscow, because in October 1905 the Tsarist empire was plagued by revolutionary disturbances. He left for Constantinople earlier than planned, where he stayed for two weeks, subsequently travelling through Asia Minor, Syria, Palestine, Egypt, Sudan, Greece, Sicily, and Tunisia. At the end of March Kuyper returned to the Netherlands for a few weeks because of his daughter Henriëtte's illness. In mid-April he left for North Africa once again to complete his journey, visiting Algiers, Morocco, Spain, and Portugal. He returned to the Netherlands on 16 June 1906.

Kuyper during his travels around the Mediterranean.

Kuyper did not make his journey like an average tourist. As a former prime minister who had often intervened in foreign affairs, he was well known internationally and welcomed with respect everywhere he went. The Dutch envoys gave him the necessary information and ensured that he was introduced to heads of state and government leaders, and gained entrance to places and ceremonies that remained out of reach for the average traveller.

Constantinople. 21 December 1906 *Pont de côté de Galata.*

The bridge across the Golden Horn in Constantinople, where Kuyper stayed from 6 to 20 November 1905, a week longer than he had initially planned. In spite of the decline of the Ottoman Empire, Kuyper was impressed by the power of Islam, which would not resign itself to the influence that the Western powers had on the Middle East. In the Dutch East Indies too, Islam was the most important factor in the rising resistance against the colonial regime.

In the Hagia Sophia Kuyper witnessed Friday evening prayers from a portico. From there he could overlook the full mosque, which made a "stunning and lasting" impression on him: "Over the entire area some beautiful, floating lighting had been installed. . . . Under that glowing sea of light one saw thousands of eastern prayer carpets on the ground stretching out in straight lines, and on every one of those carpets a 'believer' kneeling, bowing, bending over, falling down and getting up again, while calling out the prayers that were presided over by the imam. After every prayer a solemn silence reigned, and all waited until the lips of the imam began a new *rakah*, and all of a sudden one saw the whole crowd go into wild ecstasies again. Like tools, if you so wish, and yet so full of life intensely lived."

Kuyper's travels abroad were closely followed in the Dutch press, as is apparent from a
report by the correspondent of the *NRC* about his stay in Constantinople, reprinted in
De Standaard of 17 November 1905. The correspondent was able to report that the sultan
had awarded Kuyper the Grand Cross in the Order of Medjidjieeh and then added: "Dr.
Kuyper looks very well, is very cheerful and most satisfied with his travels up till now."

Illustration by Patrick Kroon in *De Ware Jacob* of 9 December 1905.

At the end of November the correspondent of the liberal daily paper *Het Vaderland* (*The Fatherland*) created a small riot in the Dutch press. He reported that Kuyper had travelled through Asia Minor in a luxury parlor carriage that had been offered to him by the sultan himself. This report gave the editorial staff the opportunity to write a vicious commentary. Calling to mind the many visits Kuyper had made abroad as prime minister, *Het Vaderland* wrote on 1 December: "Dr. Kuyper gives free rein to his old love of travel. . . . We were somewhat surprised about the enthusiasm with which our former prime minister pays visits to foreign courts. We wondered whether the high knighthood bestowed upon him by the sultan of Turkey would be as pleasing to his dear brethren if they took into account the Armenian Christian blood that has flowed. Perhaps they too have objections against the Sultan's salon car, in which Dr. Kuyper sat as his guest. Which Turkish delights go with it, we do not know."

On 2 December the Anti-Revolutionary newspaper *De Rotterdammer* was most incensed about what had been written in *Het Vaderland*: "As if Dr. Kuyper would succumb to 'Turkish delights'" — and said it was scandalous that the liberal press could not leave him alone, even abroad. Fortunately, Kuyper's own paper *De Standaard* was able to contradict the report upon the authority of the *NRC* correspondent: "The journey . . . in a salon car that was offered to him by the sultan, as was reported in a paper published in The Hague, never took place."

Visschers op het meer van Genezareth.

In Palestine Kuyper visited the holy places from the Bible, which prompted him to give lyrical testimonials. The photograph shows Lake Tiberias, also known as the Sea of Galilee, which he crossed in a boat as night fell "with six men at the oars." He gave his impressions as follows: "What affected me during the silent crossing came from above, from the hidden world of the spirits, because of its holy past conjured up in my mind. It was Jesus' name that surrounded me, that on all the shores around me and over the waters across which I glided was called out before me. Imagine he is not there, and the Sea of Galilee loses all its charm, but if you let his holy image rise up in your imagination, suddenly everything around you sparkles in a glow, as no lake in Italy or Switzerland ever matched. You see it all come to life in your mind's eye. Along those shores Jesus walked, and a multitude of many thousands followed him; from that hill there in the distance sounded the Sermon on the Mount in its quiet majesty. Those waters on which you glide along were, when they swelled up in a storm, silenced by his command. . . . To be able to contemplate such overwhelming impressions for two full hours without interruption was a balm for the soul that I had not absorbed in any other place in Palestine."

The Garden of Gethsemane and the Mount of Olives (on the left in the front of the photograph), where in great loneliness Jesus's road of suffering had begun. According to legend, the eight olive trees that Kuyper saw there were "in their roots still the same as the olive trees under whose leaves Jesus knelt down." Kuyper was given permission to take an olive branch with him from the garden, which he later gave to Queen Wilhelmina as a gift.

Below, picture postcard from Kuyper to his daughter Henriëtte, sent from Egypt, January 1906.

Onze Ex-Minister Dr. Kuyper nadert de 70, maar geeft op zijne reis in het Oosten blijk van een levenslust en een weerstandsvermogen, die menig jongmensch hem zal benijden. In Egypte, in Klein-Azië en het Heilige Land reisde hij afwisselend te paard, te voet en per as, soms in noodweer en niet zelden aan gevaren blootgesteld. In Athene logeerde hij in het hôtel „Grande Bretagne", werd hij met bijzondere onderscheiding door de autoriteiten bejegend en had hij zelfs de eer door den kroonprins van Griekenland in audiëntie te worden ontvangen. Hij bezoekt musea, oude en moderne instellingen van kunst en wetenschap, bestudeert het staatkundig leven en de toestanden in de landen, die hij bezoekt. Vermoedelijk gaat de reis over Micene, Nauplia, Korinthe, Patras naar Olympia en van daar naar het eiland Corfu. Bovenstaande foto's geven Dr Kuyper te zien, wandelende tusschen de ruïnen van den Akropolis bij Athene, in gezelschap van de jongste kinderen van den Nederlandschen zaakgelastigde te Athene, mejuffrouw Jolande van Lennep en Harold van Lennep.

In Greece Kuyper visited the Acropolis in Athens. The general public at home was kept fully informed of this excursion also.

Athene. 20.2.06.

Böhringer
KGL.HOFPHOTOGRAPH.

ATHEN.

Kuyper in Athens, with a handlebar moustache, 20 February 1906.

Because of his daughter Henriëtte's serious illness, at the end of March 1906 Kuyper abruptly broke off his journey and travelled from Tunis to the Netherlands. She had fallen ill in the United States, where she had been staying since September 1905 upon the invitation of the American writer Caroline Atwater Mason. She had received care for two weeks in the George Washington University Hospital at the beginning of March, then travelled to the Netherlands upon the advice of her American doctors, where she was admitted to the Reformed Eudokia Hospital in Rotterdam. There she made a good recovery after a successful operation. On 14 April Kuyper again left The Hague to travel south.

After his final return to the Netherlands on 16 June 1906, Kuyper began writing an account of his travels to "share at least some of my impressions with a wider audience." The result was a two-volume work of 1080 pages, not including the illustrations, which was published in 1907 and 1908 by the publishers Van Holkema en Wahrendorf in Amsterdam, entitled *Around the Old-World Sea*. The French edition *Autour de l'Ancienne Mer du Monde* was published in 1910 and 1911 by Albert Dewit in Brussels.

In the third volume of his *Kuyper-Bibliography*, Rullmann relates that the book "almost suffocated at birth." What happened? "While cleaning Dr. Kuyper's study, his maid had accidently relegated the envelopes containing the information about his travel documents to the dustbin. . . . Luckily however, three quarters of the lost documents were retrieved. And so the book could be published after all."

Om de Oude Wereldzee.

DOOR

Dᴿ. A. KUYPER,

Oud-Minister van Binnenlandsche Zaken.

INHOUD VAN HET EERSTE DEEL: Het Aziatisch Gevaar. – Rumenië. – Rusland. – De Zigeuners. – Het Joodsche Probleem. – Constantinopel. – Klein-Azië. – Syrië. – Het heilige land.
Geïllustreerd met platen in zwart en kleurendruk.

Compleet in 12 afleveringen à **50** cent.
Compleet in 2 deelen ingenaaid *f* **6.——**
Compleet in één deel gebonden „ **7.25**

Uitgave van VAN HOLKEMA & WARENDORF, te Amsterdam.

In order to draw attention to the first volume of *Around the Old-World Sea*, the publisher made use of what at the time was a new form of advertising (which would not have displeased Kuyper, who had a good sense of publicity): he ordered large posters of Kuyper's portrait to be printed and then posted in book shops. The sale of the book (5000 copies were printed) was a success. As early as 19 October 1907, just a few days after its publication, the bookstore W. ten Have in Amsterdam advertised in *De Standaard* that "Dr. Kuyper's account of his travels" was sold out at the publishers and was now available only at his store. On 23 October Ten Have announced that only the hardcover edition was available. In November the book was reprinted. The third printing followed in February 1908.

On 26 July 1906 Kuyper visited Maassluis together with his daughters Henriëtte and Jo, where he was photographed in front of the house of his birth. Kuyper visited Maassluis for the opening of a new building for the Christian school that had existed since 1860 as the "Monsieur" Van Dalen School. On this occasion it was rechristened the "Dr. A. Kuyper School."

Outside the school, Kuyper delivered a speech to a large audience in which he emphasized the importance of passing on religious beliefs not only in schools but also in the family. After all, Christianity in the Netherlands was not guaranteed to continue. He had just returned from a journey through countries where the Christian church had once flourished, but where now everything "that can possibly serve as a reminder of Christianity [has] burned down in the sand of the desert." As far as piety was concerned, Christians could follow the example of Muslims: "In those countries where Mohammed is followed, I often felt ashamed when I saw how deeply devoted they were in serving Mohammed there. And don't you dare lift one finger against the prophet — it would cost you your life! When one sees that and compares it to the little reverence that one sees here, not for a false prophet, but for the only Prophet, the Christ of God, the Anointed King, then these Muslims put one to shame."

Willem Bilderdijk (1756-1831), the tormented Romantic poet, and scholar, who turned against the rationalism of his day.

On 1 October 1906 Kuyper gave a lecture entitled *What Bilderdijk Meant to the Nation* in the Concertgebouw, on the occasion of the one hundred and fiftieth anniversary of Bilderdijk's birth. The hall was filled for the most part by Kuyper supporters, who seized the opportunity to cheer on their leader at his first major public appearance after his return, and to declare their loyalty to him after he had been so humiliatingly driven from the political stage in 1905. According to the *NRC* of 2 October, the interest in Anti-Revolutionary circles was so great that tickets to the event were scalped, often for high prices.

Hoe (Bilderdijk) in het Concertgebouw te Amsterdam gehuldigd werd.

Caricature by Albert Hahn in *Het Volk* of 5 October 1906, with the subtitle: "How (Bilderdijk) Was Honored in the Concertgebouw in Amsterdam."

Kuyper's performance was a rhetorical triumph, according to newspaper reports the following day, which sang Kuyper's praises in unison. The speech "was delivered with a glow and an oratorical talent that compelled admiration in a man of his age," wrote the *Algemeen Handelsblad* on 2 October. The Roman Catholic daily paper *De Tijd* was also surprised by the vitality of the almost sixty-nine-year-old speaker: "For two hours the indefatigable, powerful man spoke with an enviable tone of voice; for two hours he captivated his audience, demanding attention until the very last, both for his command as well as for the thoroughness of the speech itself." According to the *NRC* the speech elicited a "tumultuous ovation." The Anti-Revolutionaries were delighted. In his *Kuyper-Bibliografy* Rullmann wrote, "The imposing figure on the podium and his stately bearing as he walked to the place of honour immediately met with unbelievably enthusiastic cheers. . . . The Bilderdijk lecture, in which Kuyper brought together all the beams of light which that mighty genius emitted onto one focal point, was, in a word, beautiful, a wonderful piece both in style and content."

In giving his Bilderdijk speech, Kuyper had reported to the front lines once more. The speech had been composed with great care. His ode to Bilderdijk as the incarnation of national greatness and spiritual essence ended up as a historical legitimization of the Anti-Revolutionary movement, while neo-Calvinism was portrayed as a national power that under Kuyper's leadership wanted to inspire the people with new zeal.

TECHNISCHE HOOGESCHOOL

E SENAAT DER TECHNISCHE HOOGESCHOOL

HEEFT IN ZIJNE VERGADERING VAN 19 DECEMBER 1906

HONORIS CAUSA

HET DOCTORAAT IN DE TECHNISCHE WETENSCHAP

VERLEEND AAN

ABRAHAM KUYPER

GEBOREN TE MAASSLUIS DEN NEGEN-EN-TWINTIGSTEN OCTOBER 1837

WEGENS DE UITSTEKENDE VERDIENSTEN, DIE HIJ ZICH TEN OPZICHTE VAN DE TECHNISCHE WETENSCHAP HEEFT VERWORVEN DOOR DE STICHTING VAN HET HOOGER TECHNISCH ONDERWIJS.

DE SENAAT DER TECHNISCHE HOOGESCHOOL

VOORZITTER

B.H. Boldering SECRETARIS

On 8 January 1907, in the Remonstrant church in Delft, Kuyper was awarded an honorary degree by the Technical University which had gained academic status through his efforts. The theologian Kuyper was Delft's first honorary doctor. Among the other five laureates were Cornelis Lely, the man behind the later Zuiderzee Project, and the architect P. J. H. Cuypers, the designer of the Rijksmuseum in Amsterdam and many other neo-gothic Roman Catholic church buildings. Kuyper's honorary degree did not go undisputed among the engineers of Delft, but according to Baudet the objections against his degree were overruled on the grounds that Kuyper had, "after all, built a bridge from Dort to Rome" (that is, from Protestantism to Roman Catholicism).

Th. H. de Meester (1851-1919), Kuyper's successor as prime minister, was a brother of the well-known journalist Johan de Meester.

As a newcomer to politics, De Meester had little authority, and his Liberal cabinet (1905-1908) did not sit firmly in the saddle. This became apparent when on 9 February 1907 a cabinet crisis broke out over the budget of Minister of War H. P. Staal. Although Kuyper was satisfied with the defeat of what to his mind was an "unconstitutional cabinet," in *De Standaard* he opposed the formation of a Confessional minority cabinet because this would reduce his own chances of becoming prime minister after the regular term had elapsed. In the end, on 4 April, the Queen decided to maintain the cabinet that was in office and to accept only Staal's resignation.

DR. K.: *Dit verkiezingsbulletin mag gezien worden! Ik heb blijkbaar de kunst nog niet verleerd. Het is ook veel gemakkelijker dan regeeren.*

"This electoral bulletin will pass inspection! Apparently I have not lost my touch. It is also much easier than governing."

In the elections for the Provincial Councils in June 1907, Kuyper rediscovered his old form and led the Anti-Revolutionary campaign from *De Standaard*. The electoral victories that the Confessional parties won in the provinces of South Holland and Overijssel were significant for politics on a national level, because they enabled the Confessionals to increase their majority in the first chamber. For Kuyper this was all the more evidence that the electoral results of 1905 had not been just.

On 17 October 1907 Kuyper again took over the leadership of the ARP from Bavinck who had acted as interim chairman since the spring of 1905. Twelve days later, the return of the leader to his command post was marked once more by the exuberant celebration of his seventieth birthday on 29 October 1907. The photograph shows the decorated hall in the Building of Arts and Sciences in The Hague, where Kuyper gave a reception.

 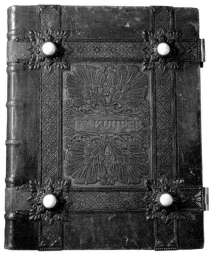

Portrait of Kuyper, painted by H. J. Haverman, donated by a number of Christian teachers.

A report of the birthday festivities can be found in the *Kuyper-Gedenkboek 1907*, which was published in 1908. The series of tributes was exceptional even for that time, featuring a long procession of speakers from all walks of life who paid homage to the guest of honor for what he had achieved in a wide range of fields. Speeches alternated with singing and the offering of presents and beautifully inscribed commemorative books, among which was an album signed by 1061 "corporations" and a "children's tribute" with the names of 35,574 grateful school children who, in part owing to Kuyper's efforts, could now receive a Christian education. Characteristic of the atmosphere during the festivities were the lines of poetry written by the Protestant poet Seerp Anema, which were sung as Kuyper came in: "Hail, oh warlike hero, / Given to us in the Lord's good grace; / Free rule and prosperous life / God through your hand has arranged."

Album with the names of organizations and persons who took part in the official homage. The album was designed by the architect and designer Jac. Ph. Wormser. The cover is decorated with knobs of ivory, each surrounded by eight red corals that are set in copper and mounted on a silver square between four copper corners.

HULDE AAN BOEHDA-ABRAHAM.

"Homage to Buddha-Abraham," drawing by Johannes Hendriks in *De Ware Jacob*, 19 October 1907.

Along with a report about the commemorative celebrations, the *Kuyper-Gedenkboek 1907* contained no less than 400 pages of press commentaries devoted to Kuyper. Needless to say, the articles from the "liberal press" were considerably more critical than those from the "Christian press." The most outspoken was *Het Volk*, which called Kuyper the "most dangerous enemy of the struggling proletariat" and wished that he might spend the rest of his days "quietly remorseful about the evil done and the suffering created." *Het Vaderland* was not to be outdone, writing that Kuyper had sown the seeds of dissension for forty years and had persistently ridiculed, maligned, and offended his enemies. However, in many commentaries there was also a note of respect for the great political rival. Thus the *Haagsche Courant* compared Kuyper to the Liberal statesman Thorbecke, and the *Nieuwe Arnhemsche Courant* wrote that it was a pity that the De Meester cabinet had not taken the opportunity to make Kuyper a minister of state. Kuyper also received birthday wishes from Domela Nieuwenhuis. In a tone that was free from even the faintest hint of animosity, he offered a considered opinion about his "esteemed opponent," in which he discussed not only the differences but also the similarities between the two: "Your life and mine have too many affinities to be ignored. You and I are both uncommonly popular and uncommonly hated. I can still remember

Domela Nieuwenhuis, F.

den Haag 29 Oktober 1907

Gewaardeerde tegenpartijder,

Misschien, ja waarschijnlijk zult gij vreemd opzien onder de vele brieven, die gij ontvangt, er ook een van mij te ontvangen, want sinds jaren staan wij vlak tegenover elkander. En dat is er niet beter op geworden. Sinds het jaar 1903 toen gij als minister de werkstaking hebt verpletterd op een alles behalve christelijke manier of liever juist op een christelijke wijze, want het was op eenzelfde wijze dat de christelijke kerk altijd optrad tegen haar vijanden. Altoos bezield in strijd met de leer van Jesus, dien gij zegt uw Heer en Heiland te zijn. Intusschen men heeft u de schuld gegeven van hetgeen alle lessen hebben gedaan. Immers in die dagen waart gij de held der liberalen en deze maakte het u ook mogelijk een wetten ervoor te krijgen. Ja, de eigenlijke schuld zat nog dieper, want het is het gezag dat u en elk gezagsman dwingt tot dergelijke stappen. Uw fout lag in het aanvaarden der regeering, al het andere vloeit voort uit die fout! Elkeen, die zich verbaagt om regeeringsman te worden, gaat al menschen verloren, want heerschen is en blijft geweld uitoefenen over anderen, die men betitelt als zijn broeders. Heerschappij uitoefenen is tiranniseeren en welk recht heeft de eene mensch om den anderen te tiranniseeren? Zoodra gij dus optradt als regeeringspersoon, waart gij een verloren man, evenals zulks het geval is geweest met den Franschen staatsman Clémenceau. Al het andere is daaruit voortgevloeid als het gevolg en de oorzaak.

how in the year 1888 a well-known man from The Hague said that our nation's peace would only be restored when three men had been beheaded: Schaepman, Kuyper, and Domela Nieuwenhuis. . . . Therefore I can easily imagine what your life is like. But your path did not cross Golgotha, as mine did; on the contrary, you ascended the throne of honor, and generally speaking one can say that suffering ennobles more than fame and greatness. Yet all of this does not detract from any appreciation of your great mental skills and principles as a rival. Yes, I have often thought, while enjoying your writings, that basically we were not so far removed from one another. There were whole passages from your writings that I could take without hesitation and which I also used in my speeches. Only the gulf of religion lay between you and me."

Family photograph, taken on the occasion of Kuyper's seventieth birthday. Sitting from left to right: Henriëtte S. S. Kuyper, C. M. J. Kuyper-Heyblom (wife of H. H. Kuyper), C. M. E. (Cato) Kuyper. Standing from left to right: J. H. (Jo) Kuyper, Abraham Kuyper (son of H. H. Kuyper), Adriana Kuyper (daughter of A. Kuyper Jr.), Guillaume Kuyper, Abraham Kuyper, Willem Kuyper (son of H. H. Kuyper), H. H. Kuyper, Abraham Kuyper Jr., and his wife, the writer H. Kuyper-van Oordt.

DE POLITIEKE WEEK.

SNEEK!
(De Amsterdammer.)

"I don't like those after all. They are too headstrong for me." Drawing by Johan Braak-ensiek in *De Amsterdammer*, 1 December 1907, about Kuyper's unsuccessful candidacy in Sneek for a seat in the chamber.

Kuyper had every reason to be satisfied with the way his anniversary celebrations had gone, but soon his path would also cross Golgotha. The first setback was the by-election for a seat in the second chamber for the district of Sneek in November 1907. Kuyper had been nominated as the candidate for the Anti-Revolutionaries there, but the Christian-Historicals in Sneek refused their support, after which he stepped down. He interpreted the way things had gone as a personal affront and began a stinging polemic in *De Standaard* against Lohman, who according to Kuyper should have brought his sympathizers in Sneek into line in time. The polemic between the two Confessional leaders ended up with Lohman breaking off all personal contacts with Kuyper, because he felt that Kuyper's last "three-star" editorial in *De Standaard* of 20 December 1907 was an attack on his integrity.

In de vestibule van Het Loo.

Vele achten zich geroepen, maar slechts weinigen
zijn uitverkoren.

The break with Lohman could not have come at a worse time, because on Saturday evening, 21 December 1907, the Liberal De Meester cabinet fell, after the war budget had been rejected by the second chamber in part because of a speech delivered by the leader of the Anti-Revolutionary parliamentary caucus, Heemskerk. The very fact that Heemskerk had acted without consulting him as party leader made it clear that Kuyper had lost control. Had he been elected as the member of Parliament for Sneek, he might have been able to avert the crisis, or at any rate play an important part in the formation of the new government. Now he was in fact an outsider and had to watch Queen Wilhelmina, strongly supported by Lohman, ask Heemskerk to form the new government. The Queen did summon Kuyper to the Loo Palace for advice, but because the crisis was of Heemskerk's doing, little remained but to recommend that he form the new government: "If the result is that a statesman from the Right *must* in the end take the formation upon himself, then it seems to me, too, that Th. Heemskerk is the man to do so."

The drawing by Albert Hahn in *De Notenkraker (The Nut Cracker)* of 19 January 1908 shows Kuyper being helped into his coat at the Loo Palace by a footman versed in Scripture saying, "Many are called, but few are chosen."

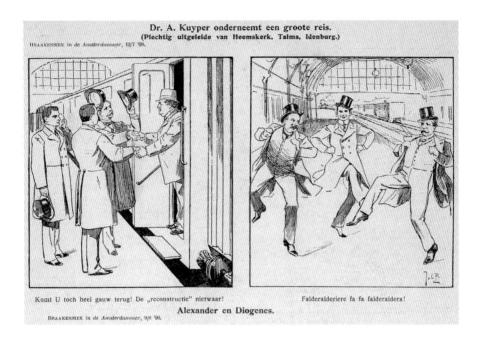

Dr. A. Kuyper onderneemt een groote reis.
(Plechtig uitgeleide van Heemskerk, Talma, Idenburg.)
BRAAKENSIEK in de Amsterdammer, 12/7 '08.

Komt U toch heel gauw terug! De „reconstructie" nietwaar!   Falderalderiere fa fa falderaidera!
Alexander en Diogenes.
BRAAKENSIEK in de Amsterdammer, 9/8 '08.

Heemskerk succeeded in forming a government, which was installed on 12 February 1908. Kuyper's confidant Idenburg, who as Governor of Surinam resided far away in Paramaribo, was prepared to become the minister for colonies again, although the question remains whether he would have accepted this position if he had known that Kuyper was upset about Heemskerk's initiatives.

Kuyper adopted a cautious attitude towards the Heemskerk cabinet. In *De Standaard* he continually insisted on a more principled government policy, which was hardly possible given the composition of the second chamber. Kuyper's reservations were further strengthened as Heemskerk refused to make promises about a reconstruction of the cabinet after the elections of 1909 that would make it possible for Kuyper to become a minister again.

In June 1908 Idenburg and his political colleague Talma tried to bring about a reconciliation between Kuyper and Heemskerk. Idenburg reported on 5 April 1932, "The result was that — at least on the outside — the relationship again improved and Dr. Kuyper, when he set out on his vacation in early July, was seen off from the station by Heemskerk, Mr. Talma, and myself." The drawing by Johan Braakensiek (*De Amsterdammer*, 12 July 1908) suggests that they were thrilled to see him leave.

§ 1. De Regeering heeft met belangstelling kennis genomen van hetgeen van verschillende zijden is aangevoerd aangaande de beginselen van het Kabinet. Zij waardeert den toon van rustige gedachtenwisseling, die daarin klinkt, en verhengt zich over de betuiging van waardeering der verzoenende houding van het Kabinet.

Zij verwondert zich echter eenerzijds, dat naar de meening van een deel der leden wellicht eene belangrijke frontverandering ware tec onstateeren: anderzijds, dat sommige leden betreurden, dat het Kabinet, vooral door het vermijden van de uitdrukking „Christe-lijke beginselen", eenigen grond had gegeven voor de onderstel-ling, dat het de principieële onderscheiding tusschen de Christe-lijke beginselen en die van daaraan tegenovergestelde richtingen had losgelaten en dat het dus eene eenigszins andere scha-keering der partijen ter rechterzijde vertegenwoordigde dan het Ministerie Kuyper. Zij betuigt haar dank aan de leden, die klaarblijkelijk hebben verstaan, dat het Kabinet zich omtrent zijne beginselen duidelijk heeft uitgesproken.

Dit is geschied, toen de Minister van Binnenlandsche Zaken op 10 Maart namens de Regeering verklaarde, dat zij wenschte het bewind te voeren overeenkomstig de beginselen, levende in de partijen der rechterzijde. Dat de uitdrukking „Christelijke beginselen" die beginselen duidelijker zoude hebben aange-duid, kan niet worden toegegeven. Ieder, en zij, die tot de rechterzijde behooren, zeker niet het minst, weten, dat inderdaad de partijen der rechterzijde, van eigen tekortkoming zich be-wust, niettemin zich ten doel stellen om hunne staatkunde door de Christelijke beginselen te doen beheerschen.

Twijfel aan de besliste overtuiging der Regeering aangaande de noodzakelijkheid daarvan was dus aanstonds uitgesloten, en zoo die twijfel niettemin bij eenigen gerezen is, de Regeering wijst iedere verantwoordelijkheid daarvoor af.

De omstandigheden, waaronder het Kabinet optrad, dwongen tot de keuze der op 10 Maart gebezigde woorden. Het Kabinet, homogeen met de rechterzijde, moest rekenschap geven, waarom het optrad, niettegenstaande de rechterzijde niet de meerderheid der Kamer uitmaakte, in tegenstelling met de linkerzijde, die wel in de meerderheid was. Frontverandering schijnt dit moeilijk te noemen, en tot welke veronderstellingen op die wijze grond werd gegeven kan niet worden bevroed.

Zeker was geen grond gegeven voor de onderstelling dat het Kabinet de principieele onderscheiding tusschen de Christelijke beginselen en die van daaraan tegenovergestelde richtingen had

Heemskerk did his best to improve relations, seeing to it that on 29 August 1908, on the recommendation of the cabinet, Kuyper was appointed minister of state, an honorary title that was only granted to the most prominent politicians.

Two months later Heemskerk made a most unusual constitutional gesture by al-lowing Kuyper to rewrite the government's memorandum on the 1909 state budget. Kuyper took the opportunity to bring the antithesis to the forefront once again. Kuyper had insisted on this emphasis as a condition for his return to the second chamber, to which he had been elected in the districts of Sneek and Ommen in October 1908. Af-ter he had refused Sneek, Kuyper stalled on the election for Ommen until Heemskerk acquiesced on the memorandum. On 10 November 1908 Kuyper wrote to the electoral association in Ommen that it would have been distasteful to "have to oppose a friendly cabinet. If I had had to decide before the memorandum had seen the light of day, then I would probably have had to refuse; now I feel free to accept."

The photograph shows the memorandum, with Kuyper's notes. The introductory paragraph in particular was heavily edited.

In the autumn of 1908 Kuyper published three major works in which he again demonstrated his vitality and versatility. In September Van Holkema & Warendorf published the first volume of his four-volume *Parliamentary Speeches* (from the period 1894-1901), which was followed in October by the second volume of *Around the Old-World Sea*. In the same month J. H. Kok in Kampen published the two-volume collection of devotionals *To Be Near unto God*, which Kuyper had published in *De Heraut* between 1901 and 1906. The photograph shows the Korean translation of 1986, by S. K. Chung.

In June 1909 the elections for the second chamber were due to be held. And as before, the Anti-Revolutionary election campaign again started with a massive and demonstrative convention, which was held on 22 April 1909 in the Tivoli in Utrecht. Kuyper's speech to the delegates was entitled *We, Calvinists . . .*, and as was often the case centered around an important historical event, this time the commemoration of the four hundredth anniversary of Calvin's birth (10 July 1509).

The photograph shows the podium in Tivoli with Kuyper in the middle behind the committee table, flanked by Bavinck (right) and Verweijck (left).

D^R. A. KUYPER IN DE CARICATUUR

MET EEN VOORREDE VAN D^R. KUYPER ZELF.

ABRAHAM de GEWELDIGE

AMSTERDAM — VAN HOLKEMA & WARENDORF.

The collection *Dr. Kuyper in Caricatures*, with the cover portrait of *"Abraham de geweld-ige,"* drawn by Albert Hahn. (*Geweldige* can be translated as "great," "terrible," or "tre-mendous.")

Perhaps the most surprising fact about this collection of caricatures is that Kuyper himself wrote the preface for the book, published by his Amsterdam publisher Van Holkema & Warendorf. The drawings made during the first decades of Kuyper's public life were almost completely absent, while the most malicious caricatures of later years had been omitted entirely. The publication was a success as an election stunt. Moreover, in his preface Kuyper pointed out that according to this publication he was still very much alive and kicking as a politician: "Political, personal caricatures are meant to fin-ish you off as a statesman and should, say, after ten years of hunting, at least have put you out of action for good. For how long should I not have been dead, according to this artistic calculation? And all the more, as I was only acting as Scapegoat. I was always the one to have done wrong; as one man they repeatedly attacked me from every corner. . . . But this collection in particular will now provide the evidence that this plot has *not* suc-ceeded, and that I was too tough for these gentlemen."

Kuyper had close ties with Belgium. He often visited Brussels, sympathized with the Flemish movement, and kept in touch with prominent politicians and scholars there. Since August 1903 he had been a foreign honorary member of the Royal Flemish Academy for Language and Literature. On 10 May 1909 he received an honorary doctorate in political and social sciences from the University of Leuven. Because of the electoral campaign, Kuyper was not able to receive the official document in person, but after the ceremony the dean of the Law Faculty, J. van den Heuvel, wrote to him: "At the academic meeting of 10 May, your name was read aloud and received with unanimous and particularly warm rounds of applause."

It was especially because of Kuyper's campaign strategy that the Confessional parties won the 1909 elections for the second chamber with a clear majority. After the second ballot on 23 June they held 60 of the 100 seats. The clear winners were the Anti-Revolutionaries, who went from fifteen to twenty-three seats, while the Roman Catholics stayed at twenty-five seats, and the Christian-Historicals climbed from nine to twelve. The Anti-Revolutionary press was jubilant: "The rehabilitation of our great leader Dr. Kuyper, who masterfully led us to our victory, is truly complete."

If expectations had been raised that Kuyper might become a member of the cabinet, the council of ministers had decided already on 24 June that the cabinet would continue "without any reconstruction owing to the admittance of Dr. Kuyper." The principal motive for this decision was that Kuyper was too controversial, which could lead to bitterness within the opposition and to tensions within the coalition. Because Heemskerk understood that the cabinet's decision was not a pleasant one for the Anti-Revolutionary leader, he asked Idenburg to inform Kuyper. Idenburg complied with the request in a letter of 29 June (see illustration), but in order to spare his elderly friend he offered another motivation for the cabinet's decision. According to Idenburg, the cabinet had taken into consideration "that Dr. Kuyper cannot be seated in a cabinet which he was not instructed to form and of which he is not the spokesman."

Het lintje.

Een moderne Laokoön-groep.

By the time Kuyper received this letter, he must have known that his quest to become a minster again had already failed for other reasons: he had already become discredited by painful revelations in the Socialist daily paper *Het Volk*.

Under the caption "Dr. Kuyper's Trade in Decorations," on Sunday, 27 June 1909, *Het Volk* published an interview with Pieter Tideman, a lawyer from Haarlem, which marked the beginning of what became known as the "decorations affair." Tideman charged that in 1903, at Kuyper's behest and in his capacity as a minister, a royal honor had been conferred on the salesman R. A. L. Lehmann, who donated a substantial sum to the electoral coffers of the ARP shortly afterwards. The donation had been made through Kuyper, who despite his position as minister had remained party chairman. Rudolf Lehmann's brother, E. A. Lehmann, who had also donated funds to the ARP, had been recommended for a decoration by Kuyper, but this was said not to have taken place because of the resignation of the Kuyper administration in the summer of 1905. In their efforts, the Lehmanns had asked Mathilde Westmeijer to act as a mediator. She was an unofficial agent of the ARP, and thus connected to Kuyper. The Lehmanns paid her for her services. In order to strengthen his accusation of corruption, Tideman also published a number of letters from, or in the name of, Kuyper to Mathilde Westmeijer, to which Tideman had access as her lawyer.

In the above drawing "The Decoration" by Braakensiek, published in *De Amsterdammer* on 4 July 1909, Mathilde Westmeijer, Kuyper, and Rudolf Lehmann are portrayed in a re-creation of the famous statue *Laocoön and His Sons*, wrestling with ribbons and medals instead of sea serpents.

Kuyper responded immediately to the sensational interview in *Het Volk*. Already on 29 June he had *De Standaard* include a "Statement," dated 28 June, in which he took up the accusations point by point and denied any connection between the financial support and the decoration. When Tideman subsequently made new accusations, Kuyper stated in *De Standaard* of 9 July 1909 that he would respond only when all the "presumed evidence" had been made known. After that he went abroad for his annual holiday, returning to the Netherlands on 5 September.

The lawyer from Haarlem, Pieter Tideman (1871-1943), was an impetuous man with strong opinions and polemical tendencies. As a student in the 1890s he had played a role in conflicts regarding the progressive literary paper *De Nieuwe Gids*. As a Remonstrant, but in particular as a Free Liberal, Tideman wanted nothing to do with Kuyper's politics, and he developed a personal aversion to the Anti-Revolutionary leader. He went to *Het Volk* because he wanted to prevent Kuyper from becoming a minister again, a step which in hindsight was unnecessary because the cabinet itself had already come to the conclusion on 24 June that "the return of Dr. Kuyper to power" was not desirable.

„De decoratie was alleszins gerechtveerdigd."

"Not So? The decoration was justified in every respect." Drawing by Tjerk Bottema in *De Notenkraker*, 1909, one of the many caricatures that were published regarding the decorations affair.

The interview in *Het Volk* came as a real bombshell and created much commotion in the press. No one had expected that the Anti-Revolutionary leader who was apparently so above reproach would defend himself against such accusations. Kuyper's "Statement" in *De Standaard* of 29 June 1909 was generally regarded as insufficient, and the months of silence that followed led to much criticism even among his fellow party members. Although the Anti-Revolutionaries believed that the attack on Kuyper was for the most part a political conspiracy by the Socialists and the Liberals, the facts in themselves were serious enough. Without doubting his good faith and good intentions, they realized that Kuyper had apparently made mistakes, had been careless and rash — in short, had shown himself to be sinful. That was why old friends such as Hovy, Bavinck, and Rutgers urged him to explain matters and not to leave "our people" in the dark any longer.

"Mathilde Westmeijer in Her Boudoir," photograph in the illustrated magazine *Het Leven (Life)*, 11 September 1909.

Mathilda Maria Antonia Westmeijer (1874-1945), who played such a notorious role in the decorations affair, was an enterprising woman who enjoyed living in luxury and knew how to manipulate people. With a fragile appearance, including a limp, she knew how to gain sympathy by presenting herself as a vulnerable, unhappy woman who needed help and protection. Kuyper was not insensitive to her charms, although the tone and content of their correspondence give no reason whatsoever to suppose that an illicit relationship took place. It does seem, however, that Kuyper supported her financially on various occasions.

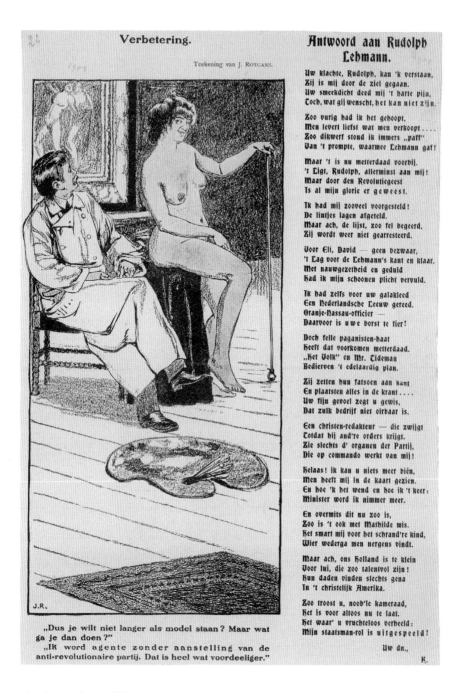

The decorations affair was a source of much amusement in the Liberal and Socialist press, where the relationship between Kuyper and Mathilde Westmeijer lent itself to all kinds of innuendos and insinuations. Kuyper believed that these rumors were spread to strike *him* in particular. The caption for the drawing by J. Rotgans in the *Nederland-sche Spectator* of September 1909 is a reference to Kuyper's statement in *De Standaard*, in which he had described Mathilde Westmeijer as an "unofficial agent for the elections."

R. A. L. Lehmann (1870-1928) as consul-general of Greece, 1897.

A wealthy merchant from Amsterdam, R. A. L. Lehmann was a descendant of a Jewish family from Germany that in the course of the nineteenth century had become wealthy in the Amsterdam tobacco trade. Baptized in the Dutch Reformed Church, Lehmann strove for social recognition and status. As consul-general of Greece in Amsterdam he used his substantial fortune to obtain a large number of foreign honors. In 1906 he tried in vain to gain admittance to the Dutch peerage. In April 1909, just before the decorations affair became public, he donated two ambulances to the Dutch Red Cross in the (futile) hope of receiving membership in the Order of the Netherlands Lion. However, by a royal decree on 1 May 1909 he was appointed as an honorary member of the Dutch Red Cross.

Hoeve de laster wee gaa dorru,
't sa alton nog we se de engela om my her.
K̄

While Kuyper was caught up in the decorations affair, his friend and confidant Idenburg departed for the Dutch East Indies, where he had been appointed as governor-general (1909-1916). The photograph, taken upon Idenburg's departure on 21 October 1909, shows from left to right: Kuyper, Lohman, Idenburg, his son Piet Idenburg, M. E. Idenburg-Duetz, and J. H. Kuyper.

Note by Kuyper in answer to an anonymous abusive letter about the decorations affair: "How far slander dares to go. And yet, there are still guardian angels around me." Also in a note to a supporter from that same time, Kuyper described the accusations as "slanderous talk": "It is all entirely made up. . . . This is how they slandered Luther, how they slandered Calvin, even making our dear Savior out as a glutton and a wine-bibber. The Lord is judge. He will do right by this affair."

Het boetekleed ontsiert den man niet!

Spiegeltje, spiegeltje in de hand,
Wie is er 't boetvaardigst in heel het land?

Not until 18 November 1909 during the general political deliberations in the second chamber did Kuyper make a "Further Statement" about the decorations affair. In it he showed that there had been sufficient grounds for awarding R. A. L. Lehmann the decoration: he had given financial aid for the repatriation to the Netherlands of fellow countrymen who had fought in the Boer War and who had been sent to Saint Helena as prisoners of war by the English. However, he also admitted that in his dealings with the brothers Lehmann and Mathilde Westmeijer he had been imprudent and had become entangled in the threads of a scheme that he had not clearly discerned. He concluded his speech with the famous words: "Even though sackcloth disgraces not the man, I may have sinned against the standards of due caution and wise policy."

For *De Amsterdammer* of 28 November 1909 Johan Braakensiek drew a caricature of Kuyper in a hair shirt, with the lines: "Mirror, mirror in the hand/Who is the most penitential in our land?" The Rev. Hendrik Pierson had also been irritated by the way in which Kuyper had acted. On 29 November 1909 he wrote to De Savornin Lohman: "That someone like Kuyper is satisfied with having come through the thicket more or less in one piece, is a complete mystery to me. . . . And then the expression at the end: 'Sackcloth disgraces not the man.' He who truly does penitence and wears the appropriate clothes does not look at himself in a mirror!"

The leader of the Social Democratic parliamentary caucus, P. J. Troelstra, led the attacks on Kuyper in the second chamber and initially succeeded in driving the Confessional parties into retreat. However, his proposal to conduct a parliamentary investigation into the decorations affair was rejected by the second chamber on 25 May 1910. Still, at the insistence of Lohman, who disapproved of Kuyper's behavior but protected him in Parliament, a commission of independent politicians was formed to investigate the allegations of corruption.

The former minister for foreign affairs, the Free Liberal W. H. de Beaufort, also spoke out against instituting a parliamentary investigation, because he believed that the most important facts were known and was "not inclined to root around in the mire." In his diaries he was most critical of Kuyper, whom he described as imperious, a vulgar demagogue, an impudent fanatic, a mishmash of vanity and inconsistency, a boaster, an actor, an irresponsible party booster, and a diva. De Beaufort summed up his aristocratic aversion with the scornful words, "Dr. Kuyper is the type of politician to come from a democratic society based on the American model."

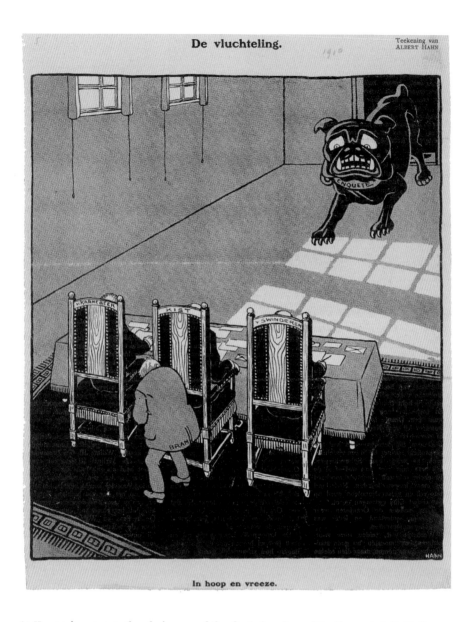

De vluchteling.

Teekening van ALBERT HAHN

In hoop en vreeze.

At Kuyper's request, the chairman of the first chamber of Parliament, J. E. N. Baron Schimmelpenninck van der Oye formed a commission, consisting of the Christian-Historical Vice-President of the Council of State P. J. van Swinderen, the Liberal H. J. Kist, who was former attorney-general for the Court of Justice in Amsterdam and a member of the first chamber, and A. P. C. van Karnebeek, former minister for foreign affairs and a member of the second chamber for the Free Liberals.

As illustrated in the caricature by Albert Hahn, *De Notenkraker*, 13 February 1910, the Social Democrats believed that the commission had been set up to prevent a parliamentary investigation and hush up the matter. Their main objection was against the fact that the commission was not authorized to question witnesses under oath.

HET LINTJE
DE FEITEN DER KUYPER=ZAAK

DOOR

ED. POLAK
REDACTEUR VAN „HET VOLK"

Brochurenhandel der S. D. A. P. - Keizersgracht 378, Amsterdam - 1910

A *Het Volk* journalist, Eduard Polak, made a list of the "facts about the Kuyper case," but despite all the negative publicity the coalition parties managed to strengthen their position during the elections for the States-General in June 1910. The Liberals suffered a heavy defeat, losing twenty-four seats: sixteen to the Confessionals and eight to the Social Democrats. In the preceding weeks Kuyper had skillfully played on the anti-Socialist feelings that existed among the conservative Liberals, and had, practically on a daily basis, emphasized in *De Standaard* that the Liberals had let themselves be led by Troelstra as "leader of the opposition."

§ 2. Mejuffrouw M. Westmeijer.

Niet onwaarschijnlijk met de bedoeling, om op het ge-
beurde een voor mij min aangenaam licht te doen vallen,
is in de Pers gedurig de figuur van Mej. Westmeijer op
den voorgrond geschoven, en wel in het beeld van eene
dame van „verdachte reputatie". Haar eer werd aangetast,
niet om haar, maar om mij te treffen. Ik stel er daarom
prijs op, hare aanraking met mij nader toe te lichten.

Toen ik in het begin van 1902 te Amsterdam een gebouw was
gaan zien voor een Rijksstichting en er den nacht moest over-
blijven, meldde Mejuffrouw Westmeijer zich den volgenden
morgen, vlak voor mijn vertrek, aan mijn hotel aan. Wat ze te
verzoeken had, kwam in 't kort hierop neer: Dat hare
familie eenige jaren geleden uit hooggaanden financieelen
nood was gered door zekeren heer R. Lehmann, en dat diens
oude moeder haar in vertrouwen had geklaagd, dat haar
zoon wel meer dan ééne vreemde ridderorde bezat, maar
nog altoos geen van zijn eigen land. En dat zij, juffrouw
Westmeijer, nu, uit dankbaarheid voor wat de heer L.
voor haar ouders deed, eens kwam vragen, of hier niets
aan te doen was; een verzoek, dat zij aandrong met er
op te wijzen, dat hij ook op ander terrein zooveel goeds
deed; een bewering ten bewijze waarvan zij eenige papieren
op tafel legde. Daar ik geen tijd had, antwoordde ik haar
kortaf, dat dit alles niets te beteekenen had, want dat eene
ridderorde alleen voor *nationale verdiensten* kon worden
gegeven; en zij vertrok.

The printed memorandum, furnished with forty-one appendices, in which Kuyper told
his version of the decorations affair. The memorandum was not made public, but sent
exclusively to the members of the commission.

DE DECORATIE-QUAESTIE.

Wij zijn in staat gesteld mede te deelen een afschrift van het Rapport der Commissie, die zich heeft willen belasten met een onderzoek der bekende Decoratie-zaak.

Het rapport, gericht aan den Hoogwelgeboren Heer J. E. N. Baron Schimmelpenninck van der Oye van Hoevelaken, voorzitter van de Eerste Kamer der Staten-Generaal, luidt als volgt:

's-Gravenhage 14 Juli 1910.

»Hoog Welgeboren Heer!«

De Commissie, die zich op Uwe uitnoodiging geconstitueerd heeft teneinde »ingevolge een verzoek van Dr. A. Kuyper, na onderzoek haar oordeel uittespreken in zake de sinds einde Juni des vorigen jaars uitgestrooide beschuldiging; als zou hij zich, tijdens hij Minister van Binnenlandsche Zaken was, schuldig gemaakt hebben aan corruptie", heeft de eer u hierbij het resultaat van haar onderzoek mede te deelen.

De commissie heeft bij haar onderzoek, behalve van de door den druk openbaar gemaakte stukken, waaronder ook de op de zaak betrekkelijke Kamerverslagen, gebruik gemaakt van een haar door Dr. Kuyper toegezonden memorie met bijlagen, waaronder brieven van verschillende personen in originali, voorts van schriftelijke inlichtingen die zij van onderscheidene personen gevraagd en verkregen heeft, eindelijk van haar door mej. M. Westmeijer mondeling verstrekte inlichtingen.

Zij is van meening, dat de tegen Dr. Kuyper uitgebrachte beschuldiging zich concentreert in de quaestie van de ridderorden voor de heeren Lehmann, en spreekt haar oordeel uit als volgt:

1o. Voor wat aangaat de bepalingen van het Wetboek van Strafrecht, dat Dr. Kuyper vrij uitgaat, aangezien niet gebleken is van eenige aanduiding, dat hij ten eigen bate geld heeft aangenomen van de heeren Lehmann.

2o. in aanmerking nemende, dat de tegen Dr. A. Kuyper gerichte beschuldiging ook betrof het geven van ridderorden in verband met geldelijke bijdragen aan de antirevolutionaire partijkas voor verkiezingsdoeleinden, iets dat, al valt het niet onder de strafwet, als corruptie is gequalificeerd: ten eerste, dat, voor wat den heer R. Lehmann betreft, die, naar aanleiding van zijne ruime bijdragen ten behoeve van het herstel der Hollandsche kerk te Colombo en van het repatrieeren der op St. Helena verblijvende krijgsgevangenen, den 31 Aug. 1903, gedecoreerd werd, niet gebleken is van eenige reden om te twijfelen aan de verzekering van Dr. Kuyper en van hem zelven, dat hij voor het eerst in Mei 1904, dus geruimen tijd na de decoreering, geld voor de partijkas heeft gegeven;

dat het onder 2o. bedoelde verband ook niet af te leiden is uit de omstandigheid, dat het aanwijzen van daden, waardoor de heer R. Lehmann zich voor het nationaal belang verdienstelijk kon maken, plaats had ingevolge een verzoek van Mej. M. Westmeyer, wier ijverige bemoeiingen ter inzameling van gelden voor de partijkas en wier geldelijke verplichtingen aan den heer R. Lehmann, aan Dr. Kuyper bekend waren.

Immers naar het oordeel van de commissie zou door deze omstandigheid in aanmerking te nemen het verband in den zin van corruptie te ver gezocht zijn, terwijl er geen twijfel kan zijn, dat Dr. Kuyper, ook afgezien van eenige betrekking tot mej. M. Westmeyer, als agente zonder aanstelling, bijzonder belang stelde in het herstel der Kerk te Colombo en het repatrieeren der Krijgsgevangenen op St. Helena;

ten andere, dat voor wat den heer E. A. Lehmann aangaat, de zaak zich anders voordoet. De poging toch van Dr. Kuyper om hem voor eene decoratie te doen voordragen, heeft plaats gehad, nadat Dr. Kuyper gelden van hem had aangenomen voor de partijkas, en zonder dat hij zich door eenige speciale daad verdienstelijk had gemaakt voor het nationaal belang.

Deze feiten op zich zelf leveren echter, naar het oordeel der commissie, nog geen grond op om corruptie aan te nemen en van het innerlijk verband tusschen die feiten is de Commissie bij haar onderzoek niet gebleken. Overigens is, naar haar oordeel, de voorspraak van Dr. Kuyper bij een zijner ambtgenooten, ten gunste van den heer E. A. Lehmann, niet te beschouwen als een ambtsdaad.

Met bijzondere hoogachting,
De commissie voornoemd:
w.g. VAN SWINDEREN.
» H. J. KIST.
» VAN KARNEBEEK.

Voor eensluidend afschrift:
SCHIMMELPENNINCK v. D. OYE
v. HOEVELAKEN.

In its report of 14 July 1910, published in the daily newspapers on 23 August 1910, the commission concluded that there was insufficient evidence to support the presumption that Kuyper had acted corruptly in the decorations affair. Although the commission did conclude that Kuyper had recommended E. A. Lehmann for a decoration *after* he had donated money to the party funds of the ARP, *without* having done anything for the greater good of the nation, the honorary council stopped short of calling this corruption, because "connections between the facts . . . have not come to light."

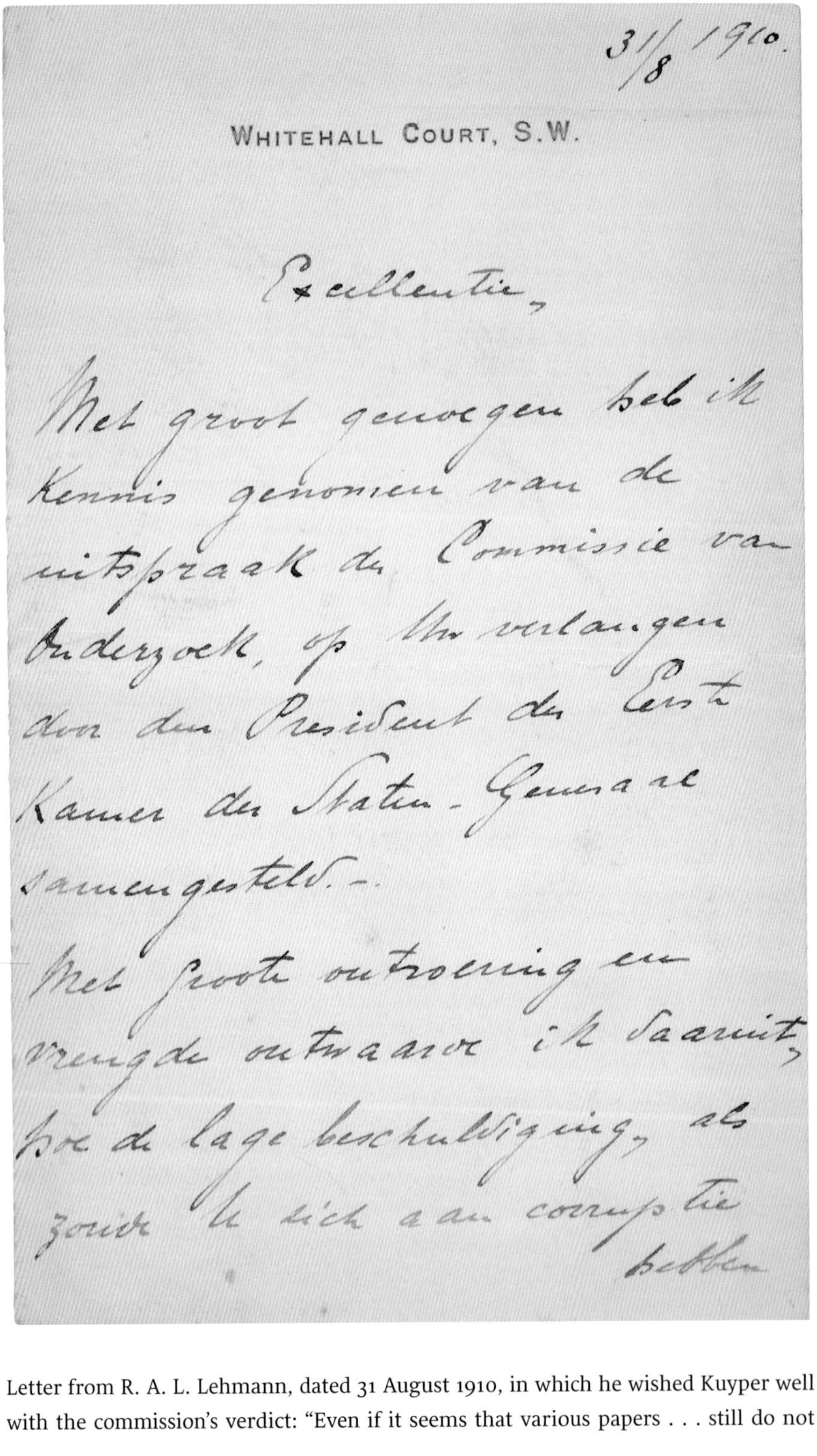

31/8 1910.

WHITEHALL COURT, S.W.

Excellentie,

Met groot genoegen heb ik
kennis genomen van de
uitspraak der Commissie van
Onderzoek, op Uw verlangen
door den President der Eerste
Kamer der Staten-Generaal
samengesteld. –

Met groote ontroering en
vreugde ontwaar ik daaruit,
hoe de lage beschuldiging, als
zoude U zich aan corruptie
hebben

Letter from R. A. L. Lehmann, dated 31 August 1910, in which he wished Kuyper well with the commission's verdict: "Even if it seems that various papers . . . still do not want to accept this outcome that is so favourable for Your Excellency, and even if they do continue their attacks, what does it matter? The commission, consisting of people whose verdict is above every suspicion, has clearly found you not guilty of corruption as charged."

Idenburg was less satisfied with the verdict. On 28 September 1910 he wrote to F. L. Rutgers, "I cannot say that the commission's report pleases me much. It undoubtedly reflects the charitable sentiments of its members, but the remark — I think from Liberal quarters — that the report does not contain the verdict Dr. Kuyper's friends so wanted, namely, that there is no question of corruption, is alas true. Of course, one cannot approve of everything Dr. Kuyper has done — that is certainly not necessary after he himself admitted to having erred — but the declaration against the charge of corruption could have been stronger. Now I am most interested to see what Dr. Kuyper's position in the second chamber will be. These are difficult years for our good friend."

Dr. J. D. C. van Heeckeren van Kell, 1854-1931.

This was indeed a difficult time for Kuyper, because in addition to the decorations affair, in 1910 he was also under fire in the Van Heeckeren case, which also originated from the time of his ministry. Baron van Heeckeren van Kell was an Anti-Revolutionary diplomat who, as envoy to the Scandinavian courts (1899-1909), had initially enjoyed Kuyper's trust. Although Minister Melvil van Lynden wanted to discharge him, the cabinet kept Van Heeckeren in office, and with Kuyper's help even appointed him as a member of the first chamber (1904-1910).

This combination of positions, still possible at that time, had unpleasant consequences when in the autumn of 1905 the envoy was passed over for a promotion by the De Meester cabinet. Van Heeckeren, a man who thought highly of himself and who always felt badly treated, now could not resist the temptation to find fault with Foreign Office policy, which brought him as a diplomat into conflict with his superiors. Although this impossible situation was brought to an end when Van Heeckeren resigned as an envoy in the autumn of 1909, in the first chamber he continued to bombard the Foreign Minister with memorandums. He particularly caused a stir with the repeated assertion that the German Kaiser, in a 1904 letter to Queen Wilhelmina, had hinted at the occupation of Dutch territory in case of a European war if the Dutch coastal fortresses were not brought into a good state of defense against England.

De zaak Van Heeckeren—Kuyper bijgelegd.

Hoe dankbaar is mijn kleine hond.....

Van Heeckeren brought the case up for discussion again on 9 February 1910 in a secret session of the First Chamber, after which Minister of Foreign Affairs De Marees van Swinderen openly contradicted him. On 15 February Van Heeckeren responded with the statement that Prime Minister Kuyper had informed him at the time of the Kaiser's letter. In *De Standaard* of 15 and 18 March 1910 Kuyper disputed this statement, but he contradicted himself often enough that the Liberal press cast doubt on his credibility. In this case too, Kuyper was raked over the coals. The publicity surrounding the Van Heeckeren case continued until the beginning of July, when the Confessional-led first chamber declared the case closed and Van Heeckeren himself was not reelected as a member of Parliament after the elections of June 1910.

De ondergeteekende ee verklaart hiermede op heden, geheel on
verplicht, een bedrag van duizend gulden van D'. A. Kuyper
ontvangen te hebben, alsmede geenerlei pretentie, welke
dan ook, op Zijne Excellentie, noch op den heer Jacques
Deen te hebben, en in de toekomst nooit eenige pretentie
op Zijne Excellentie te zullen erkennen, of in rekening te zullen
brengen, dan naar schrijven door Zijne Excellentie zelf in
afgegeven en mits op naam ondertekend, na deze dag en heden.

's Gravenhage 18 April 1914.

Mathilde Westmeijl

With the commission's verdict the decorations affair disappeared from the headlines, but the aftereffects of the case lingered for years. Because Mathilde Westmeijer had not given incriminating testimony against Kuyper and R. Lehmann as a witness before the council, she was able once more to capitalize on the scandal. According to the statement reproduced here and drafted by Kuyper personally, the last payment (of 1000 guilders) to Mathilde Westmeijer took place on 18 April 1914. As a favor in return, she stated that she no longer had any claims on Kuyper.

CHAPTER X

The Final Years, 1910-1920

Kuyper's old age was not free of tragedy. His reputation had suffered from the decorations affair and his political position had been weakened, but Kuyper did not yet contemplate stepping down. As party leader, member of Parliament, and opinion maker in *De Standaard,* he remained a force to be reckoned with, as the Heemskerk cabinet witnessed on more than one occasion. In coalition circles he was increasingly regarded as a "nuisance" who disturbed relations by his willful behavior. Although Kuyper resigned as a member of the second chamber in September 1912 because of increasing deafness, a year later he was appointed as a member of the first chamber. From a strategic point of view this was a sensible move, because after the elections of June 1913 the Confessional parties were a minority in the second chamber, while in the first chamber they retained a majority. Then during the cabinet formation of 1918, Kuyper caused problems with his opposition to the formation of the Ruijs de Beerenbrouck cabinet. Only after being persuaded by his future successor Colijn and by Idenburg was Kuyper prepared to accept the cabinet.

Kuyper was still idolized by the average Anti-Revolutionary, but his position as leader of the ARP came under pressure when a younger generation of politicians came onto the scene. In a sense it was thanks to Kuyper's pioneering work that talented men were now ready to take over his task. But instead of being pleased about this, he regarded them mainly as a threat to his leadership, which he found difficult to relinquish. As he grew older, Kuyper tended to interpret every contradiction as insubordination towards the leadership given to him by God. This attitude was reinforced by his continual concern about the signs of weakening and watering down that he thought he perceived everywhere, even at his own Free University. In 1915 the internal differences led to an open pamphlet war within the ARP. He never came into conflict with Idenburg or Colijn, however, in part because Kuyper respected their unique abilities, but it was significant that they also sometimes preferred to consult Lohman rather than the old party leader.

Despite his old age, Kuyper did not slow his pace of publishing. In addition to theological works such as *Our Worship* (1911) and the three-volume *Pro Rege* (1911-12), he published a host of speeches and smaller publications in which he discussed matters of current importance, such as colonial affairs (1912), the position of women (1914), and the First World War (1917). In his two-volume work *Anti-Revolutionary Politics* (1916-17) he again offered an elucidation of Anti-Revolutionary principles, as he had done at the outset of his political career.

Unlike Lohman, Kuyper did not play a great role during the "Pacification" of 1917, the historic compromise concerning the school question and the franchise that came about under the leadership of the Liberal cabinet of Cort van der Linden. The settlement of the two issues did not meet with Kuyper's approval in all respects, but in a sense it was the crowning glory of his work and heralded decades of Confessional domination in national affairs. In his last speech to the party convention, *What Now?*, of 2 May 1918, which he was not able to deliver himself, Kuyper addressed the question of which direction the ARP should go after the conclusion of the school struggle. He emphasized once more that for Christian politics the social issue was the main challenge. The second Christian Social Congress, which was organized upon Kuyper's initiative in March 1919, should also be seen in this light.

On his doctor's advice, Kuyper had to stop working for *De Standaard* in December 1919, but he could in no way be persuaded to officially resign. In September 1920 he tendered his resignation as a member of the first chamber. After that his condition slowly deteriorated. He died on Monday, 8 November, at approximately five o'clock in the afternoon, in the presence of his children and of Idenburg, who had attended to him spiritually on his deathbed. On Friday, 12 November, he was laid to rest in Oud Eik en Duinen cemetery in The Hague.

Heemskerk as Prime Minister.

During these final years the relationship between Kuyper and the Heemskerk cabinet remained difficult. Particularly after the departure of the conciliatory Idenburg to the Dutch East Indies, regular conflicts occurred between Kuyper, who as in the past during the Mackay cabinet complained about the lack of consultation, and the cabinet, which did not want to be led by Kuyper's directives in *De Standaard*.

Anti-Revolutionary Minister for Industry, Agriculture, and Trade A. S. Talma (1864-1916) was regularly criticized by Kuyper because in social matters he preferred his own approach. At one time, when Kuyper was a minister, he had tried to bring about a *total* revision of labor law, while Talma preferred a *separate* revision for each branch of industry, such as the baker's law, the mason's law, and the dockworker's law. Kuyper expressed his disapproval of this approach in *De Standaard* and did not vote during the discussion of the baker's law, which was rejected by the second chamber on 5 June 1912.

After two cabinet shuffles, Anti-Revolutionary member of the second chamber Hendrik Colijn (1869-1944) was appointed minister of war on 4 January 1911. On 14 May 1912 he was also appointed as the minister of the Navy. Like Idenburg, Colijn had been a soldier in the Dutch East Indies, where he had made a name for himself as the right-hand man of Governor-General J. B. van Heutsz. The energetic and confident Colijn soon gained authority as a member of the cabinet and also built up a good relationship with Kuyper — for example, by informing him of his policy plans in advance. The energetic way in which Colijn presented his military bill in the second chamber elicited words of praise from Kuyper in *De Standaard* of 6 June 1911: "The Minister has almost performed magic!"

Een opzienbarend krantenbericht geïllustreerd.

De ex=minister Dr. Kuyper te Brussel gearresteerd.

Reuter's Bureau seinde verleden Donderdag over de heele wereld van uit zijn Brusselsch agentschap: „Hedenmorgen om halftw alf vormde er zich een groote oploop op de Place Brouckere, waar men voor een raam van het hôtel Métropole een spiernaakten man heen en weer zag loopen. Die meneer was niemand anders dan dr. Kuyper, oud-minister-president van Nederland. Dz heer Kuyper werd door de politie naar het politie-bureau in de Rue de la Fiancée gebracht en vandaar naar het commissariaat van het vierde arrondissement. Vele getuigen, die gehoord werden, stonden in voor de juistheid van het feit. De heer Kuyper, ondervraagd, erkende het feit, doch zeide aldus in zijn kamer op en neer te wandelen op voorschrift van zijn dokter. Hij wist niet, dat men hem van het plein af zien kon. Proces-verbaal is opgemaakt."

De ex-minister Dr. Abraham Kuyper voor het hotel Métropole op de Place Brouckere. Het gemerkte raam op de tweede verdieping is dat van de kamer van Dr. Kuyper, waarachter de ontkleede oud-staatsman het eerst door een tram-conducteur ontdekt werd.

Illustration in the weekly paper *Het Leven* of 26 September 1911.

In the autumn of 1911 Kuyper caused quite a stir. During a stay in Brussels, on Thursday, 21 September 1911, he was taken away by the police for questioning after he had been observed that morning standing naked in front of the window of his room at the hotel Métropole on the Brouckèreplein. Apparently the spectacle had lasted long enough for "a large crowd" to gather, as Reuters reported. Kuyper stated to the police that he did gymnastics in the nude on the advice of a doctor and had not noticed that he was visible from the square. That brought the incident to an end in Brussels, but the liberal press in the Netherlands still had weeks of fun about "Adam Kuyper" and in its commentaries recalled the decorations affair. For two weeks *Het Leven* devoted a full-page comic strip in rhyme to "Dr. Kuyper's Kneipp cure" [Kneipp was a Bavarian priest and a proponent of naturopathic medicine]. On 22 September *Het Volk* wrote, "Apart from that, no one need be surprised about the man's lack of clothes. During recent years he had taken off so many old togs and thrown them into a corner that he hardly has anything left to cover his nakedness. Even the sackcloth seems to have gotten lost."

J. H. de Waal Malefijt, 1852-1931.

Idenburg's successor as the minister for colonial affairs, the Anti-Revolutionary J. H. de Waal Malefijt, was regularly criticized in *De Standaard*. On 6 December 1911 Kuyper launched an attack on the minister because he was said not to take the promotion of Christian education in the Dutch East Indies seriously enough. In April 1912 Kuyper published the pamphlet *Coerced* in which he explained his opinions at length.

In a letter to Idenburg written on 22 April 1912, De Waal Malefijt unburdened himself about Kuyper's pamphlet: "It is really an insincere and false piece. What I have been able to do since my appointment has been carefully ignored. My words and arguments are either not mentioned at all or twisted beyond all recognition. Mean articles from liberal papers are quoted at will. Colijn praised to heaven — at my expense — and last but not least, the person of Dr. K. presented as the incarnation of innocence, mercy and truth. Against all this I am powerless and must now watch how in Wiesbaden [where Kuyper had gone on vacation] Dr. K. digests the winnings that the pamphlet brought him. He departed on Saturday, and on Friday evening I received the pamphlet as a farewell gesture."

Bergum 5 April 1912

Excellentie!

Nu onze „Kuyperweek" (wil mij dit karakteristieke, uit den volksmond overgenomen woord ten goede houden), nu deze week met haar emotie en met haar beslommering voor den Secretaris van het Comité achter den rug is, zij het mij toegestaan, U persoonlijk nog eens mijn diepgevoelden dank te betuigen voor Uwe komst naar het Noorden. Zoo iets in staat was, den moed er weer in te brengen bij ons volk, dan was het Uw bezielend woord. En U hebt het zelf kunnen zien, dat dit woord zijne uitwerking niet gemist heeft. En niet alleen Uw woord deed het, maar Uwe verschijning zelve te midden Uwer getrouwe Friezen deed de geestdrift ontvlammen. Den man voor ons te zien, die voor ons gestreden, maar

With the average Anti-Revolutionary, Kuyper was still as popular as ever and was regarded as a martyr for the good cause. Kuyper enjoyed his supporters' adoration and even encouraged it so that he could continue to wield political influence. In March and April of 1912 he spoke at party conferences in Leeuwarden, Groningen, and Rotterdam, where he was fervently applauded. In his speech *Delivered from the House of Bondage* he compared the political emancipation of the "little people" with the exodus from Egypt — and implicitly himself with Moses. It was a truly triumphal march. In his diary, the Liberal De Beaufort scornfully wrote: "Everywhere great crowds at the stations in Leeuwarden and Groningen where Kuyper is greeted like a king, and escorted to his guesthouse amid cheers from the jubilant crowd."

On 5 April, the secretary of the ARP in the province of Friesland, J. D. de Vries, described to Kuyper the impression Kuyper had made in Leeuwarden on his fellow party members: "If anything could give our people courage once more, then it was your inspiring word. . . . And not only your word did so, but your very appearance amidst the loyal Frisians stirred up enthusiasm. To see the man in front of us who had fought but had also suffered for us, who brought us to where we are now, who in God's hand was *the* means to lead us out of the house of bondage — it provoked in us an unprecedented emotion. . . . It was a shame that on the railway platform in Leeuwarden things got a bit too boisterous, and yet there was also a good side to that, a charming side. . . . The Anti-Revolutionaries, who had often suffered pain for the slander leveled at you, felt a need to show their emotions."

L. F. Duymaer van Twist als Kapitein (1906).

As secretary of the parliamentary caucus in the chamber, treasurer of the Central Committee, and member of the second chamber from 1901 until 1946, the Anti-Revolutionary L. F. Duymaer van Twist (1865-1961) was an important link between Kuyper and the party. He was so devoted to him that he was sometimes called "Dr. Kuyper's shield-bearer." Typical of his loyalty was that he moved from Bezuidenhoutse-weg to Kanaalstraat in The Hague, because it was important to Kuyper that the treasurer of the Central Committee live in his neighborhood.

At the fortieth anniversary of *De Standaard*, Kuyper was celebrated as the paper's founder and editor-in-chief during a meeting held on 8 April 1912 in the Hall of Arts and Sciences in Utrecht. The photograph shows an overview of the hall with Kuyper seated in the middle of the dais; to the right, dressed in white, a ladies' choir from Amsterdam.

Although the fête was not on the same grand scale as in 1897 and 1907, according to De Beaufort "the most profuse adulation" took place. De Beaufort did not fail to see the irony, given the decorations affair, when Kuyper received not only an amount of money that was to go to a Kuyper fund for the dissemination of Anti-Revolutionary principles, but also a small chest for his decorations: "It seems like anything goes as far as Kuyper is concerned. . . . Who could have thought this up? Perhaps someone who wanted to see just how far one can go in venerating Kuyper. But if so, he can rest assured, because the general public has taken even this veneration most seriously."

Album with congratulations, presented to Kuyper on the occasion of the fortieth anniversary of *De Standaard*. At the top of the title page are printed the portraits of Calvin and Groen van Prinsterer, at the bottom on the left the building that housed *De Standaard*, and at the bottom on the right the "turret" in The Hague where Kuyper resided as prime minister.

At the festivities the only ministers present on behalf of the Heemskerk cabinet were Colijn and Talma. Heemskerk and De Waal Malefijt did not attend. De Waal Malefijt believed that Kuyper wanted to confirm his political leadership with the jubilee celebrations. On 8 April 1912 he wrote to Idenburg: "While I write this, in Utrecht the celebrations are taking place marking the fortieth anniversary of *De Standaard*. Mr. Verweijck has already spent months drumming up the necessary people for it. During the last few weeks Dr. Kuyper himself went on the road and intends to continue to do so. As a result, I think there will be quite some enthusiasm, and the ovation that is so sorely hoped for will fall to him. . . . As far as national politics are concerned, one can be sure that Dr. Kuyper will take the leadership upon himself during the elections. In fact, all he does is prepare himself for them. He takes great pains to take care of his body by way of gymnastics in the nude, massage, frequent walks, abstinence from alcoholic beverages, a vegetarian diet, many medical consultations, etc. And with success. He goes to the second chamber for five minutes a day. By appearing everywhere, he offers proof that he still feels young and powerful."

The building that housed *De Standaard* on the Nieuwezijds Voorburgwal, which at the time was *the* newspaper street in Amsterdam. Next to it, the statistics for advertisements and subscriptions in the period 1909-1920. During the First World War the paper did badly, after which Colijn reorganized it, making it possible for the paper to be published along more commercial lines.

Kuyper in an open carriage on his way to the thirty-second annual meeting of the Free University in Haarlem, 4 July 1912 where he spoke about the foundation of the Free University as "an article of faith." Seated next to him is the pastor from Haarlem, W. Ringnalda. As in his speech *Delivered from the House of Bondage,* in *An Article of Faith* Kuyper looked back to what had been achieved and warned against weakening.

From the summer of 1912 onwards, Kuyper underwent health treatment at Dr. Lahmann's Weisser Hirsch Sanatorium near Dresden every year. The German physician Heinrich Lahmann (1860-1905) was one of the pioneers in the field of natural medicine and nutrition. In 1888 he founded his sanatorium, whose therapy included massage, light therapy, baths, enemas, dietary rules, and remedial gymnastics. As a sanatorium, Weisser Hirsch soon became legendary and attracted thousands of visitors from the upper classes. In 1913 it welcomed 7400 "cure-guests," of whom half were foreigners. Even writers such as Franz Kafka and Lodewijk van Deyssel took treatment there.

The photograph shows the "Herrenbad" (Gentlemen's baths) of Weisser Hirsch.

Teekening van Alb. Hahn, speciaal voor de Holl. Revue.
„Denk er om Theo, al is mijn *gehoor* niet goed meer, ik *zie* nog uitstekend".

Drawing by Albert Hahn, *De Hollandsche Revue*, autumn 1912, with the caption: "Don't forget, Theo, even though I can no longer hear very well, I can still see perfectly."

After he had taken his first treatment in Weisser Hirsch, Kuyper announced in *De Standaard* of 9 September 1912 that because of increasing deafness he was going to resign as a member of the second chamber. With the announcement came medical statements by ear specialist Felix Panse from Dresden and the chief physician of Lahmann's Sanatorium. Panse wrote: "In any case, I can certainly rule out that His Excellency Kuyper will be able to continue to act as a parliamentary representative, particularly in a role as party leader, because it is impossible for him to follow a highly charged debate. It would not only have a detrimental effect on his hearing disorder but would also be damaging to his general health."

De Waal Malefijt wrote to Idenburg, 17 September 1912: "Dr. Kuyper's resignation came as a surprise to everyone. . . . I myself believe that his desire for more freedom, even from the cabinet, was part of his decision." Idenburg also expressed his surprise, although Kuyper had already told him of his intentions on 4 August. On 24 September 1912 he wrote to Colijn: "What does Kuyper's resignation from the parliamentary club mean? Is this *reculer pour mieux sauter* ['backing away to leap higher'] or is it a threat of strike?" According to the caricature by Johan Braakensiek depicted above, Kuyper's influence had not nearly run out.

28 SEPTEMBER 1912   — 46e JAARGANG —   NO. 25

DR. A. KUYPER

bij zijn uittreden uit de Tweede Kamer der Staten-Generaal, voor de „Katholieke Illustratie" opgenomen in zijn studeervertrek ten huize Kanaalstraat 5, te 's-Gravenhage.

The *Katholieke Illustratie* featured Kuyper's portrait on its cover and praised Kuyper's achievements in the political field. In his commentary the editor-in-chief described one of his personal memories: "It was at one of the congresses for tradespeople, held in Rotterdam, when the prime minister had the staff of the congress introduced to him. . . . The magical power surrounding the name was even greater then than it is now: Dr. Kuyper . . . . Then I saw the colossus for the first time: a small, agile, square little man, well-mannered and *worldly,* with a large head on broad shoulders — actually quite different than we had expected. But what suddenly captured our attention, and what won us over to him, was the look in his eye that struck each one of us as we were introduced to him — it was the *charm* that this brilliant, powerful man put into the few words with which he greeted each one of us."

In autumn of 1912 the Dutch Red Cross sent three ambulances to Greece, Bulgaria, and Turkey to offer medical assistance in the war between Turkey and the Balkan states. The photograph shows Kuyper on the occasion of the departure of the ambulance service for Turkey, which left for Constantinople on Friday, 22 November 1912. His daughter Jo (second from the right) was part of the ambulance crew as head nurse. The photograph also shows Minister for War Colijn (to the left of Kuyper) and Henriëtte Kuyper (to the far right).

After the ambulances had returned in May 1913, ten members of the crew were awarded royal decorations. Among those honored were not only Jo Kuyper (Knight of the Order of Orange-Nassau) but also R. A. L. Lehmann (Knight of the Order of the Dutch Lion), who had supported the expedition with the generous sum of 40,000 guilders and had also acted as head of the ambulance service in Greece. At first the cabinet refused to decorate Lehmann because it was afraid that this would dig up the decorations affair again, which was hardly desirable just before the elections of June 1913. However, after heavy lobbying by Prince Hendrik as chairman of the Dutch Red Cross, the cabinet changed its mind.

In the elections of 1913 the coalition parties were defeated, after which, on 9 September 1913, a liberally-oriented cabinet was installed under the leadership of P. W. A. Cort van der Linden (1846-1935), with whom Kuyper was on good terms.

On 16 September 1913 Kuyper was sworn in as member of the first chamber of Parliament, where he was less encumbered by his bad hearing than in the much more rowdy second chamber. Since the Confessional parties had a majority in the first chamber, Kuyper was indirectly able to exert some influence on the cabinet's policies.

Marble bust of Kuyper made in 1905 by the sculptor Toon Dupuis, and presented by Kuyper to the Free University in May 1913. In September 1913 the bust was placed in the Senaatszaal (Senate Room) in the building of the Free University at Keizersgracht 162 in Amsterdam. The bust had already been offered to the Free University in 1906, but the offer had met with opposition from F. L. Rutgers because Kuyper was portrayed in a minister's uniform and not in an academic robe.

Cartoon about "The Bust," *Het Leven*, 22 July 1913.

On 11 July 1913 *Het Volk* revealed that the bust of Kuyper had been made upon the initiative of J. C. Veltman, a volunteer for the town clerk's office in Almelo, who hoped that the effort might lead to his becoming a mayor. On the basis of a written statement by Veltman, the paper suggested that Kuyper had acted in a corrupt way. However, proof of this was never provided. It was true that Veltman had been appointed as mayor of Kattendijke, but only in December 1905 (thus after Kuyper's resignation) by the new minister for home affairs.

Het Volk further suggested that Kuyper had paid for the bust himself. This was indeed true, but there was more to the story. Kuyper himself had indicated that he did not want a bronze bust but rather a marble one, which turned out to cost more than estimated. He was prepared to pay for part of the extra costs if necessary, but in November 1906 refused to pay the thousand guilders that Veltman demanded. In 1910, Veltman, who had ended up in financial difficulties and had also been dismissed as mayor, went into action again. Threatening to bring the case to public attention, he demanded a sum

Het leven in caricatuur.

De Buste.

1. De Maecenas:
   „Inderdaad, voor 'n fraaie buste heb ik altijd veel gevoeld."

2. De afwaschbare Buste:
   „Zie zoo — daar zit geen smetje meer op.... boffer!"

3. Baas boven baas:
   „Pardon — ik ga vóór u — zooals u ziet, ambiëer ik 'n ministersplaats."

4. Voor de kast met oude plunje:
   „Welk costuum zou ik voor m'n buste kiezen."

5. In de antieken-gallerij:
   „Sakkerloot — wat hadden die kerels 'n baantjes te vergeven!"

6. Bij den buste-ontwikkelaar, ('n gruwelijk misverstand.)
   „Och dokter — zoudt u mij niet eens kunnen helpen....?"

of almost 9000 guilders from Kuyper in compensation. In response, Kuyper called in the help of the lawyer and Liberal politician J. D. Veegens, who looked after Kuyper's interests when Veltman went bankrupt and the bust ended up among his assets. Since Kuyper wanted to prevent the bust from being sold at public auction, in the end he was prepared to pay 2000 guilders for it. In June 1911 the case was settled. After that it took two more years before the bust was transferred to the Free University.

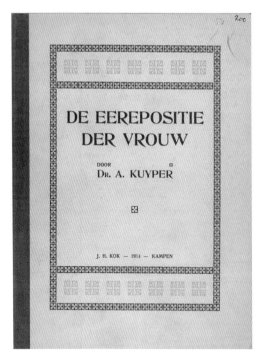

Kuyper continued working as a journalist and publicist until late in life. In *The Woman's Position of Honor* (1914), a number of his articles from *De Standaard* concerning women's emancipation and suffrage were published as a collection. Kuyper believed that "a woman in public life was *not* equal to a man" and that "the power, the calling and the honor of womankind" lay outside the political sphere. That was why he was also against women's suffrage, a point of view that resonated within the ARP for a long time. The party accepted the inevitable triumph of women's suffrage in 1921, but the report by the Idenburg commission that year, which refused to give actual endorsement to suffrage, would not be revoked by the ARP until 1935. And even then it took until 1963 before Jacqueline Rutgers (a granddaughter of F. L. Rutgers) was elected as the first woman member of the second chamber for the ARP.

J. H. Kok (1871-1940) was the foremost publisher of Kuyper's work after the Höveker and Wormser firm in Amsterdam went bankrupt in July 1907. In the auction of that publisher's assets on 12 December 1907, Kok had also obtained copyright to Kuyper's publications which had previously been published by Höveker and Wormser.

WIJ ZIJN . . . . NEDERLANDERS!

(Nadruk verb·

"We are . . . Netherlanders!" Drawing by Louis Raemaekers, *De Telegraaf,* August 1914. Kuyper, Goeman Borgesius, Lohman, and Troelstra engage in a joint handshake.

At the beginning of August 1914 the First World War broke out, which would last for four years and change the situation in Europe completely. Although as a neutral power the Netherlands managed to stay out of the conflict, the economic effects were obvious. Another effect was that political differences receded for the time being. The parties agreed to a truce of national unity, "God's peace." On 3 August the first and second chambers approved mobilization funds by the largest possible majority, and emergency legislation was proposed which would give the government far-reaching powers.

Mobilization in Amsterdam, August 1914. When the First World War broke out, Kuyper was on holiday in Germany and did not return to the Netherlands until 6 August. On 18 August 1914 he wrote to Idenburg, "I have been extremely nervous. I struggled for four days to get from Munich to Kleve [on the Dutch-German border], and that with my right hand in a wrap because it is sprained."

Not until 15 August did Kuyper publish an article in *De Standaard* entitled "Neutral — of course." In it he argued that the war was not a struggle about religious or political principles, but "actually a struggle for *power*." Great care had to be taken not to endanger the neutrality of the Netherlands. That was the reason that *De Standaard* had at first refused to comment. Despite this call for reticence, Kuyper soon gave evidence of strong pro-German sentiments, which were dictated in particular by the English actions against the Boers in South Africa. He was on good terms with the German envoy in The Hague, the orientalist Dr. Friedrich Rosen, and exchanged politely worded notes with Wilhelm II. On 13 February 1917, the Kaiser sent a portrait of Luther to Kuyper.

Kuyper on 3 March 1915 leaving the Nieuwe Oosterbegraafplaats in Amsterdam after the funeral of his old friend and comrade Willem Hovy, who had died in Zeist on 27 February 1915. To Kuyper's left, Hovy's son-in-law, W. H. de Savornin Lohman. At the family's request, Kuyper was the only one to speak at the grave.

Bijvoegsel van

De Nieuwe
Amsterdammer

No 20   26 Juni. 1918.

onafhankelijk nederlandsch weekblad
onder redactie van Mr H.P.L. Wiessing

ABRAHAM: — 'T *IS* ME ZOON NIET!!

Every now and again Kuyper bared his teeth in the first chamber. On 17 June 1915 the first chamber voted down a bill for the regulation of oaths as submitted by Minister for Justice B. Ort. The Confessional parties objected to the bill on principle, because it allowed for a choice between an oath and a promise.

H. Koffyberg (1871-1925), former student of Kuyper and a minister in Muiden and Muiderberg.

In February 1915 the Calvinist pastor H. Koffyberg published the pamphlet *You, Calvinists . . . Open Letter to the Anti-Revolutionary Party Concerning the Observations about the War in 'De Standaard,'* in which he criticized Kuyper's articles about the world war as un-Calvinist, unscriptural, and one-sidedly pro-German. Koffyberg's pamphlet met with much approval, even in the Anti-Revolutionary daily paper *De Rotterdammer,* which under the leadership of professors from the Free University, A. Anema and P. A. Diepenhorst, followed an independent agenda.

In March 1915 Kuyper himself reacted to the brochure with a series of "three-stars" in *De Standaard.* In those short articles he blamed Koffyberg the "officer" for inciting the troops against the "general" (Kuyper) and "damaging the core of the whole indispensable party order." Koffyberg defended himself in the pamphlet *"Agitation?"* (April 1915), in which he asked whether every criticism of the leadership should be regarded as a personal attack on the leader: "Is freedom of speech . . . no longer possible in our Anti-Revolutionary Party?"

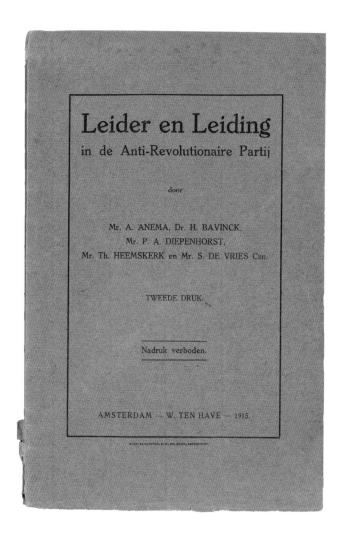

Leider en Leiding
in de Anti-Revolutionaire Partij

door

Mr. A. ANEMA, Dr. H. BAVINCK,
Mr. P. A. DIEPENHORST,
Mr. Th. HEEMSKERK en Mr. S. DE VRIES Czn.

TWEEDE DRUK.

Nadruk verboden.

AMSTERDAM — W. TEN HAVE — 1915.

Although Kuyper did not deem Koffyberg's second pamphlet worthy of a review, he decided to open the attack on a broader front. From 26 April until 5 July he published fifty-three "three-stars" in *De Standaard* in which he discussed the high and low points in the history of the ARP, defended his leadership, and denounced the divisions and lack of discipline within the party. He singled out Heemskerk and his cabinet in particular.

Kuyper's articles in *De Standaard* resulted in an open conflict within the ARP. Heemskerk defended himself in the pamphlet *A Word about Dr. A. Kuyper's Numerous "Three-Stars"* (September 1915). Kuyper responded by publishing his "three-stars" as a collection in the pamphlet *Three-Stars* (October 1915), which sported the subtitle *Editio castigata*, because he had left out a number of accusations directed at Heemskerk. Next, in November 1915, on Herman Bavinck's initiative, the so-called "five gentlemen" — Bavinck, A. Anema, P. A. Diepenhorst, Theo Heemskerk, and S. de Vries — published the pamphlet *Leader and Leadership in the Anti-Revolutionary Party*, in which they detailed their objections to Kuyper's leadership.

De vijf verlichte knapen: „Wij gelooven niet meer aan Sinterklaas!"

Caricature by Johan Braakensiek published in *De Amsterdammer* on 5 December 1915 about the conflict between Kuyper and the "five gentlemen" that had troubled the ARP for some time. On the right are the "five enlightened knaves" who no longer believe in Sinterklaas (Kuyper); to the left, Koffyberg is being stuffed into a sack by "Zwarte Piet" (in Dutch tradition, Sinterklaas's assistant, who punishes bad children by kidnapping them).

On 23 January 1916 Idenburg wrote to his wife: "I am sorry that Dr. K. is so put out by Anema & Co's pamphlet. Here and there something was written that might easily have been omitted, but on the whole it is a good pamphlet. It expresses what intellectuals and the public at large feel and discuss. Now that Kuyper has started to take his case to the public domain, he should have known that the public would give him an answer."

Prof. A. Anema (1872-1966) and Prof. P. A. Diepenhorst (1879-1953), both professors at the Law faculty of the Free University since 1904, belonged to the younger generation of intellectuals within the ARP who refused to accept Kuyper's authoritarian leadership style. Diepenhorst was also the political editor-in-chief of the Anti-Revolutionary daily paper *De Rotterdammer*, which often wrote against Kuyper's *De Standaard*.

Idenburg to Kuyper on 19 January 1916: "The sorrow that now overcomes you is consequence and fruit of your work, of course. More than anyone, *you* have worked for the revival of the Reformed principles, and have thereby strengthened your pupils' individuality and their sense of responsibility toward God. More than any other, *you* have worked to promote education at every level, and have thereby formed a group of men who are used to carrying out their own scholarly work. Your assistants used to be made up completely of followers; now some of them cannot limit themselves to following alone, but believe that they can form their own opinions and ask for an audience for those opinions. . . . I sometimes get the impression that you do not fully account for *those* fruits of your labor; that you do not fully realize that leadership over highly educated men brings with it different responsibilities than leadership over a large crowd; and that because of this, you perceive attacks against your person where this is not remotely the case; that as a result, alas, many who could be of great support do *not* cooperate with you."

At Kuyper's behest, on 26 February 1916, at his home on Kanaalstraat in The Hague, Kuyper and his five opponents discussed their disagreements. The meeting brought a measure of rapprochement but did not resolve the conflict. It was agreed that the controversy about Kuyper's pamphlets and the "five gentlemen" would be put before a board of arbitration. However, this board was never established, because the parties could not agree on the arbitration procedure.

The photograph (*Het Leven*, 7 March 1916) shows three of the "five gentlemen" as they approach Kuyper's house: from left to right, Diepenhorst, Heemskerk, and De Vries.

Kuyper on a visit to Budapest (April 1916), where his daughters Jo and Henriëtte (visible in the background) worked as head nurse and head of the household staff respectively for the Dutch ambulance service in Austria-Hungary that had left Amsterdam on 28 December 1915. The experience led Henriëtte to write the book *Hungary in Wartime: In and around the Dutch Ambulance Service in Budapest (Including a Short Visit to Vienna).*

Kuyper with his granddaughter Adriana, a daughter of his son Abraham Kuyper Jr. and the writer Hendrika Kuyper-van Oordt, 1916. Kuyper was sorry that he had only two grandsons. When in 1914 another granddaughter was born, he wrote to Idenburg: "Again a girl. Now I have among my grandchildren five girls and two boys. I do find the generations that come after me to be important. That's why it is rather a disappointment."

A sprightly Kuyper on his way to congratulate Cort van der Linden on his seventieth birthday, *De Spiegel*, 14 May 1916. The week before, Kuyper had published his two thousandth devotional in *De Heraut*.

In July 1916 the publishing house Kok in Kampen published the first volume of *Anti-Revolutionary Politics, with Further Explanation of "Our Program,"* in which Kuyper, almost fifty years after the publication of *Our Program*, once more rendered an account of the principles and practices of Anti-Revolutionary political theory. The second volume was published in March 1917. The work had earlier been published in twenty-one separate installments, the first one on 1 September 1915. It gave him the opportunity to record his political legacy in a comprehensive fashion.

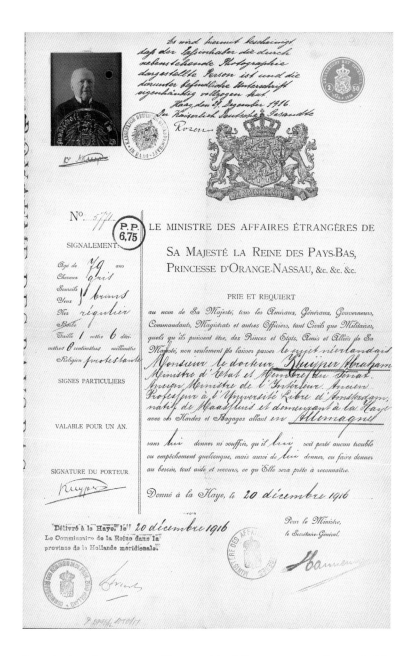

Even during the war years, Kuyper visited Germany annually to take his treatment at Weisser Hirsch, the last time in 1918. In 1917 Idenburg also went for a cure in Weisser Hirsch, while in 1918 Kuyper was accompanied by Mrs. Idenburg and his youngest daughter, Cato.

The photograph shows the passport issued by the Foreign Service, 16 December 1916. Kuyper had resolved to take a week's vacation abroad again in early 1917, as he was used to doing. However, the trip to Cologne he had planned could not take place because he contracted bronchitis, and after that, pneumonia.

A. C. E. Mond-Kuyper.

In January and February 1917 Kuyper was seriously ill. Although a planned operation turned out not to be necessary at the last minute, it took a long time before he had recovered and could continue his work, and he was never quite the same again. On 3 February 1917, while he was recovering from a serious illness, he wrote to his eldest sister, Anna Mond-Kuyper, "Dearest Anna, I am not really allowed to write yet. However, my heart compels me to thank you heartily for your dear letter, which refreshed me so much. I am in God's hands. What he has ordained for me, I await with quiet humility. The situation is still fraught with troubles. And yet he is my savior. May the Lord also have mercy on you. Your most affectionate brother."

Kuyper's youngest sister, Jeannette Jacqueline Rammelman Elsevier-Kuyper (1847-1941), with her husband, Jacques Rammelman Elsevier (1846-1921), a notary public in Arnhem. She wrote a booklet with memories of the years of her brother's youth and was an honorary guest at the Kuyper memorial that was held on 29 October 1937 in the Concertgebouw in Amsterdam.

First page of the birthday guestbook for Kuyper's eightieth birthday, 29 October 1917, with various well-known names. The reception was held in the afternoon at Kuyper's house. His family doctor had allowed the reception, as long as Kuyper remained seated when receiving his guests. On behalf of the anniversary committee, Idenburg offered him a sum of money towards a fund for the establishment of a Kuyper chair in the history and philosophy of Anti-Revolutionary political theory at the Free University. The plans for the foundation of a Kuyper chair were not implemented until the centennial anniversary of the Free University in 1980.

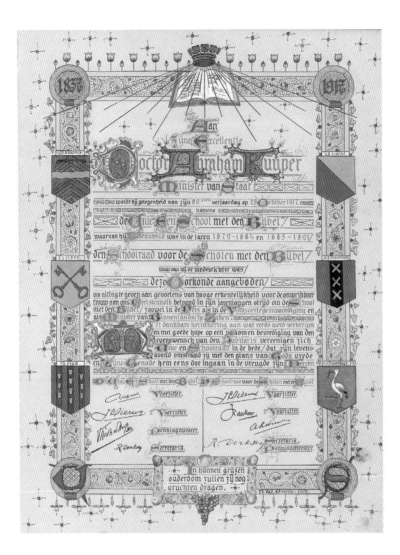

Certificate for Kuyper on the occasion of his eightieth birthday, presented to him by the "School with the Bible" Association and the School Council for the Schools with the Bible. The constitutional reform of 1917 had just ended the discrimination against religious schools that Kuyper had fought throughout his political career.

This constitutional reform is also known as the Pacification of 1917, because it resolved two issues that had dominated Dutch politics for a long time: the school question and the question of electoral suffrage. Suffrage was extended to include universal suffrage for men (voting rights for women would follow in 1919), while with the substitution of proportional representation for the constituency voting system, the electoral system became organized along very different lines. In addition, the constitution opened the way for the complete financial equality of state education and private elementary schools, which would become law in 1920 under the Christian-Historical education minister Johannes Theodoor de Visser.

Kuyper at eighty. The portrait was made upon the request of his publisher, J. H. Kok, who included it in the publication of Kuyper's speech, *The Little People,* to the ARP convention on 23 November 1917 in the Tivoli, Utrecht. The meeting of delegates was held to amend the statutes of the ARP in accordance with the amended electoral system. Kuyper would rather have seen the introduction of "householder franchise," which the Anti-Revolutionaries had championed.

Six months later, on 2 May 1918, with an eye to the elections for the second chamber of July 1918, a meeting of delegates was again convened in the Tivoli. This time Kuyper could not attend the meeting for health reasons, which meant that his speech to the delegates was read by Idenburg in his capacity as deputy chairman. In this speech entitled *What Now?* Kuyper posed the question as to how Christian politics should develop now that the school struggle had ended. Kuyper believed that placing "the Social labor issue in the full and proper context of our Anti-Revolutionary politics" would reinvigorate the ARP.

DE PERSTENTOONSTELLING IN DEN HAAG.

Ter gelegenheid van het zilveren jubileum van de Haagsche Journalisten-vereeniging wordt te 's-Gravenhage een Perstentoon
stelling gehouden. Onze foto geeft een groep van genoodigden en leden der H. J. V. Zittend, v. l. n. r.: De burgemeeste
van 's-Gravenhage; Dr. A. Kuyper; Mr. Van Bolhuys, voorzitter der H. J. V.; Mr. D. Fock, voorzitter der Tweede Kamer.

Kuyper with the mayor of The Hague, H. A. van Karnebeek, at the opening of the press exhibition at the Pulchri Studio in The Hague, Saturday, 8 June 1918, organized by the Journalists' Association of The Hague. This appears to be the only occasion when Kuyper was filmed.

Ch. J. M. Ruijs de Beerenbrouck (1873-1936).

At the elections of 3 July 1918, the first under the new electoral system, the three major Christian parties won 50 of the 100 parliamentary seats. The Roman Catholics (from 25 to 30 seats) were the biggest winners. After a difficult cabinet formation, a Confessional cabinet was installed on 9 September that was led for the first time by a Roman Catholic, Ruijs de Beerenbrouck. His father had been a minister during the Mackay cabinet. From Weisser Hirsch, Kuyper opposed the formation of a right-wing cabinet in vain. In his opinion it had too narrow a basis in Parliament and would be dominated by Roman Catholic ministers.

In the end Kuyper gave in to the combined pressure of Idenburg and Colijn, who believed that the ARP could not remain outside the cabinet. That Idenburg, as minister for colonial affairs, became a member of the cabinet was particularly disappointing to Kuyper, because it meant that Idenburg would not be able to succeed him as leader of the ARP.

Disappointed about what had occurred during the cabinet formation, on 31 October 1918 Kuyper sent a letter to the ARP Central Committee in which he announced his resignation as party chairman. Subsequently, on 25 November the Central Committee appointed Colijn as temporary chairman of the ARP. Colijn had been the director of the Batavian Petroleum Company since 1914, but remained well-informed about political developments in the Netherlands, partly through his membership in the first chamber. Colijn accepted the appointment on 27 December 1918, but emphasized that it was temporary and that he thought Idenburg was the right man for the job. In saying this he struck the right chord with Kuyper; in *De Standaard* Kuyper seemed pleased with his successor.

After the meeting of delegates of the ARP had formally elected Colijn as party chairman on 13 April 1920, *De Groene* published a drawing by Johan Braakensiek of "Colijn wearing Kuyper's prophet's mantle" with the caption: "Would it stain my new coat if I continued in that business?"

De Spiegel
WEEKILLUSTRATIE VOOR HET CHRISTELIJK GEZIN

DE AARDE IS DES HEEREN

WAAR EN KLAAR

23 November 1918 | Uitgave van W. KIRCHNER, Bloemgracht 133, Telephoon 4449, AMSTERDAM | 13ᵈᵉ Jaargang - No. 8

GROOTE HULDEBETUIGING AAN HET KONINKLIJK HUIS EN DE REGEERING OP HET MALIEVELD TE 's-GRAVENHAGE.

Het was 'n ontroerende plechtigheid, waarbij bleek van den hechten band, die Nederland en Oranje houdt saamgesnoerd. Op de *bovenste photo* ziet men de Ministers voor het rijtuig van de Koningin. — *Onderaan* de Koninklijke Familie in het rijtuig.

Photo's Vlaar van Weeren.

After the defeat of Germany and the German Kaiser's flight to the Netherlands in November 1918, Troelstra declared in Parliament that the Netherlands was also ripe for revolution. Soon it became clear that he was wrong. On 18 November 1918 a large demonstration took place on the Malieveld in The Hague in which the crowd professed loyalty to the House of Orange and other lawful authorities. That evening a demonstration also took place in front of Kuyper's house on Kanaalstraat by Frisian troops, who sang the "Wilhelmus" and the Frisian national anthem. Kuyper, who had come outside, addressed them and at the end asked them to sing one of his favorite psalms: "Blessed is the nation who listens to Your voice."

The Second Christian Social Congress was held in Amsterdam 10-13 March 1919; Kuyper had already called for such a gathering in 1914. However, Kuyper refused to be appointed as the honorary chairman of the congress, because the organizing committee had also offered such a position to Savornin Lohman. Kuyper did not attend the congress; instead, on 12 March, he delivered his last great oration in the first chamber, on the topic of "our colonies in the archipelago."

The photograph shows the executive committee of the congress. Diepenhorst, who acted as chairman, is seated in the middle. In the back row are students of the Free University, who were appointed to keep order.

In 1919 Kuyper did not visit Weisser Hirsch again, but spent the summer months at the Bethesda Medical Baths in Laag-Soeren in the Veluwe, which Lohman had recommended to him. Bethesda was the first health resort in the Netherlands, founded in 1849 by the Amsterdam merchant P. N. J. van Breukelerwaard.

In December 1919 Kuyper had to relinquish his journalistic activities for *De Standaard* because of declining health. His doctor was brought in to persuade him to resign, and duly forbade him to have anything more to do with the newspaper. His last "three-star" appeared in *De Standaard* of 18 December 1919 and was dedicated to the resignation of L. J. Plemp van Duiveland as editor-in-chief of the *Nieuwe Courant*.

R. C. Verweijck to Colijn, 28 November 1919: "You probably already know that Dr. Kuyper's health had been deteriorating during the past few weeks. This has been noticeable in his copy for some time already, and as a result it often required special attention; but during the last few days the situation has become somewhat worrying. I have heard that the calcification of blood vessels increases rapidly; it is quite possible that very shortly his work will come to an end. Currently he is still working regularly, now and then even very well; however, I had to intervene and leave out of the paper a couple of 'three-stars' that made no sense at all. Yesterday I had a conversation with the eldest son, who aims to have the physician forbid him to do any kind of work whatsoever. I also had a conversation with Mr. De Vlugt about the matter last night. He will also take it upon himself today to insist on the physician's forbidding any further work."

In name Kuyper remained editor-in-chief, but the editorial work fell to a group consisting of Colijn, Idenburg, Anema, J. Schouten, J. A. de Wilde, and A. Zijlstra.

Toward the end of their lives Kuyper and Lohman made peace, after having had conflicts repeatedly since 1905. On 26 December 1919, when he heard that Kuyper was feeling "a bit under the weather," Lohman wrote, "Although a reconciliation between us in

the flesh could not take place, I will never be able to forget that we both served the same Lord, each in his own way; that we will both need the same garments for the Wedding Feast, and that we will thereby recognize that we may sit together at the same Table. All that prevented us from meeting will then be forgotten, because our eyes will then be better opened. Whatever you have done *for and to me,* for that I thank you, and for that by which I have unnecessarily hurt you, I ask forgiveness."

Kuyper answered Lohman on 28 December 1919: "Let me thank you most heartily and sincerely for yesterday's letter. For me it was as if a prayer, uttered so often, had finally been heard. And I praise God that after so many years of having awaited brotherhood and reconciliation, it has thus finally come, and in such a loyal and truly Christian way. Your letter is a gift for which I thank not only you, but also my God."

Kuyper out walking with his daughter Jo, end of April 1920. The *Katholieke Illustratie* reported on 1 May 1920: "Despite the inclement weather, he was really dressed for summer."

Aan de Eerste Kamer van de Staten-Generaal

Ondergeteekende, Dr. A. KUYPER, bevestigt hierbij de aan
de Kamer gedane mededeeling en heeft de eer bij deze zijn ontslag
als lid der Kamer te nemen.

's-Gravenhage, 21 September 1920.

For health reasons, Idenburg resigned as minister for colonial affairs on 13 November 1919. In April 1920 he was appointed as second chairman of the ARP. In that capacity the leadership of the ARP in fact rested with him, because Colijn, in order to continue his work for the Batavian Petroleum Company, had moved to London in December 1919, leaving many matters to Idenburg. Idenburg saw to it that Kuyper was informed of what went on, and consulted him about current issues, such as relations with the Roman Catholic party, the colonial question, and women's suffrage, which within the ARP was a controversial issue. As Kuyper's end drew nearer, Idenburg visited him more and more often to guide him spiritually. The booklet *The Autumn of Dr. A. Kuyper's Life*, which Henriëtte and Jo Kuyper published in 1921, included a description of these visits: "During the entire period that my father was ill, Mr. Idenburg was a regular visitor. Visiting the sick is an art, or rather a gift . . . and Mr. Idenburg possesses this gift in high degree. His visits were never too short, never too long, never tiring — on the contrary, always refreshing. I often noticed how my father looked forward all day to the arrival of Mr. Idenburg. . . . And the nearer the end of my father's life came, the stronger his desire was to have his friend with him."

On 21 September 1920 Kuyper resigned his membership in the first chamber of Parliament.

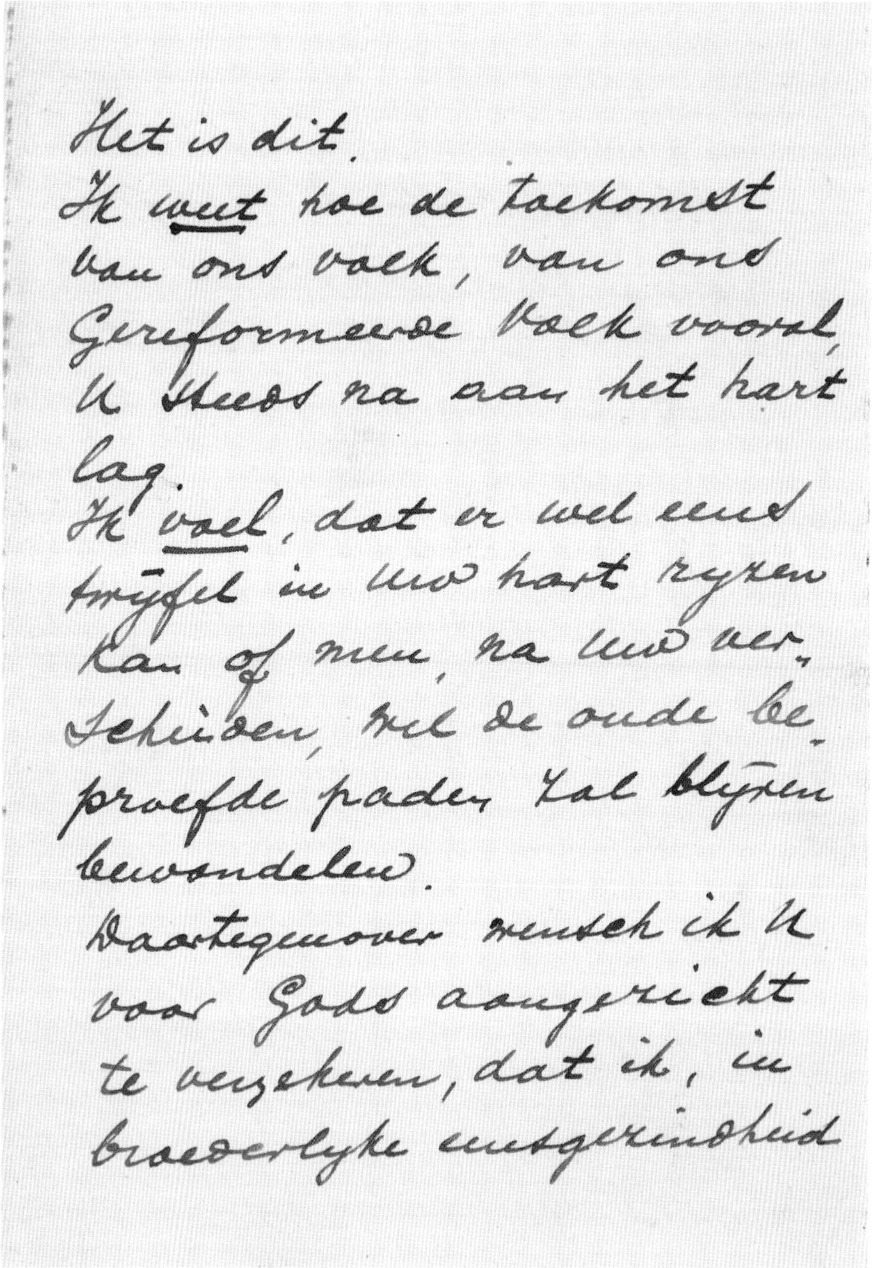

Het is dit.

Ik weet hoe de toekomst
van ons volk, van ons
Gereformeerde volk vooral,
U steeds na aan het hart
lag.

Ik voel, dat er wel eens
twijfel in Uw hart rijzen
kan of men, na Uw ver-
scheiden, wel de oude be-
proefde paden zal blijven
bewandelen.

Daartegenover wensch ik U
voor Gods aangezicht
te verzekeren, dat ik, in
broederlyke eensgezindheid

Letter from Colijn to Kuyper, 17 October 1920, in which he gave Kuyper his assurance that together with Idenburg he would use all his powers "to keep our people on the paths that you showed." One of his daughters read the letter at Kuyper's sickbed and later wrote, "My father listened to this letter with rising interest and increasing joy, and soon requested me to thank Mr. Colijn warmly on his behalf and to say to him that this letter had lightened his heart."

met u mee, e bidt voor u.

Ee blijde oogopslag, die bewees

hoezee hij dit waardeerde.

5 Nov. den geheele dag zeer

onrustig e in de war.

Hr Idenburg drukte hem slechts

even de hand.

6 Nov. eerst onrustig, toen veel alles

gelaten, ge controleerd door opening

in 't schut. Stil... rustiger

geworden Tegen den middag

verandering. wezenloose blik,

dee op alsnel, pols veel minder

Hr. Idenburg afgetelefoneerd.

savonds 10 uur dokter getelefo-

neer komen, liet het ernstig in.

e wordt besloten volgende morgen

vroeg broer te telefoneeren.

7 Nov. Zondag. snachts om 2 uur

nog even bij hem geweest. toestand

was achteruit gegaan, ik durfde

Diary entries of Henriëtte Kuyper about her father's last days. Some of the notes were used in *The Autumn of Dr. A. Kuyper's Life.*

404   THE FINAL YEARS, 1910-1920

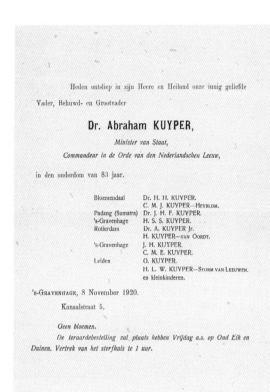

On Monday, 8 November 1920, at about five o'clock in the afternoon, Kuyper died in the presence of his children and Idenburg. After Kuyper's death, Idenburg read a few verses from 2 Corinthians 5, including these words: "For we know that if our earthly tabernacle is destroyed, we have a building from God, a house not made with hands, eternal in the heavens."

Kuyper on his deathbed. Above his bed hangs the picture of Christ crucified that he bought as a student. During the turbulent days of the railway workers' strike in 1903, Kuyper wrote to his daughter Jo, then working at the missionary hospital in Yogyakarta: "My calling is high, my task is glorious, and above my bed hangs a picture of the crucifixion, and when I look upon it, it seems that every evening the Lord asks: 'What is your struggle compared to my cup?' Serving him is so uplifting and glorious."

Two photographs of Kuyper's funeral on 12 November 1920. At the grave, Heemskerk spoke on behalf of the government, Colijn on behalf of the Anti-Revolutionary Party, R. H. Woltjer on behalf of the Free University, K. Dijk on behalf of the *Gereformeerde* churches, and Idenburg as a friend, after which Kuyper's son Herman expressed his appreciation on behalf of the family.

Idenburg wrote to his daughter then living in the Dutch East Indies on 13 November 1920: "The funeral was truly solemn and dignified. The turnout from all parts of the country was large. According to conservative estimates, 20,000 to 30,000 people lined the road; at the churchyard there were more than 10,000. It was well organized, and the Anti-Revolutionary supporters behaved in an exemplary way. No restlessness, no pushing and shoving, no complaints — great solemnity, deeply felt sadness, warm gratitude to God. The same was true for Kuyper's deathbed. He did not suffer, was clearly accepting, and passed on peacefully without the slightest struggle."

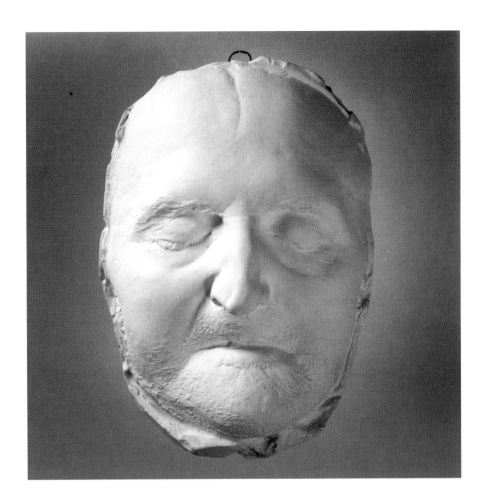

Kuyper's death mask.

Kuyper's grave in the cemetery of Oud Eik en Duinen in The Hague.

Literary Sources

G. Abma and J. de Bruijn, eds., *Hoedemaker herdacht*. Ten Have, Baarn 1989.

C. Augustijn, J. H. Prins, and H. E. S. Woldring, eds., *Abraham Kuyper. Zijn volksdeel, zijn invloed*. Meinema, Delft 1987.

C. Augustijn and J. Vree, *Abraham Kuyper: vast en veranderlijk. De ontwikkeling van zijn denken*. Meinema, Zoetermeer 1998.

W. Bakker, "Kuypers afscheid van het Leidse gymnasium," *Gereformeerd Theologisch Tijdschrift* 81 (1981): 1-21.

W. Bakker et al., eds., *De Doleantie van 1886 en haar geschiedenis*. J. H. Kok, Kampen 1986.

J. A. A. H. de Beaufort, *Vijftig jaren uit onze geschiedenis*. 2 vols. P. N. van Kampen en Zoon, Amsterdam 1928.

W. H. de Beaufort, *Dagboeken en aantekeningen, 1868-1918*, ed. J. P. de Valk and M. Van Faassen. 2 vols. Instituut voor Nederlandse Geschiedenis, 's-Gravenhage 1993.

A. Bornebroek, *Een heer in een volkspartij. Theodoor Heemskerk (1852-1932), ministerpresident en minister van Justitie*. Aksant, Amsterdam 2006.

D. Bos, *In dienst van het Koninkrijk. Beroepsontwikkeling van hervormde predikanten in negentiende-eeuws Nederland*. Bert Bakker, Amsterdam 1999.

J. D. Bratt, ed., *Abraham Kuyper: A Centennial Reader*. Eerdmans, Grand Rapids 1998.

Th. B. F. M. Brinkel, J. de Bruijn, and A. Postma, eds., *Het kabinet-Mackay. Opstellen over de eerste christelijke coalitie (1888-1891)*. Arbor, Baarn 1990.

J. de Bruijn and G. Puchinger, eds., *Briefwisseling Kuyper-Idenburg*. T. Wever, Franeker 1985.

J. de Bruijn, "Calvinism and Romanticism: Abraham Kuyper as a Calvinist Politician," in Luis E. Lugo, ed., *Religion, Pluralism and Public Life: Abraham Kuyper's Legacy for the Twenty-First Century*. Eerdmans, Grand Rapids 2000, 45-58.

J. de Bruijn, *"Kuyper ist ein Luegner." De kabinetsformatie van 1901*. Free University, Amsterdam 2001.

J. de Bruijn, "De poëzie van het vervallene. Abraham Kuyper in Constantinopel," in J. P. Henrichs, ed., *Passage Istanbul*. Uitgeverij Bas Lubberhuizen, Amsterdam 2001.

J. de Bruijn, " 'Weg met zóó onzedelijke constitutie!' Abraham Kuyper, volkspetitionnement en spoorwegstaking," in A. van de Beek and W. M. van Laar, eds., *Sola Gratia. Bron voor de reformatie en uitdaging voor nu*. Boekencentrum, Zoetermeer 2004, 118-25.

J. de Bruijn, *Het boetekleed ontsiert de man niet. Abraham Kuyper en de Lintjesaffaire (1909-1910)*. Bert Bakker, Amsterdam 2005.

J. de Bruijn, "Abraham Kuyper en de Bilderdijkherdenking van 1906," in M. van Hattum, et al., eds., *Een eeuw rare kostgangers. Vereniging Het Bilderdijk-Museum 1908-2008*. EON Pers, Amstelveen 2008, 8-29.

J. de Bruijn, *Wilhelmina formeert. De Kabinetscrisis van 1907/1908*. Boom, Amsterdam 2011.

J. de Bruijn, *De Sabel van Colyn. Biografische opstellan aver rcligie en politiek in Nederland*. Verlorem, Hilversum 2011.

H. Colijn, *Levensbericht van dr. A. Kuyper*. J. H. Kok, Kampen 1923.

A. Th. van Deursen, *Een hoeksteen in het verzuild bestel. De Free University 1880-2005*. Bert Bakker, Amsterdam 2005.

P. A. Diepenhorst, *Dr. A. Kuyper*. F. Bohn, Haarlem 1931.

C. K. Elout, *De heeren in Den Haag*. Illustrations by Louis Raemaekers. Jacob van Campen, Amsterdam 1913.

C. K. Elout, *Figuren en momenten uit de politiek van Koningin Wilhelmina's tijd*. Algemeen Handelsblad, Amsterdam 1938.

Gedenkboek opgedragen aan prof. dr. A. Kuyper bij zijn vijfentwintigjarig jubileum als hoofdredacteur van "De Standaard," 1872 — 1 april — 1897. G. J. C. Gerdes, Amsterdam 1897.

Gedenkboek ter herinnering aan het overlijden van dr. A. Kuyper en de sprake die daarbij uit de pers voortkwam. W. ten Have, Amsterdam 1921.

Geen vergeefs woord. Verzamelde deputatenredevoeringen. J. H. Kok, Kampen 1951.

K. Groot, *Kuyper en Kohlbrugge in hun wederzijds contact*. Bosch en Keuning, Baarn 1956.

G. Harinck and M. Urbanus, eds., *Ik voel steeds meer dat ik hier zijn moest. Amerikaanse brieven van Abraham Kuyper aan zijn vrouw en kinderen (1898)*. Free University, Amsterdam 2004.

P. S. Heslam, *Creating a Christian Worldview: Abraham Kuyper's Lectures on Calvinism*. Eerdmans, Grand Rapids 1998.

R. Janssens, *De opbouw van de Antirevolutionaire Partij, 1850-1888*. Verloren, Hilversum 2001.

H. J. de Jonge, "Kuyper en de disputaties geleid door Cobet," in *Gereformeerd Theologisch Tijdschrift* 81 (1981): 22-35.

P. Kasteel, *Abraham Kuyper*. J. H. Kok, Kampen 1938.

G. van Klinken, *Actieve burgers. Nederlanders en hun politieke partijen, 1870-1918*. Wereldbibliotheek, Amsterdam 2003.

J. Koch, *Abraham Kuyper. Een biografie*. Boom, Amsterdam 2006.

C. A. J. van Koppen, *De Geuzen van de negentiende eeuw. Abraham Kuyper en Zuid-Afrika*. Innerc, Wormer 1992.

D. Th. Kuiper and G. J. Schutte, eds., *Het kabinet-Kuyper (1901-1905)*. Meinema, Zoetermeer 2001.

Tj. Kuipers, *Abraham Kuyper: An Annotated Bibliography, 1857-2007*. Brill, Leiden/Boston 2011.

H. S. S. Kuyper and J. H. Kuyper, eds., *Herinneringen van de oude garde aan den persoon en den levensarbeid van dr. A. Kuyper*. W. ten Have, Amsterdam 1922.

H. S. S. and J. H. Kuyper, *De levensavond van dr. A. Kuyper*. J. H. Kok, Kampen 1921.

Kuyper in de caricatuur. 100 uitgezochte caricaturen. Met een brief van dr. A. Kuyper. Van Holkema & Warendorf, Amsterdam 1909.

Kuyper-gedenkboek 1907, bevattende een overzicht van de feestviering op dinsdag 29 october 1907 ter gelegenheid van den zeventigsten verjaardag van prof. dr. A. Kuyper, oud-minister van Binnenlandsche Zaken, te 's-Gravenhage, benevens een verzameling van tal van courantenartikelen uit binnenen buitenland, dat jubileum betreffende. 's-Gravenhage 1908.

H. J. Langman, *Kuyper en de volkskerk.* J. H. Kok, Kampen 1950.

H. van Malsen, *Alexander Frederik de Savornin Lohman. Karakterschets.* D. van Aken, Terneuzen 1924.

O. de Moor and A. M. de Moor-Ringnalda, *Een Maassluizer jongen wordt minister-president. Het leven van dr. Abraham Kuyper 1837 — 29 october — 1937.* C. F. Callenbach, Nijkerk 1937.

L. Praamsma, *Abraham Kuyper als kerkhistoricus.* J. H. Kok, Kampen 1945.

G. Puchinger and N. Scheps, *Gesprek over de onbekende Kuyper.* J. H. Kok, Kampen 1971.

G. Puchinger, *Ontmoetingen met antirevolutionairen.* Terra, Zutphen 1981.

G. Puchinger, *Nederlandse minister-presidenten van de twintigste eeuw.* Sijthoff, Amsterdam 1984.

G. Puchinger, *Abraham Kuyper. De jonge Kuyper (1837-1867).* T. Wever, Franeker 1987.

G. Puchinger, *Kuyper-herdenking 1987. De religieuze Kuyper.* J. H. Kok, Kampen 1987.

A. J. Rasker, *De Nederlandse Hervormde Kerk vanaf 1795.* J. H. Kok, Kampen 1986.

S. J. Ridderbos, *De theologische cultuurbeschouwing van Abraham Kuyper.* J. H. Kok, Kampen 1947.

C. de Ru, *De strijd over het hoger onderwijs tijdens het ministerie-Kuyper.* J. H. Kok, Kampen 1953.

J. C. Rullmann, *De strijd voor kerkherstel in de Nederlandsch Hervormde Kerk der XIXe eeuw historisch geschetst.* W. Kirchner, Amsterdam 1915.

J. C. Rullmann, *De Doleantie in de Nederlandsch Hervormde Kerk der XIXe eeuw historisch geschetst.* W. Kirchner, Amsterdam 1916.

J. C. Rullmann, *Abraham Kuyper. Een levensschets.* J. H. Kok, Kampen 1928.

J. C. Rullmann, *Kuyper-Bibliografie.* 3 vols. Js. Bootsma, 's-Gravenhage 1923; J. H. Kok, Kampen 1929, 1940.

A. J. C. Rüter, *De spoorwegstakingen van 1903. Een spiegel der arbeidersbeweging in Nederland.* Brill, Leiden 1935.

W. H. de Savornin Lohman, *Dr. A. Kuyper.* H. D. Tjeenk Willink, Haarlem 1889.

L. W. G. Scholten, et al., eds., *Dr. A. Kuyper 1837-1937. Gedenkboek uitgegeven bij gelegenheid van de herdenking op 29 october 1937 van het feit dat dr. A. Kuyper honderd jaar geleden te Maassluis geboren werd.* J. H. Kok, Kampen 1937.

G. J. Schutte, *De Free University en Zuid-Afrika, 1880-2005.* 2 vols. Meinema, Zoetermeer 2005.

H. Smitskamp, *Een keerpunt in de voorgeschiedenis der Free University.* J. H. Kok, Kampen 1961.

J. Stellingwerff, *Dr. Abraham Kuyper en de Free University.* J. H. Kok, Kampen 1987.

L. C. Suttorp, *Jhr. mr. Alexander Frederik de Savornin Lohman, 1837-1924*. A. A. M. Stols,
's-Gravenhage 1948.

J. Voerman, *Het conflict Kuyper-Heemskerk*. Libertas, Utrecht 1954.

J. Vree, *Kuyper in de kiem. De precalvinistische periode van Abraham Kuyper, 1848-1874*. Verloren, Hilversum 2006.

J. Vree and J. Zwaan, eds., *Abraham Kuyper's* Commentatio *(1860): The Young Kuyper on Calvin, a Lasco and the Church*. 2 vols. Brill, Leiden/Boston 2005.

Jac. van Weringh, *Het maatschappijbeeld van Abraham Kuyper*. Van Gorcum, Assen 1967.

W. F. A. Winckel, *Leven en arbeid van dr. A. Kuyper*. W. ten Have, Amsterdam 1919.

L. G. Zwanenburg, *Gerrit Jan Vos Az. Het recht van de Kerk*. J. H. Kok, Kampen 1978.

Sources of Photographic Material

Most of the photographic material used in this publication came from the archives of the Historical Documentation Center for Dutch Protestantism of the Free University in Amsterdam. The remaining illustrations were put at the author's disposal by the private persons and organizations listed below, with a statement of the corresponding page numbers in the book.

Academisch Historisch Museum, Leiden 14, 19

A Lasco Bibliothek, Emden 28, 50

Bilderdijk Museum, Amsterdam 315

A. A. W. Bolland MA, Amsterdam 262

Gemeentearchief, Leiden 12, 16

Gemeentelijke Archiefdienst, Utrecht 59, 62, 113

Groninger Universiteitsmuseum, Groningen 65

Mr. P. W. Koffijberg, Amsterdam 379

Ms. A. Kruger, Amsterdam 270

Mondriaanhuis, Amersfoort 183

Museum Freriks, Winterswijk 182

Nationaal Archief, 's-Gravenhage 257

Princeton Theological Seminary, Princeton (New Jersey, USA) 238, 239, 242

Rijksbureau voor Kunsthistorische Documentatie, 's-Gravenhage 184

Rijksmuseum Het Catharijneconvent, Utrecht 159

Stadsarchief, Amsterdam 77, 88, 120

Universiteitsbibliotheek, Free University, Amsterdam 29, 196

Universiteitsmuseum, Utrecht 64

Mr. O. W. A. baron van Verschuer, Beesd 45

Verschönerungsverein Weisser Hirsch, Dresden 367

Index

Abdoel Hamid II, Sultan of Turkey, 306, 307
Amorie van der Hoeven, A. des, Jr., 23
Anders, P., 225
Anema, A., 379-82, 399
Asch van Wijck, T. A. J. van, 271, 279
Atwater Mason, C., 311

Baltus, Pietje, 51-52, 90
Barger, G., 68
Baudet, H., 317
Bavinck, H., 178, 222, 224, 320, 330, 337, 380
Beaufort, W. H. de, 235, 253, 262, 343, 359, 362
Beelaerts van Blokland, G. J. F., 165
Beets, Cornelis, 58
Beets, Nicolaas, 57-58, 69, 71, 88, 148, 197
Bergansius, J. W., 198, 271
Bergh, L. Ph. C. van den, 14
Bergh, W. van den, 156
Bilderdijk, W., 315-16
Bismarck, O. von, 49
Boetzelaer, G. H. L., Baron van, 173
Boissevain, Charles, vii, 230, 232
Bottema, Tj., 337
Braakensiek, Johan, 194, 210, 253, 265, 274, 287, 290, 298, 325, 327, 334, 342, 368, 381, 395
Bredius, A., 272
Breukelerwaard, P. N. J. van, 398
Bronsveld, A. W., 69, 117-18, 125, 148, 231
Bronsveld-Vitringa, S. Ch. C., 69
Bruine, J. R. de, 9
Burke, E., 79
Busken Huet, C., 227
Bylandt van Mariënweerd, O. W. A. Graaf van, 42, 45

Calvin, John, 1, 29-30, 51, 213, 330, 341, 363
Chantepie de la Saussaye, D., 71, 88, 98
Chung, S. K., 329
Cobet, C. G., 20
Colijn, H., 272, 353, 356, 358, 363, 365, 368, 370, 394, 395, 399, 402, 403, 406

Cort van der Linden, P. W. A., 235, 354, 371, 386
Costa, I. da, 134, 225
Cremer, J. T., 235
Cuypers, P. J. H., 317

Deen, J., 230
Deyssel, Lodewijk van, 367
Dicey, A. V., 245
Diepenhorst, P. A., 379-83, 397
Dijk, K., 406
Dilloo, F. W. J., 133, 145
Doedes, J. I., 64
Domela Nieuwenhuis, F., 163, 165, 189, 197, 283, 288, 322-23
Dupuis, Toon, 299, 372
Duymaer van Twist, L. F., 361

Ellis, A. G., 271
Elout, C. K., 262
Elout van Soeterwoude, P. J., 111-12, 116, 127, 153
Emma, Queen, 197, 236, 268, 294

Fabius, D. P. D., 133, 157, 164
Fabius, J. C., 173
Felix, J. W., 73, 173
Fox, Charles, 79
Fruin, R. J., 14, 50, 129

Galilei, Galileo, 122
Geer, D. J. de, 273
Geer van Jutphaas, B. J. L., Baron de, 107-8
Geldorp, P. J. van, 231, 288
George V, King of Hanover, 50
Gleichman, J. G., 192
Goeman Borgesius, H., 235, 375
Gorissen, W. J., 73
Gratama, B. J., 107
Groen van Prinsterer, G., 41-42, 49, 55-56, 70-71, 80, 81, 85, 88, 91, 94, 96, 100, 106, 112, 179, 190, 196, 209, 363